Title: Tetherstones

Date of first publication: 1923

Author: Ethel M. Dell (1881-1939)

Date first posted: June 14, 2015

Date last updated: June 14, 2015

Faded Page eBook #20150640

This ebook was produced by: Marcia Brooks, Al Haines, Alex White & the
online Distributed Proofreaders Canada team at http://www.pgdpcanada.net

BY ETHEL M. DELL

<hr size=2 width="20%" align=center>

The Way of an Eagle

The Knave of Diamonds

The Rocks of Valpré

The Swindler, and Other Stories

The Keeper of the Door

Bars of Iron

The Hundredth Chance

The Safety Curtain, and Other Stories

Greatheart

The Lamp in the Desert

The Tidal Wave

The Top of the World

The Obstacle Race

The Odds and Other Stories

Charles Rex

<hr size=2 width="100%" align=center>

Tetherstones

By
Ethel M. Dell

First Published 1923
Republished 2023

CONTENTS

PART I

CHAPTER I
THE MACHINE

Twelve deep notes sounded from the clock-tower of the Cathedral, and the Bishop's secretary dropped her hands from her typewriter and turned her face to the open window with a quick sigh. The Bishop's garden lay sleeping in the sunshine—the pure white of lilies and royal blue of delphiniums mingling together as the wrought silks on the fringe of an altar-cloth. The age-worn stone of the Cathedral rose beyond it, and the arch of the cloisters gave a glimpse of the quiet burial-ground within. A great cluster of purple stone-crop rioted over one corner of the arch, and the secretary's tired eyes rested upon it with a touch of wistfulness as though the splendour of it were somewhat overwhelming. She herself was so slight, so insignificant, so altogether negligible a quality, a being wholly out of place in the midst of such glorious surroundings. But yet she loved them, and her happiest hours were those she spent with her little sketching-block in various corners of that wonderful garden. It was only that the purple flower seemed somehow to be the symbol to her of all that was out of reach. Her youth was slipping from her, and she had never lived.

The tired lines about the brown eyes were growing daily more marked. The little tender curve about the lips was becoming a droop. The brown hair that grew so softly about her forehead gleamed unexpectedly white here and there.

"Yes, I'm getting old," said Frances Thorold. "Old and tired and dull." She stretched up her arms with a sudden movement, and for a second her hands were clenched. Then they fell to her sides.

"I suppose we are all slaves," she said, "of one kind or another. But only the rebels know it."

She turned again to her work, and for a space only the sharp click of the machine disturbed the summer silence. It had an unmistakably indignant sound as though its manipulator were out of sympathy with the words so deftly printed on the white page. The secretary's mouth became very firm as she proceeded, the brown eyes narrowed and grew hard.

Suddenly she lettered an impatient exclamation and looked up. "Oh, these platitudes!" she said. "How are they going to help men and women to live?"

For a moment she had almost a desperate look, and then abruptly she laughed.

"Perhaps it isn't all your fault," she said to the manuscript by her side, "that you give us stones for bread. You have lived on them all your life and don't know the difference."

"How do you know?" said a voice at the window.

The secretary gave a start. Her eyes met the eyes of a man who stood against the clematis-covered window-frame looking in upon her—a careless, lounging figure as supremely at ease as a cat stretched in the sunshine.

He marked her brief confusion with a smile. "Do tell me how you know!" he said.

Her eyes fenced with his for a moment, then were proudly lowered. It was as if she drew a veil over her face.

"His lordship is not here," she remarked in a tone that was strictly official.

"So I have already observed," rejoined the new-comer, with his easy tolerance that was somehow quite distinct from familiarity. "In fact, at the present moment, I believe his lordship is in the thick of an argument with the Dean as to whether Shakespeare or Bacon wrote the Bible. It's rather an important point, you know. Have you any theories on the subject, might one ask?"

A little quiver that could hardly be described as a smile passed over the secretary's thin features, but her eyes remained upon her work.

"I don't go in for theories," she said, "or arguments. I am far too busy."

"By Jove!" he commented. "How you hate it!"

She raised her brows very slightly,—delicate brows, one of them a shade more tilted than the other, giving a quaint look of humour to a face that seldom smiled.

"I hate nothing," she said with precision, "I have no time."

"By Jove!" he said again, and chuckled as at some hidden joke.

The exasperating click of the typewriter put an end to all discussion, but it did not dislodge the intruder as was obviously intended. He merely propped himself against the grey stone-work of the window and took out his cigarette-case. His eyes dwelt with artistic appreciation upon the stately glories of the old garden, the arch of the cloisters against the summer blue, the wealth of purple flower adorning it. His face had the lines and the weather-tan of the man who has travelled far and wide, has looked upon the wonders of life and death with a certain cynical amusement, and returned almost to the starting-point with very little of value in his pack.

As the click of the typewriter persisted, he turned from his deliberate survey and gave his attention to a calm study of the woman seated behind it. His gaze was speculative, faintly humorous. There was something in that face of passive severity that aroused his curiosity. An insignificant type, it was true; but behind the insignificance there lurked something unusual that drew his interest. He wondered how long she would manage to ignore him.

On and on clicked the typewriter. The typist's lips were firmly closed, her eyes resolutely fixed upon her work. The watcher summoned his own resolution to wait upon opportunity, meditatively smoking the while.

Opportunity came at the end of some minutes of persistent clicking that might well have exasperated the most patient. The end of the page was reached, and there came a check. The secretary reached a thin, nervous hand for another sheet.

"Still more platitudes?" queried the man who leaned against the window-frame.

It would not have greatly surprised him had she made no response, but the sudden flashing upwards of her eyes came as a revelation. He straightened himself, almost as if he expected a blow.

"I am sorry," said the secretary very evenly, her eyes unswervingly upon him, "but you are disturbing me. I must ask you to go away."

He stood looking at her in frank astonishment. No woman had ever made him so simple and so compelling a request before. This from the secretary, the insignificant adjunct, the wholly undesirable and unknown etcetera of his uncle's household! There certainly was more here than met the eye!

He collected himself with an unwonted feeling of being at a disadvantage and instantly determined to save the situation at all costs. He leaned towards her, meeting the grave insistence of her look with a disarming smile. "Miss—Thorold, I haven't offended you?"

"No," said Frances Thorold briefly. "I am busy, that's all."

Her tone was official rather than ungracious, her eyes questioning rather than hostile, her whole attitude too impersonal for resentment. And yet it aroused resentment in the man. His smile vanished.

"I am sorry," he said stiffly, "to have appeared intrusive. That was not my intention. I only spoke to you because I heard your voice and imagined the hour for recreation had arrived. Pray accept my apologies!"

The firm lips relaxed a little, and a short sigh came through them. "There is no need for apology," she said. "No one apologizes to—a machine. But it has got to keep working, and it mustn't be interrupted."

"You can't work all day!" he protested.

She nodded. "I can. I do. And why not? It's what I'm here for."

Her voice had a note of challenge. Her eyes had gone beyond him. They rested upon the wealth of purple flower that crowned the coping of the cloister-arch in the hot sunshine, and again they held that wistful look as of baffled longing for the unattainable.

The man's eyes were upon her. They saw the longing. His anger passed.

"No machine will go for ever," he said, "if left to itself. The very best of them need occasional rest for adjustment and lubrication. Otherwise they run down and wear out before their time."

He was aware of the gleam of appreciation that crossed her intent face, and for the first time he marked the wary lines about her eyes. Then he met them again, and knew that he had scored a point.

She spoke in her brisk, official voice, returning to her work. "No doubt you are right. I shall have to oil it one of these days—when I have time."

"I shouldn't leave it too long," he said. "Take an engineer's advice! It's poor economy—may lead to a break-down in the end."

She adjusted the fresh page with deft care. "Thank you Mr. Rotherby. I shall remember your advice."

"And take it?" suggested Rotherby. Then, as she did not reply, "It may be dry bread, but it's better than stones, anyway."

He got what he angled for. She threw him a fleeting smile, and in a moment he caught the charm which up till then had eluded him.

It faded almost instantly as a picture fades from a screen. Only the official mask remained. Yet as he turned to depart, the gleam of satisfaction lingered in his eyes. He had made his small bid for amusement, and he had not bid in vain.

The monotonous clicking of the typewriter continued through the summer silence as the secretary pursued her task with erect head and compressed lips. With machine-like precision she tapped out the long, learned sentences, reading them mechanically, transmitting them with well-trained accuracy, aloof, uncritical, uninterested. She did not lift her eyes from her work again for a full hour.

Page after page was covered and laid aside. The Cathedral clock chimed and struck again. Then, in a quarter of an hour, there came the booming of a heavy gong through the house. Frances Thorold finished her sentence and ceased to work.

Her hands fell upon her lap, and for the moment her whole frame relaxed. She sat inert, as one utterly exhausted, her eyes closed, her head bowed.

Then, very sharply, as though at a word of rebuke, she straightened herself and began to set in order the fruits of her morning's work. She had laboured for five hours without a break, save for the brief interlude of Montague Rotherby's interruption.

At the opening of the door she rose to her feet, but continued her task without turning. The Bishop of Burminster had a well-known objection to any forms of deference from inferiors. He expressed it now as he came forward to the table at which she had worked for so long.

"Why do you rise, Miss Thorold? Pray continue your task. You waste time by these observances."

She straightened the last page and made quiet reply. "I think I have finished my task for this morning, my lord. In any case it is luncheon-time."

"You have finished?" He took up the pile of typescript with eagerness, but in a moment tossed it down again with exasperation. "You call that finished!"

"For this morning," repeated Frances Thorold, in her quiet, unmoved voice. "It is a lengthy, and a difficult, piece of work. But I hope to finish it to-night."

"It must be finished to-night," said the Bishop with decision. "It is essential that it should be handed to me for revision by nine o'clock. Kindly make a note of this, Miss Thorold! I must say I am disappointed by your rate of progress. I had hoped that work so purely mechanical would have taken far less time."

He spoke with curt impatience, but no shade of feeling showed upon his secretary's face. She said nothing whatever in reply.

The Bishop, lean, ascetic, forbidding of aspect, pulled at his clean-shaven chin with an irritable gesture. He had a bundle of letters in his hand which he flapped down upon the table before her.

"I had hoped for better things," he said. "There are these to be answered, and when is time to be found for them if your whole day is to be occupied in the typing of my treatise—a very simple piece of work, mere, rough copy, after all, which will have to be done again from beginning to end after my revision?"

"I will take your notes upon those this afternoon," said Frances. "I will have them ready for your signature in time to catch the midnight post."

"Absurd!" said the Bishop. "They must go before then."

She heard him without dismay. "Then I will do them first, and type the rest of the treatise afterwards," she said.

He made a sound of impatience. "A highly unsatisfactory method of procedure! I am afraid I cannot compliment you upon the business-like way in which you execute your duties."

He did not expect a reply to this, but as if out of space it came.

"Yet I execute them," said Frances Thorold steadily and respectfully.

He looked at her sharply, his cold grey eyes drawn to keen attention. "With very indifferent success," he commented. "Pray remember that, Miss Thorold, should the position you occupy ever tempt you to feel uplifted!"

She made no answer, and her face of utter passivity revealed nothing to his unsparing scrutiny. He passed the matter by as unworthy of further consideration. If any impertinence had been intended, he had quelled it at the outset. He did not ask for deference from his subordinates, but he demanded—and he obtained—implicit submission. He had a gift for exacting this, regarding everyone whom he employed as a mere puppet made to respond to the pulling of a string. If at any time the puppet failed to respond, it was thrown aside immediately as worthless. He was a man who had but one aim and object in life, and this he followed with untiring and wholly ruthless persistence. Before all things he desired and so far as his powers permitted he meant to achieve, the establishment of the Church as a paramount and enduring force above all other forces. With the fervour and the self-abnegation of a Jesuit, he followed unswervingly this one great idea, trampling down all lesser things, serving only the one imperative need. It was his idol, his fetish—this dream of power, and he worshipped it blindly, not realising that the temple he sought to erect was already dedicated to personal ambition rather than to the glory of God.

He worked unceasingly, with crude, fanatical endeavour—a man born out of his generation, belonging to a sterner age, and curiously at variance with the world in which he lived.

To him Frances Thorold was only a small cog-wheel of that machine which he was striving to drive for the accomplishment of his ends. The failure of such a minute portion of mechanism was of small importance to him. She had her uses, undoubtedly, but she could be replaced at almost any moment. She suited his purpose perhaps a shade better than most, but another could be very quickly fitted to the same end. He was an adept at moulding and bending the various portions of his machine to his will. Not one of them ever withstood him for long.

The rosy-faced Dean, with his funny Shakespearean hobby-horse, was as putty in his hands, and it never struck him that that same pink-cheeked curiosity was a tool infinitely more fit for the Master's use than he himself could ever be. Neither did he ever dream of the fiery scorn that burned so deeply in his secretary's silent soul as she bent herself to the burden he daily laid upon her. It would not have interested him had he known. The welfare of the dogs under the table had never been any concern of the Bishop of Burminster. They were lucky to eat of the crumbs.

And so he passed her by as unworthy of notice, merely glancing through her script and curtly noting a fault here and there, finally tossing the pages down and turning from her with a brief, "You will lunch with me, but pray be as speedy as possible and return to your work as soon as you have finished!"

That was his method of exacting the utmost from her. Under those hard grey eyes she would spend no more than the allotted half-hour out of the office-chair.

And the sun still shone upon that garden of dreams, while the bees hummed lazily among the blue and purple flowers. And all was peace and beauty—save for the fierce fanaticism in the man's heart, and the bitter, smouldering resentment in the woman's.

CHAPTER II
THE BREAK-DOWN

Four people sat at the old oak table in the oak-raftered dining-room of the Bishop's palace that day, and no greater contrast than they presented could well have existed among beings of the same race.

Dr. Rotherby—the Bishop—sat in pre-occupied silence scanning an ecclesiastical paper while he ate. He never encouraged conversation at any meal save dinner, and his sister, Miss Rotherby, nervous, pinched, and dyspeptic, supported him dutifully in this as in every other whim. She sat with her knitting on the table beside her ready to be picked up at every spare moment, on the principle that every second was of value—a short-sighted, unimaginative woman whose whole attention was concentrated upon the accomplishment of her own salvation.

Montague Rotherby, the sunburnt man of travel, sat between the two, and wondered what he was doing there. He had just wandered home from an expedition in Central Africa, and he had come hither with the half-formed intention of writing a book on his experiences. He wanted peace and quiet for the purpose, and these surroundings had seemed ideal. The Bishop and his sister had given him welcome, and he had believed himself to be fulfilling a family duty by visiting them. But he had begun already to realize that there was something very vital lacking in the atmosphere of the Palace. The place was stiff with orthodoxy, and he himself as much a stranger as he had ever been in the most desert corner of his travels.

"Can't stand this much longer," was his thought, as he sat before the polished board on this the fourth day of his sojourn.

And then his look fell upon the secretary seated opposite to him, and his interest stirred again.

She sat, remote and silent, in the shadow of a heavy green curtain against which the pallor of her face took a ghastly hue. Her eyes were downcast, the brows above them slightly drawn, conveying somehow an impression of mute endurance to the observant onlooker. He watched her narrowly, having nothing else to occupy him, and the impression steadily grew as the meal proceeded. She scarcely touched the food before her, remaining almost statuesque in her immobility, had her obvious insignificance not precluded so stately a term. To the man who watched her, her attitude expressed more than mere passivity. She was a figure of tragedy, and as it were in spite of itself his careless soul was moved to an unwonted compassion. In silence he awaited developments.

They came, more swiftly than even he anticipated. Very suddenly the Bishop looked up from his paper.

"Miss Thorold, you have work to do. I beg you will not linger here if you have finished."

His voice came with the rasp of authority through the sultry summer quiet. The secretary started as if at the piercing of a nerve and instantly rose to leave the table. She pushed in her chair methodically, but oddly at that point her intention seemed to fail her. She stood swaying as one stricken with a curious uncertainty, gazing straight upwards with dazed eyes that ever travelled farther and farther back as if they marked the flight of an invisible bird.

Rotherby sprang to his feet, but he was too late. Even as he did so, she threw up her hands like a baffled swimmer and fell straight backwards on the polished floor. The sound of her fall mingled with the furious exclamation that leapt to Rotherby's lips—an exclamation which he certainly would not have uttered in a more reasoned moment—and he was round the table and by her side almost before the two other spectators had realized what was taking place.

"Oh, good gracious!" gasped the Bishop's sister, pushing back her chair with the gesture of one seeking to avoid contact with something obnoxious. "What is it? What is the matter?"

"It is only a faint." Curt and contemptuous came the Bishop's reply. He also pushed back his chair and rose, but with considerably more of annoyance than agitation. "Lay her in that chair, Montague! She will soon recover. She is only overcome by the heat."

"Overcome!" growled Montague, and he said it between his teeth. In that moment, cool man of the world though he was, he was angry, even furious, for the white face with its parted, colourless lips somehow excited more than pity. "She's worn out—driven to death by that accursed typewriting. Why, she's nothing but skin and bone!"

He raised the slight, inert figure with the words, holding it propped against his knee while with one hand on the dark head he pressed it forward. It was a device which he had not thought would fail, but it had no effect upon the unconscious secretary, and a sharp misgiving went through him as he realized the futility of his efforts.

He flung a brief command upwards, instinctively assuming the responsibility. "Get some brandy—quick!"

"There is no brandy in the house," said the Bishop. "But this is nothing. It will pass. Have you never seen a woman faint before?"

"Damnation!" flared forth Montague. "Do you want her to die on your hands? There is brandy in a flask in my room. Send one of the servants for it!"

"This is dreadful!" wailed Miss Rotherby hysterically. "I haven't so much as a bottle of smelling-salts in the place! She has never behaved in this extraordinary way before! What can be the matter?"

"Don't be foolish!" said the Bishop, and firmly rang the bell. "She will be herself again in five minutes. If not, we will have a doctor."

"Better send for one at once," said Montague with his fingers seeking a pulse that was almost imperceptible.

"Very well," said the Bishop stiffly. "Perhaps it would be the wisest course. Why do you kneel there? She would be far better in a chair."

"Because I won't take the responsibility of moving her," said Montague.

"This is very painful," said Miss Rotherby tremulously, gathering up her knitting. "Is there nothing to be done? You are sure she isn't dead?"

"I am not at all sure," said Montague. "I shouldn't stay if I were you. But get someone to bring me that brandy at once!"

He had his way, for there was about him a force that would not be denied. In moments of emergency he was accustomed to assert himself, but how it came about that when the brandy arrived, the Bishop himself had gone to telephone for a doctor and the Bishop's sister had faded away altogether, lamenting her inability to be of use in so serious a crisis, even Montague could not very easily have said. He was still too angry and too anxious to take much note of anything beyond the ghastly face that rested against his arm.

Impatiently he dismissed the servant who was inclined to hang over him with futile suggestions, and then realized with a grimace that he was left in sole charge of a woman whom he scarcely knew, who might die at any moment, if indeed she were not already dead.

"Damn it, she shan't!" he said to himself with grim resolution as this thought forced itself upon him. "If these miserable worms can't do anything to save her, I will."

And he applied himself with the dexterity of a steady nerve to the task of coaxing a spoonful of brandy between the livid lips.

He expected failure, but a slight tremor at the throat and then a convulsive attempt to swallow rewarded him. He lifted her higher, muttering words of encouragement of which he was hardly aware.

"That's all right. Stick to it! You're nearly through. It's good stuff that. Damn it, why didn't that fool give me the water?"

"Yes, it—does—burn!" came faintly from the quivering lips.

"It won't hurt you," declared Montague practically. "Feeling better, what? Don't move yet! Let the brandy go down first!"

Her eyelids were trembling painfully as though she sought to lift them, but could not.

"Don't try!" he advised. "You'll be all right directly."

She stirred a groping hand. "Give me—something—to hold on to!" she whispered piteously.

He gripped the cold fingers closely in his own. "That's it. Now you'll be all right. I know this sort of game—played it myself in my time. Take it easy! Don't be in a hurry! Ah, that's better. Have a cry! Best thing you can do!"

The white throat was working again, and two tears came slowly from between the closed lids and ran down the drawn face. A sob, all the more agonizing because she strove with all her strength to suppress it, escaped her, and then another and another. She turned her face into the supporting arm with a desperate gesture.

"Do forgive me! I can't help it—I can't help it!"

"All right. It's all right," he said, and put his hand again on the dark head. "Don't keep it in! It'll do you more good than brandy."

She uttered a broken laugh in the midst of her anguish, and the man's eyes kindled a little. He liked courage.

He held her for a space while she fought for self-control, and when at length she turned her face back again, he was ready with a friendly smile of approval; for he knew that her tears would be gone.

"That's right," he said. "You're better now."

"Will you help me up?" she said.

"Of course." He raised her steadily, closely watching the brown eyes, drawn with pain, that looked up to his. He saw them darken as she found her feet and was prepared for the sudden nervous clutch of her hand on his arm.

"Don't let go of me!" she said hurriedly.

He helped her to a chair by the French window. "Sit here till you feel better! It's a fairly cool corner. Is that all right?"

Her hand relaxed and fell. She lay back with a sigh. "Just for two minutes—not longer. I must get back to my work."

"It's that damned work that's done it," said Montague Rotherby, with unexpected force. "You'll have to go on sick leave—for this afternoon at least."

"Oh no," said the secretary in her voice of quiet decision. "I have no time to be ill."

Rotherby said no more, but after a pause he brought her a glass of water. She thanked him and drank, but the drawn look remained in her eyes and she moved as if afraid to turn her head.

He watched her narrowly. "You'll have a bad break-down if you don't take a rest," he said.

She smiled faintly. "Oh no. I shall be all right. It's just—the heat."

"It's nothing of the kind," he returned. "It's overwork, and you know it. You'll either kill yourself or go stark staring mad if you keep on."

She laughed again at that, and though faint, her laughter had a ring of indomitable resolution. "Oh, indeed I shall not. I know exactly what my capabilities are. I have been unlucky to-day, but I am in reality much stronger than I seem."

He turned from her with the hint of a shrug. "No doubt you know your own business best, and of course I fully recognise that it is no part of mine to give advice."

"Oh, please!" she said gently.

That was all; but spoken in a tone that brought him back to her with a sharp turn. He looked at her, and was amazed at himself because the faint smile in her tired eyes gave him a new sensation.

"Wasn't that what you meant?" he said, after a moment.

"No," she made quiet answer. "I never mean that to the people who show me kindness. It happens—much too seldom."

She spoke with a dignity that was above pathos, but none the less was he touched. It was as if she had lifted the official mask to give him a glimpse of her soul, and in that glimpse he beheld something which he certainly had not expected to see. Again, almost against his will, was he stirred to a curious reverence.

"You must have had a pretty rotten time of it," he said.

To which she made no reply, though in her silence he found no sign of ungraciousness, and was more attracted than repelled thereby.

He remained beside her without speaking until the irritable, uneven tread of feet in the corridor warned them of the Bishop's return; then again he looked at her and found her eyes upon him.

"Thank you very much for all your kindness," she said. "Please—will you go now?"

"You wish it?" he said.

"Yes." Just the one word, spoken with absolute simplicity!

He lingered on the step. "I shall see you again?"

He saw her brows move upwards very slightly. "Quite possibly," she said.

He turned from her with finality. "I shall," he said, and passed out without a backward glance into the hot sunshine of the Palace garden.

CHAPTER III
A BUSINESS PROPOSITION

There was a sheet of water in the Palace garden, fed by a bubbling spring. Cypress and old yew trees grew along its banks, and here and there the crumbling ruins of an old monastery that had once adjoined the Cathedral showed ivy-covered along the path that wound beside it. It was said that the frocked figure of an ancient friar was wont to pace this path in the moonlight, but none who believed the superstition ever had the courage to verify it.

Montague Rotherby, wandering thither late that night after the rest of the household had retired, had no thought for apparitions of any description. He was wrapt in his own meditations, and neither the beauty of the place nor its eeriness appealed to him. He was beginning to realize that he had come to the wrong quarter for the peace his soul desired. A few brief, wholly dispassionate, words from his uncle's lips had made it quite clear to him that it was possible even for a man of his undeniable position in the world to outstay his welcome, and, being possessed of a considerable amount of pride, Montague needed no second hint to be gone.

But very curiously he found an inner influence at war with his resolution. He knew very well what had actuated the Bishop in giving him that very decided hint, and that very motive was now strangely urging him in the opposite direction.

To admit that he was attracted by that very insignificant and wholly unimportant person, the Bishop's secretary, was of course too preposterous for a man of his standing. The bare idea brought a cynical twist to his lips. But she had undeniably awakened his compassion—a matter for wonder but not for repudiation. Insignificant she might be, but the dumb endurance of her had aroused his admiration. He wanted to stop and see fair play.

Pacing to and fro beside the dark waters, he reviewed the situation. It was no business of his, of course, and perhaps he was a fool to suffer himself to take an interest in so comparatively slight a matter. It was not his way to waste time over the grievances of outsiders. But this woman—somehow this woman with her dark, tragic eyes had taken hold of his imagination. Scoff though he might, he could not thrust the thought of her out of his mind. Possibly her treatment of himself was one of the chief factors in her favour. For Montague Rotherby was accustomed to deference from those whom he regarded as social inferiors. It was true that he had taken her at a disadvantage that morning, but the very fact of his notice was generally enough to gain him a standing wherever he sought for one. To be held at a distance by one so obviously beneath him was a novel sensation that half-piqued and half-amused him. And she needed a champion too, yet scorned to enlist him on her side. It was wholly against her will that she had gained his sympathy. Though perfectly courteous, she had made it abundantly clear that she had no desire to be placed under any obligation to him. And, mainly for that reason, he was conscious of a wish to help her.

"She'll sink if I don't," he muttered to himself, and forgot to question as to what on earth it mattered to him whether she sank or swam.

This was the problem that vexed his soul as he paced up and down in the moonlight on that summer night, and as he walked the resolution grew up within him not to leave until he had had the chance of speech with her again. She might refuse to grant it to him, might seek to avoid him. Instinct told him that she would; but he was a man to whom opposition was as a draught of wine, and it had never been his experience to be withstood for long by a woman. It would amuse him to overcome her resistance.

So ran his thoughts, and he smiled to himself as he began to retrace his steps. In a contest such as this might prove to be, the issue was assured and could not take long of achievement; but it looked as if he might have to put a strain on the Bishop's hospitality for a few days even yet. Somehow that reflection appealed to his cynical sense of humour. It seemed then that he was to sacrifice his pride to this odd will-o'-the-wisp that had suddenly gleamed at him from the eyes of a woman in whom he really took no interest whatever—one, moreover, who would probably resent any attempt on his part to befriend her. Recalling her low words of dismissal, he decided that this attitude was far the most likely one for her to adopt, but the probability did not dismay him. A hunter of known repute, he was not easily to be diverted from his quarry, and, sub-consciously he was aware of possibilities in the situation that might develop into actualities undreamed-of at the commencement.

In any case he intended to satisfy himself that the possibilities no longer existed before he abandoned the quest. With no avowed end in view, he determined to follow his inclination wherever it might lead. She had given him a new sensation and—though perhaps it was not wholly a pleasant one—he desired to develop it further. To a man of his experience new sensations were scarce.

The effect of the moonlight, filtering through the boughs of the yew and striking upon the dark water, sent a thrill of artistic pleasure through his soul. He stood still to appreciate it with all the home-coming joy of the wanderer. What a picture for an artist's brush! He possessed a certain gift in that direction himself, but he had merely cultivated it as a refuge from boredom and it had never carried him very far. But to-night the romance and the beauty appealed to him with peculiar force, and he stood before it with something of reverence. Then, very softly chiming, there came the sound of the Cathedral clock, followed after a solemn pause by eleven deep strokes.

He counted them mechanically till the last one died away, then turned to retrace his steps, realizing with a shrug the lateness of the hour.

It was thus that he saw her standing in the moonlight—a slender figure, oddly girlish considering the impression she had made upon him that day, the face in profile, clear-cut, with a Madonna-like purity of outline that caught his artistic sense afresh. He realized in an instant that she was unaware of him, and stood motionless, watching her, afraid to move lest he should disturb her.

She had come to the edge of the water and was gazing up the rippling pathway that the moonlight flung from the farther shore to her feet. Her stillness had that statuesque quality that he had marked before in her, and, oddly, here in the moonlight he no longer found her insignificant. It was as if in this world of silver radiance she had mysteriously come into her own, and the man's spirit stirred within him, quickening his pulses. He wanted to call to her as one calls to his mate.

Perhaps some hidden telepathy warned her of his presence, perhaps she heard the call, unuttered though it was, for even as that unaccountable thrill went through him she moved, turned with a strange deliberation and faced him. She showed no surprise, spoke no word, her silence and her passivity surrounding her as though with a magic circle which none might cross without her leave. The mantle of her unobtrusiveness had fallen from her. She stood, superbly erect, queen-like in her pose and the unconscious dignity of her aloofness.

And Montague Rotherby was actually at a loss before her, uncertain whether to go or stay. It was a very transient feeling, banished by the swift assertion of his pride; but it had been there, and later he smiled ironically over the memory of his discomfiture. He had called to her too urgently, and she had replied with instant dismissal, though no word had passed between them.

Now, with determination and a certain audacity, he ignored her dismissal and took words for his weapon. With a smile he came towards her, he crossed the magic circle, protecting himself with the shield of the commonplace.

"I thought we should meet again," he said. "Are you better?"

She thrust past his shield with something of contempt. "I certainly did not expect to meet you—or anyone—here," she said.

His smile became almost a laugh. Did she think him so easily repulsed?

"No?" he said easily. "Yet we probably came—both of us—with the same intention. Tell me what happened after I left you this afternoon! I tried to find out from his lordship, but was badly snubbed for my pains, which I think you will admit was hardly fair treatment."

He saw her face change very slightly at his words, but she made no verbal response to them.

"I am quite well again," she said guardedly, after a moment. "Please do not trouble yourself any further about me! It is sheer waste of time."

"Oh, impossible!" he exclaimed gallantly; then, seeing her look, "No, seriously, Miss Thorold, I refuse to be put off like that. I've no right whatever—as you have every right to point out—but I must insist upon knowing what happened. I won't rest till I know."

She looked at him for a few seconds, her dark eyes very intent as though they searched behind every word he uttered for a hidden motive; then abruptly, with the gesture of one who submits either from indifference or of necessity, she made brief reply.

"What happened was a visit from the doctor and a solemn warning that I must take a rest as soon as his lordship can conveniently release me from my duties."

"Ah!" said Montague.

He had expected it, but somehow her method of conveying the news—though he realized it to be characteristic—took him by surprise. Perhaps, remembering that he had held her in her weakness a few hours before while she had wept against his arm, he had hoped for greater intimacy in the telling. As it was, he found himself actually hesitating as to how to receive it.

She certainly did not ask for sympathy, this woman of the curt speech and tired eyes. Rather she repudiated the bare notion. Yet was he conscious of a keen desire to offer it.

He stood in silence for a moment or two, bracing himself for a distinct effort.

"Does it mean very much to you?" he asked at length.

Her short laugh grated upon him. It had the sound of a wrong chord. She had smiled at him that morning, and he had felt her charm. Her laughter should have been sheer music.

Her voice had the same hard quality as she answered him. "No more than it does to most people when they lose their livelihood, I should say."

But, strangely, her words gave him courage to pass the barrier. He spoke as one worker to another.

"What damnable luck!" he said.

Perhaps they were the most sincere words he had yet spoken, and they pierced her armour. He saw her chin quiver suddenly. She turned her face from him.

"I shall worry through," she said, and her voice was brisk and business-like, wholly free from emotion. "I'm not afraid of that."

But she was afraid, and he knew it. And something within him leapt to the knowledge. He knew that he had found the weak joint.

"Oh, there's always a way out," he said. "I've been in some tight corners myself, and I've proved that every time." He broke off, with his eyes upon the rippling pathway of moonlight that stretched to their feet. Then, abruptly as she herself had spoken: "Is the Bishop going to do anything to make things easier?" he asked.

She made a small choking sound and produced a laugh. "Good heavens!" she said. "Do you really imagine I would let him if he would?"

"Why not?" said Montague boldly. "You've worked hard for him. If he has any sense of what is fitting, he will regard it in the light of a debt."

"Will he?" said Frances Thorold sardonically.

"If he hasn't the decency to do that—" said Montague.

She turned upon him in a flash and he saw that her bosom was heaving.

"Do you think I would take his charity?" she said. "Or anyone else's? I'd rather—far rather—starve—as I have before!"

"Good God!" said Montague.

He met the fierce fire of her eyes with a swift kindling of admiration in his own. Somehow in that moment she was magnificent. She was like a statue of Victory in the midst of defeat. Then he saw the fire die down, and marked it with regret.

"Good night," she said abruptly. "I am going in."

He thrust out his hand to her with a quickness of impulse he did not stop to question. "Please wait a minute!" he said. "Surely you are not afraid of my offering you charity?"

He smiled as he said it—the smile of confident friendship. There were moments when Montague Rotherby, with the true gambler's spirit, staked all upon one cast. And this was one of them. But—possessing also a considerable knowledge of human nature—he had small fear for the result. He knew before he put down his stake that he was dealing with a woman of too generous a temperament to make him suffer complete failure. Also, he was too old and too cynical a player to care greatly whether he won or lost. He was beginning to admit that she attracted him. But after all, what of it? It was only boredom that lent romance to this moonlight scene. In three days—in less—he could banish it from his mind. There were other scenes awaiting his careless coming, other players also . . . higher stakes. . . .

The thought was still running in his mind even as he felt the quick grip of her slender hand in his. He had not expected complete victory. It took him by surprise.

"You are far too good," she said, and he heard the quiver of emotion that she no longer sought to suppress in her voice, "too understanding, to offer me that."

He squeezed her hand in answer. "I'm offering you friendship," he said.

"Thank you," she said gently.

He smiled into her eyes. "It may be of an unorthodox kind, but that we can't help—under the circumstances. It's genuine anyway."

"I am sure of that," she said.

He wondered what made her sure, and was conscious of a moment's discomfiture, but swiftly fortified himself with the reflection that she was no girl, and if she were still lacking in experience of the ways of the world, that was her affair, not his. On second thoughts he did not believe her to be lacking in this respect. She had shown too much caution in her treatment of his earlier advances.

He released her hand, but he stood very close to her in the shadow of the cypress-tree. "And now—as a friend," he said, "will you tell me what you think of doing?"

She made no movement away from him. Possibly she had not the strength to turn away from the only human being in the world who had offered to stand by her in her hour of need. She answered him with a simplicity that must have shown him clearly how completely she had banished all doubt.

"I really haven't an idea what I shall do—what I can do, in fact, if my health gives way—unless," a piteous quiver of laughter sounded in her voice, "I go into the country and learn to milk cows. There seem to be more cows than anything else in this part of the world."

"But have you no resources at all?" he questioned. "No people?"

"But one doesn't turn to one's people for help," said Frances in her quiet way. "My parents both died long ago. I was dependent in my girlhood upon a married brother—a business man—with a family. I soon broke away, and there is no going back. It wouldn't be fair to anyone."

"Of course not," said Montague. "But wouldn't he tide you over this crisis?"

"While I learn to milk cows you mean?" The laughter in her voice sounded less precarious now. "I couldn't possibly ask him. He has sons to educate, and a wife whom I can't abide. It wouldn't be fair."

"But must you milk cows?" he questioned. "Is there nothing you can do to fill in time—till you get another secretary's job?"

"Ah! And when will that be? Secretary's jobs are not easily come by. I have only had one other, and then my employer died and I was out of work for months. That is why I can't afford to be out of work now. I've had no time to save."

She spoke without pathos, a mere statement of fact. He liked her for it. Her simple courage combined with her businesslike expression thereof attracted him more and more. Whatever hard blows Fate might have in store for her, he was convinced that she would endure them unflinching, would stand on her feet to the very end. It was refreshing to meet this sort of woman. With all the present-day talk of woman's independence he had seldom found her independent when hurt. He was beginning to realize wherein this woman's fascination lay. It was in the fact that whatever happened to herself she would accept responsibility. Whatever her losses might be, she would borrow no man's counters. She was answerable to none, and she held herself strong enough to hold her own.

That impression came upon him very forcibly as he talked with her, and it was to remain with him for all time. Here was a woman who made no claim of equality or independence, but—she stood alone.

"You are marvellously brave," he said, and he uttered the words almost involuntarily. "It makes me all the keener to be of use." He paused. "You know, I could be of use if you would allow me."

"In what way?" she said.

He hesitated. "You won't be angry—turn me down unheard?"

"You don't realize that I have great reason to be grateful to you," she said.

"You haven't," he returned quickly. "I am not much of a philanthropist. I don't pretend to take an interest in people who fail to interest me. I am no better than the majority, Miss Thorold, worse than a good many."

He saw her faint smile. "But better than some," she suggested.

He smiled in answer. "Well, perhaps,—better than some. Is there really nothing you can do to fill in time for the present? Because—I can find you another secretary's job later on, if that is what you really want."

"Can you?" she said. "But how?"

He was aware of a momentary embarrassment, and showed it. "It's entirely a business proposition. I am just home from Africa. I am going to write a book on travel and sport. I've got my notes, heaps of 'em. It's just a matter of sorting and arranging in a fairly digestible form. I shall want a secretary, and I have an idea we would arrive at an arrangement not injurious to either of us. You can help me if you will—if you care to—and I should think myself lucky to get anyone so efficient."

"How do you know I am efficient?" she asked in her straight, direct way.

He laughed a little. "Oh, that! Well, mainly by the way you headed me off this morning when I showed a disposition to interrupt the progress of your work."

"I see." She spoke quietly, without elation. His suggestion seemed to excite no surprise in her, and he wondered a little while he waited for more. "Do you want me to decide at once?" she asked.

"Don't you want to?" he continued. "You have no one—apparently—to consult but yourself."

"That is true. But—" she spoke gravely—"it takes a little while to consult even oneself sometimes. What if I took up work with you and found I did not like it?"

"You would be under no obligation to stop," he said, aware of a sudden, inexplicable desire to overcome her objections. "And you would be no worse off than you are at present. But—I flatter myself you would like it. I think the work would interest you. I am convinced at least that it would not bore you."

"That consideration would not influence me one way or the other," she said. "There are always drawbacks of some description to every walk of life, and boredom—well, boredom is by no means the worst of them."

"There I disagree with you," said Rotherby boldly. "If you can honestly say that, then you have never really lived."

"That is quite true," said Frances. "I never have."

He gave her a sudden, hard look. "Don't you want to?" he said.

She uttered her faint laugh, avoiding his eyes. "I don't—especially—want to starve," she said. "But—I assure you I would rather do that than fail to earn my keep."

"I fully realize that," he said. "Will you give me a trial then, or let me give you one? I don't know how you put these things, but it means the same thing, I believe."

"Oh no!" said Frances. "It means something very different. And neither you nor I had better make up our minds to-night. You are very kind, but very rash; and I think by to-morrow morning you may regret this. In any case, let us wait till then!"

"For your satisfaction or mine?" he said.

"For both." Prompt and steady came her reply, but he was disconcerted no longer.

"Will you tell me one thing?" he said.

Her eyes came to his. "Certainly if I can."

"Only this." He spoke quickly, with a certain mastery. "If by to-morrow I have not changed my mind, shall you accept my offer?"

She raised her brows slightly. "Why do you ask me that?"

"Because I want to know what to expect. I want to know if you make that condition for your sake or mine." Unhesitatingly he went to the point. He was very nearly sure of her, but still not quite.

She paused for some seconds before she answered him. He wondered if she were seeking a means of escape. Then very calmly she gave him her reply, and he knew that the game was his.

"I have said it was for both, because if you repent of the bargain, so shall I. But—if you do not repent, then I shall accept your offer with gratitude. But you have acted upon impulse, and I think you ought to take time to consider."

"It rests with me then?" said Rotherby.

"Yes, it rests with you." Quietly, even coldly, she yielded the point. "Of course, as you say, if you decide to take me, it will only be on trial. And if I fail to satisfy you, we are not worse off than we are at present. But please do not decide before to-morrow!"

The words were a request. The tone was almost a command. He could ignore neither, and he swept her a deep bow.

"Madam, your wishes in this matter shall be respected. To-morrow then—we decide!"

"Thank you," said Frances quietly.

She turned to go, but suddenly stopped short. He was aware of a change in her—a tremor of agitation.

"Ah!" she said, under her breath.

She was looking out of the shadow into the moonlight, and swiftly his eyes followed hers.

A figure in black was walking slowly and quite noiselessly over the grass by the side of the path.

"Who on earth—" began Montague.

She silenced him with a rapid gesture. "Hush! It is the Bishop!"

He reflected later that from her point of view it might have been wiser to have ignored the warning and have gone forth openly to meet the advancing intruder. But—perhaps it was the romance of the hour, perhaps merely her impulse communicating itself to him—or even, it might have been some deeper motive, barely acknowledged as yet that actuated him—whatever the influence at work, he obeyed her, drawing back in silence against the trunk of the yew tree.

And so, like two conspirators trapped in that haunted garden, they drew close together in the depth of the shadow and dumbly watched the black-gowned figure advance over the moonlit grass.

CHAPTER IV
THE ACCUSER

He came very slowly, with priest-like dignity, yet in his deliberation of movement there was purpose. It was seldom that the Bishop of Burminster performed any action without a definite end in view. There was indeed something almost fatalistic in all that he did. The wandering friar himself who was said to haunt that sleeping garden could not have moved with greater assurance or more studied detachment of pose.

The man and the woman watching him from their hiding-place drew closer together as if in some fashion his coming inspired them with awe. It was true that Montague Rotherby's lips bore a smile of cynical amusement, as though the situation appealed more to his sense of humour than to any other emotion. But it was not any humorous impulse that moved him to put his hand suddenly and reassuringly through the tense thin arm of the secretary and closely grip it.

She started sharply at his touch, made for a moment as if she would free herself, then stiffened and stood in rigid immobility.

For the Bishop was drawing nearer, and there was resolution as well as protection in Montague's hold.

Slowly came the advancing figure, and the tension of the two who waited grew acute. Though he smiled, Montague's teeth were clenched, and there was a glitter of ferocity in his eyes. He formed his plan of action while he waited. If the Bishop passed them by, he would release his companion instantly, bid her begone, and himself cover her retreat.

It was the only feasible plan, and in the morning she would thank him. In the morning she would realize that circumstances had placed her in his debt, and she would be ready to meet the obligation in accordance with his views. She certainly could not flout him or even keep him at a distance after this. Without forcing himself upon her, he had become her intimate friend, and she was not a woman to repudiate an obligation. She would acknowledge with gratitude all that he had done for her.

He no longer questioned with himself as to wherein lay the attraction that drew him. The attraction was there, and he responded to it, without scruple, as he had responded to such all his life. After all, it was no responsibility of his what she chose to do with her life. It was not likely that he was the first man to come into her existence. She knew very well what she was doing, and if she relaxed her guard he had no hesitation in storming her defence. After all, it was but a game, and women were quite as adroit in their moves as men, even more so in some cases, he reflected, though in this one it had certainly so far not been a difficult contest.

Swiftly the thoughts succeeded each other as he watched with a grim vigilance the advancing figure.

The Bishop was close to them now, almost abreast of them. He could see the harsh lines on the thin, ascetic countenance. There was something mediæval about that iron visage, something that was reminiscent of the Inquisition. This was the type of man who would torture and slay for the fulfilment of an ideal—a man of stern fanaticism, capable of the highest sacrifice, but incapable of that which even a dog may show to his master—the Divine offering of love.

Now he had reached the old yew in the shadow of which they stood, as if he had attained his destination he stood still.

Montague felt a sharp shiver run through his companion's arm, and he gripped it more closely, with a steady, warning pressure. The Bishop was not looking in their direction. There was yet a chance that he might pass on and leave them unobserved. The situation was ridiculous. They had no reason for concealing themselves. But the instinct, old as mankind, that prompts the two whom Fate has thrown together to avoid the intrusion of a third, the unacknowledged dread of being caught in an equivocal position, the half-formed wish to protect that gleaming, iridescent wonder that is called Romance from the sacrilegious touch of the outside world, all of these impulses had conspired to bring about this absurd concealment which the man found both gratifying and exasperating. To be discovered now would be humiliating, but if the critical moment passed and they were left in peace he recognized that another powerful link would be added to the chain that some caprice had induced him to forge.

As for the woman, he had no clue to her thoughts. He only knew that with her whole soul she hoped to escape undetected.

The Bishop had turned towards the edge of the lake, and was standing there in sombre reflection.

"What on earth is he thinking about?" questioned Montague with himself. "He can't know we are here! He wouldn't play such a cad's game as that."

Nevertheless his heart misgave him. He had no faith in the Bishop's sense of fair play. In his own weird fashion he believed him to be even more unscrupulous than he was himself. That any beauty of scene held him in that trance-like stillness he did not believe. He was merely thinking out some fell design for the glory of the fetish he worshipped.

Montague began to grow impatient. Were they to be kept there in suspense all night while he worked out his fantastic problems? He began to consider the possibility of making a move unheard and unseen while the Bishop remained wrapt in meditation. He had passed so close to them without seeing them that it seemed more than possible that an escape could be accomplished without any very serious risk.

He pressed his companion's arm and was aware of her eyes strangely luminous in the shadow turned towards him in enquiry. By some trick of the moonlight, the pale features took on a sudden unexpected beauty. He saw her in that moment not as the woman she was, faded and weary with the long harassment of overwork and anxiety, but as the woman she might have been, vivid, enchanting, young. . . . The illusion was so arresting that he forgot his purpose and stood, gazing upon her, bound by a spell that he had not known for years.

There came a sound through the magic stillness—the soft chiming of the quarter from the Cathedral tower. The Bishop stirred as if a hand had been laid upon him, stirred and turned.

His face was in the full moonlight, and it was the face of a denunciatory prophet. He spoke in hollow tones that reached them like a voice of doom.

"As I thought!" he said. "As I might have known! You may come out of your hiding-place. No subterfuge will serve either of you. Go—both of you! Let me never see you again!"

"Damnation!" said Montague.

The vision flashed away from him. He saw only the red fire of his wrath. Then, strangely, the vision returned. He saw her again—a woman of amazing possibilities, a woman to dream about, a woman to love. . . .

He took her cold hand very firmly into his own and led her forth.

She tried to resist him, to free herself. He knew that later. At the time he realized but the one overmastering determination to vindicate himself and her in the eyes of the denunciatory prophet. He strode forward and confronted him.

"Damnation!" he said again, and he flung the word with all the force of his fury. "Who are you to dare to speak to either of us in this strain? What the devil do you mean by it?"

He spoke as one man speaking to another, but the calm gesture of the Bishop's uplifted hand dispelled the situation before it could be established.

"Who am I?" he said. "I am a priest of the Lord to whom profanity is no more than the vapouring of fools. How do I dare to speak to you thus? I have never flinched from my duty in the bold rebuke of vice. What do I mean? I mean that you and this woman have been detected by me on the very verge of sin. And I tell you to go, because I cannot stop your sinning until you have endured your hell and—if God is merciful—begun to work out your own salvation."

"The man is mad!" said Montague.

A moment before, he had been in a mood to take him by the throat, but now he paused, arrested by the fanatical fervour of the Bishop's speech. Quite suddenly he realized that neither argument nor indignation would have the smallest effect. And, curiously, his anger cooled. Any other man he would have hurled into the placid waters of the lake without an instant's hesitation. But this man was different. Almost involuntarily he accorded him the indulgence which the abnormal can practically always command.

He turned very quietly to the woman whose hand had closed convulsively in his own, but who stood beside him, immobile and emotionless as a statue.

"Miss Thorold," he said, "I must apologize to you for—quite inadvertently—placing you in this extraordinary situation. The whole thing is too monstrous for discussion. I only ask you to believe that I regret it from the bottom of my heart, and I beg that you will not allow anything so outrageous to prejudice you with regard to the future."

Her eyes were downcast. She heard him without raising them. And still no shade of feeling crossed her death-white face as she made reply.

"I am not likely to do that," she said coldly and proudly. "I am not likely to blame you for showing kindness to me in the house of one whom mercy and humanity are unknown. I do not hold you responsible for another man's wickedness."

It was a challenge, clearly and unhesitatingly spoken, and Montague marvelled at the icy courage of her, the biting disdain. As she spoke, she drew her hand from his, and paused, facing him, not deigning to look upon her accuser; then, as he spoke no word, calmly, regally, with head erect but eyes cast down, she walked away over the moonlit grass, and so passed out of their sight.

CHAPTER V
THE HOLIDAY

The soft thudding of cows' feet through the red mud of a Devon lane—the chirruping call of a girl's voice in their rear—the warning note of a blackbird in the hedge—and the magic fragrance of honeysuckle everywhere! Was ever summer day so fair? Was ever world so green?

"Drat that young Minnie! If she hasn't taken the wrong turning again!" cried the voice that had chirruped to the herd, and there followed a chuckling laugh that had in it that indescribable sweetness of tone which is peculiar only to those of a contented mind.

It took Frances Thorold by storm—that laugh. She got up swiftly from her knoll, sketching block in hand, to peer over the hedge.

The hedge was ragged and the lane was deep, but she caught a glimpse of the red cows, trooping by, and of the pink dress and wildly untidy hair of their attendant. Then there came a sharp whistle, and a dog went scampering by, audible but unseen in the leafy depth of the lane. There followed a blundering check among the animals, and then again the clear, happy voice calling to order and the equally cheery bark of the dog.

"That'll do, Roger! Come back!" cried the bright voice. "Minnie won't do it again till next time, so you needn't scold. Now, Penelope, what are you stopping for? Get on, old girl! Don't hold up the traffic! Ah, here's a motor-car!"

It was not annoyance so much as a certain comic resignation that characterized the last sentence. The buzz of an engine and the sharp grinding of brakes upon skidding wheels succeeded it, and Frances, still peering over the ragged hedge, flushed suddenly and deeply, almost to the colour of the sorrel that grew about her feet.

She made a small movement as though she would withdraw herself, but some stronger motive kept her where she was. The car came grinding to a standstill almost abreast of her, and she heard the animals go blundering past.

"Thank you, sir," called the fresh voice, with its irresistible trill of gaiety. "Sorry we take up so much room."

"Don't mention it! You're as much right as I—if not more," called back the driver of the car.

Frances stirred then, stirred and drew back. She left her green vantage-ground and sat down again on the bank. Her eyes returned to her sketching-block, and she began to work industriously. The hot colour receded slowly from her face. It took on a still, mask-like expression as though carved in marble. But the tired look had wholly left it, and the drawn lines about the mouth were barely perceptible. They looked now as if they sought to repress a smile.

She chose a tiny paint-brush from her box, and began to work with minute care. The sketch under her hand was an exquisite thing, delicate as a miniature—just a brown stream with stepping-stones and beyond them the corner of an old thatched barn—Devon in summer-time. The babble of the stream and the buzz of a million insects were in that tender little sketch with its starry, meadow flowers and soft grey shadows. She had revelled in the making of it, and now it was nearly finished.

She had counted upon finishing it that afternoon, but for some reason, after that episode in the lane, her hand seemed to have lost its cunning. With the fine brush between her fingers she stopped, for her hand was shaking. A faint frown, swiftly banished, drew her brows, and then one of them went up at a humorous angle, and she began to smile.

The next moment very quietly she returned the brush unused to its box, laid both sketching-block and paints aside, and clasped her hands about her knees, waiting.

The commotion in the lane had wholly ceased, but there was a sound of feet squelching in the mud on the other side of the hedge. Frances turned her head to listen. Finally, the smile still about her lips, she spoke.

"Are you looking for someone?"

"By Jove!" cried back a voice in swift and hearty response. "So you're there, are you? I thought I couldn't be wrong—through a stream and past a barn, and down a hill—what damnable hills they are too in this part of the world! How on earth does one get up there?"

Quite concisely and without agitation she made reply. "One usually goes to the bottom of the hill, opens a gate and walks up on the other side."

"Oh, that's too much to ask," protested the voice below her. "Isn't there some hole where one can get through?"

"If one doesn't mind spoiling one's clothes," said Frances.

"Oh, damn the clothes—this infernal mud too for that matter! Here goes!"

There followed sounds of a leap and a scramble—a violent shaking of the nut-trees and brambles that composed the hedge—and finally a man's face, laughing and triumphant, appeared above the confusion.

"By gad," he said, "you look as if you were on a throne!"

She smiled at him, without rising. "It is quite a comfortable perch. I come here every day. In fact," she indicated the sketching-block by her side. "This is how I amuse myself."

He came to her, carrying a trail of honeysuckle which he laid at her feet. "May I share the throne?" he said.

She looked at him, not touching the flowers, her smile faintly quizzical. "You can sit on a corner of this rug if you like. It is rather a ragged affair, but it serves its purpose."

She indicated the corner furthest from her, and Rotherby dropped down upon it with a satisfied air. "Oh, this is a loafer's paradise. How are you getting on, Miss Thorold? You look—" he regarded her critically—"you look like one who has bathed in magic dew."

She met his look, her own wholly impersonal. "I feel rather like that," she said. "It has been a wonderful fortnight. I am quite ready for work."

He leaned upon his elbow, still carelessly watching her. "Have you learnt to milk cows yet?" he asked.

"Well, no!" She laughed a little. "But I have several times watched the operation. You saw that girl just now, driving the cows back to pasture for the night. She comes from such a dear old farm on the moor called Tetherstones. I have stood at the door of the cowshed and watched her. She is wonderfully quick at it."

"Is she going to give you lessons?" he said idly.

"I haven't got to the point of asking her yet. We only pass the time of day when we meet."

Frances picked up her sketching-block again. Her hand was quite steady now.

"May I see?" said Rotherby.

"When it is finished," she said.

"No, now, please!" His tone had a hint of imperiousness.

She leaned forward with the faintest possible suggestion of indulgence, such as one might show to a child, and gave it to him.

He took it in silence, studied it at first casually, then more closely, with growing interest, finally looked up at her.

"You ought to find a ready market for this sort of thing. It's exquisite."

She coloured then vividly, almost painfully, and the man's eyes kindled, watching her.

"Do you really think that?" she asked in a low voice.

"Of course I do. It isn't to my interest to say it, is it? You've mistaken your vocation."

He smiled with the words and gave her back the sketch.

"It isn't a paying game—except for the chosen few. But I believe I could find you a market for this sort of thing. I had no idea you were so talented."

"It has always been my pastime," said Frances rather wistfully. "But I couldn't make a living at it."

"You could augment a living," he said.

"Ah! But one needs interest for that. And I—" she hesitated—"I don't think I am very good at pushing my wares."

He laughed. "Well, I'll supply the interest—such as it is. I'll do my best anyway. You go on sketching for a bit, and I'll come and look on and admire. Shall I?"

She gave him a steady look. "When are you going to begin your book?"

"Oh, that!" he spoke with easy assurance. "That'll have to keep for a bit. I'm not in the mood for it yet. By and by,—in the winter——"

Her face changed a little. "In that case," she said, slowly, "I ought to set about finding another post."

"Oh, rot!" said Montague with lightness. "Why?"

She turned from her steady regard of him, and looked down at the sketch in her hand. "Because," she said, her voice chill and constrained as was its habit in moments of emotion, "I haven't money to carry me on till then. I shouldn't have wasted this fortnight if I had known."

"It hasn't been wasted," argued Montague, still careless and unimpressed. "You couldn't have done without it."

She did not lift her eyes. "It is quite true I needed a rest," she said, "but I could have employed the time in trying to find another post. I could have advertised. I could have answered advertisements."

"And ended up as you are now minus the cost of the postage," said Montague.

She took up her brush again. "Yes, that is quite possible; but I should have had the satisfaction of knowing that I had done my best."

"You've done much more for yourself by just taking a rest and sketching," said Montague. "Have you done any besides this?"

She answered him with her eyes upon her work. "Three."

"Will you let me see them?"

"If you wish."

"When?"

"Whenever you like."

"May I come round to-night then—sometime after dinner? I went round to your diggings just now. It was the old woman who sent me on here. Extraordinary old witch! Does she make you comfortable?"

"The place is quite clean," said Frances.

"That's non-committal. What's the food like?"

"I don't suppose you would care for it. It is quite plain, but it is good. It suits me all right, and it suits my purse."

He pounced upon the words. "Then why in heaven's name worry? A little extra holiday never hurt anyone, and you have got your sketching."

"I can't afford it," said Frances.

"But if you can sell some of your work."

"I can't," she said.

"Well, I can for you. It's the same thing. Look here, Miss Thorold! You're not being reasonable."

She turned again and faced him. Her eyes were very quiet, quite inscrutable.

"It is not that I am unreasonble, Mr. Rotherby," she said. "It is simply you—who do not understand."

There was stubbornness in his answering look. "I understand perfectly," he said. "I know what you are afraid of. But if you will only leave things to me, it won't happen. After all, you promised to be my secretary, didn't you? You can't seriously mean to let me down?"

"I!" Her eyes widened and darkened in genuine surprise. "I don't think you can very well accuse me of that," she said.

"Can't I? In spite of the fact that you are threatening to throw me over?" There was a bantering note in his voice, but his look was wary.

"I must think of myself," she said. "You forget I have got to make my living."

"No, I haven't forgotten. But there are more ways than one of doing that." His look fell suddenly to the trailing honeysuckle at her feet and dwelt there with an odd abstraction. "Surely you can fill in time as I have suggested," he said. "You won't be a loser in the end."

"I like to feel I am standing on firm ground," said Frances Thorold, and returned to her sketch with an air of finality as though thereby the subject were closed.

Montague took out a cigarette-case and opened it, offering it to her with the same abstracted air.

She shook her head without looking at him. "No, thank you. I've never taken to it. I've never had time."

"It seems to me that you have never had time for anything that's worth doing," he said, as he took one himself.

"That is true," she said in her brief way.

There fell a silence between them. Montague leaned upon his elbow smoking, his eyes half-closed, but still curiously fixed upon the long spray of honeysuckle as though the flowers presented to him some problem.

Frances worked gravely at her sketch, just as she had worked in the Bishop's room at Burminster a fortnight before, too deeply absorbed to spare any attention for any interest outside that upon which she was engaged. It was her way to concentrate thus.

Suddenly through the summer silence there came a sound—the voice of a little child singing in the lane below—an unintelligible song, without tune, but strangely sweet, as the first soft song of a twittering bird in the dawning.

Frances lifted her head. She looked at Montague. "Did you leave your car in the lane?"

"I did," he said, wondering a little at the sudden anxiety in her eyes.

"Ah!" She was on her feet with the word, her sketching almost flung aside. "She'll run into it."

"Absurd!" he protested. "Not if she has eyes to see!"

"Ah!" Frances said again. "She hasn't!"

She was gone even while she spoke, springing for the gap through which he had forced his way a few minutes earlier, calling as she went in tones tender, musical, such as he had never believed her capable of uttering. "Mind, little darling! Mind! Wait till I come to you!"

She was gone from his sight. He heard her slipping down the bank into the mud of the lane. He heard the child's voice lifted in wonder but not in fear.

"You are the pretty lady who came to see the cows. May I hold your hand?"

And Frances' answering voice with a deep throb in it that oddly made the listening man stiffen as one who listens to undreamt-of music:—"Of course you shall, sweetheart. We will walk up the road together and find some honeysuckle."

The man's eyes came swiftly downwards to the flowers that trailed neglected where her feet had been. So she did love honeysuckle after all! With a movement of violence half-suppressed he snatched up the pink and white blossoms and threw them away.

CHAPTER VI
THE CAPTURE

The description that Frances had given of the lodging she had found for herself in that little Devon village on the edge of the moors gave a very fair impression of the hospitality she enjoyed. The place was scrupulously clean, and, beyond this, quite comfortless. The fare was cottage fare of the very plainest. Her hostess—a stiff-limbed old creature, toothless, ungracious—was content to bestow upon her lodger the bare necessaries of life and no more.

"I can boil you up some hot water to wash in, but it'll be an extra," expressed her general attitude towards all things. And Frances, being unable to afford the luxury here implied, contented herself with the sweet, soft moorland water as it came from the pump at the cottage-door. In fact, she very often pumped her own in preference to accepting the grumbling ministrations of the old woman.

But she had been happy during that fortnight of enforced rest after leaving the Palace. The solitude and the boundless leisure of her days had brought healing to her tired soul. She was beginning to feel equipped to face the world afresh. She was looking forward to taking up secretarial work again of an infinitely more congenial character. Her first instinctive hesitation was past. She was prepared to take refuge once more in professional absorption, resolutely banishing all misgivings regarding the man who had hidden with her in the Bishop's garden and had taken his stand beside her in the Bishop's presence.

They had been cast forth,—she thought of it sometimes still with the tremor of a smile—they had been driven out as Adam and Eve, and neither of them would ever enter that garden again. Their intercourse since that night had been of the very briefest. Rotherby had obtained from her an address by which he could find her at any time. His attitude had been as business-like as her own, and she had been reassured. She had agreed to take a three weeks' holiday before entering upon her new duties, and now had come this. He had followed her to tell her that he would not now need her until the winter.

It had been a blow. She could not deny it. But already busily she was making her plans. He would have to understand clearly that she could not wait; but he had shown her great kindness, and if he really desired her services, she would try to find some temporary work till he should be ready. She wondered, as she sorted out her sketches in the little bare sitting-room in preparation for his coming that evening, if he really did need her, or if he had merely obeyed the impulse of the moment and had now repented. She recalled his careless gallantry which might well cover a certain discomfiture at having placed himself in a difficult position, his obvious desire to help her still by whatever means that might come to hand. Yes, it was impossible to formulate any complaint against him. He had been kind—too kind. He had allowed his sympathies to carry him away. But they should not carry him any farther. On that point she was determined. He should see her sketches—since he wished to see them—but no persuasion on his part should induce her to look upon them as a means of livelihood. She would make him understand very clearly that she could accept no benefits from him in this direction. As she had said, she must feel firm ground under her feet, and only by a fixed employment could she obtain this.

So ran her thoughts on that summer evening as she waited for his coming with a curious mixture of eagerness and reluctance. She marvelled at the kindness of heart that had prompted his interest in her. If she had been—as she once had been—an ardent, animated girl, it would have been a different matter. But she had no illusions concerning herself. Her youth was gone, had fled by like a streak of sunshine on a grey hillside, and only the greyness remained. It was thus that she viewed herself, and that any charm could possibly have outlived those years of drudgery she did not for a moment suspect. That any part of her character could in any fashion hold an appeal for such a man as Montague Rotherby she could not, and did not, believe. Pity—pity, alone—had actuated him, and he chose to veil his pity—for her sake—in the light homage which he would have paid to any woman whom he found attractive. Something in the situation, as she thus viewed it, struck a humorous note within her. How odd of him to imagine that a woman of her shrewdness could fail to understand! Ah, well, the least she could do was to let him continue his cheery course without betraying her knowledge of the motive that drove him. She would not be so ungrateful as to let him imagine that she saw through his kindly device. Only she must be firm, she must stand upon solid ground, she must—whatever the issue—assert the independence that she held as her most precious possession. Whatever he thought of her, he should never deem her helpless.

There came the click of the garden-gate, and she started with a sharp jerk of every pulse. Again, before she could check it the hot colour rushed upwards to her face and temples. She stood, strangely tense, listening.

He came up the path with his easy saunter. She knew it for the step of a man of the world. None of the village men walked thus—with this particular species of leisurely decision, unhurried assurance. He strolled between the line of hollyhocks and sunflowers and spied her by the window.

"Ah! Hullo! May I come in this way?"

He stepped over the low sill into the room. It was growing dusk. The air was extraordinarily sweet.

"There's a mist on the moors to-night," he said. "Can you smell it?"

"Yes," said Frances.

She gave him no word of greeting. Somehow the occasion was too unconventional for that. Or was it merely the manner of his entrance—the supreme confidence of his intimacy with her—that made conventional things impossible? He entered her presence without parley, because—obviously—he knew she would be glad to see him. The breath caught oddly in her throat. Was she glad?

The tension of her limbs passed, but she was aware of it still mentally,—a curious constraint from which she could not break free. She laid her sketches before him almost without words.

He took them and looked at them one after another with obvious interest. "You've got the atmosphere!" he said. "And the charm! They're like yourself, Miss Thorold. No, it isn't idle flattery. It's there, but one can't tell where it lies. Ah, what's this?"

He was looking at the last of the pictures with an even closer interest.

"That is the little blind child at Tetherstones," she said. "It is only an impression—not good at all. I couldn't get the appeal of her—only the prettiness. It isn't even finished."

"What, the child you went to in the lane this morning? But this is clever. You must finish this. You've got her on the stepping-stones too. She doesn't cross those alone surely!"

"Oh, yes, she goes everywhere, poor mite. She is just seven and wonderfully brave. Sure-footed, too! She wanders about quite alone."

"Poor kid!" Rotherby laid the sketch aside and turned to her. "Miss Thorold, I've come for a talk—a real talk. Don't freeze me!"

She smiled almost in spite of herself, and the thought came to her that he must have had a very winning personality as a boy. Gleams of the boy still shone out now and again as it were between the joints of his manhood's armour.

"Sit down!" she said. "Sit down and talk!"

But Rotherby would not sit. He began to pace the narrow room restlessly, impatiently.

"You accused me of letting you down this morning," he said, "and I protest against that. It wasn't fair. You've got a wrong impression of me."

"I!" said Frances.

"Yes, you!" He met her surprise with a certain ruthlessness. "I know it sounded like the other way round, but it wasn't actually. In your heart you felt I'd played you a dirty trick—let you down. Own up! Didn't you?"

She replied with that slight humorous lift of the eyebrow that was characteristic of her, "I really didn't put it quite like that—even in my heart, Mr. Rotherby. I owe you too much for that."

He flung round as if at the prick of a goad. "What do you owe me? Nothing whatever! Let's talk sense, Miss Thorold! You don't owe me anything—except perhaps some sort of reparation for the restless nights you have made me go through."

Dead silence followed his words, uttered on the edge of a laugh that somehow had a dangerous note. He had his back to her as he uttered them, but in the silence he turned again and came back, treading lightly, with something of a spring.

Frances stood quite straight and motionless, with that characteristic pose of hers that was in some inexplicable fashion endowed with majesty. She did not attempt to answer or avoid him as he returned. She only faced him very steadily in the failing light.

"Do you know what I mean?" he said, stopping before her.

She made a slight movement of negation, but she did not speak. She stood as one awaiting an explanation.

He bent towards her. "Don't you know what I mean, you wonderful woman? Haven't you known from the very beginning—you Circe—you enchantress?"

His arms came out to her with the words. He caught the slim shoulders, and in a moment he had her against his breast.

"Oh!" gasped Frances, and said no more, for he pressed her so closely to him that no further words could come.

She did not resist him. Burningly, afterwards, she remembered her submission, remembered how, panting, her lips met his, and were held and crushed till blindly she fought for breath but not for freedom. It all came like a fevered dream. One moment she had been a woman of the world—a business woman—cold, collected, calm; the next she a girl again, living, palpitating, thrilling to the rapture which all her life she had missed, drinking the ecstasy of the moment as only those who have been parched with thirst can drink. She was as it were borne on a great wave of amazed exultation. That he should love her—that he should love her! Ah, the marvel of it—and the gladness that was like to pain!

He was speaking now, speaking with lips that yet touched her own. "So now I have caught you—my white flame—my wandering will-o'-the-wisp! How dared you refuse my flowers this morning? How dared you? How dared you?"

He kissed her between each question, hotly, with a passion that would not be denied. And she lay there in his arms, quivering, helpless, wildly rejoicing in the overwhelming mastery of the great flood-tide on which she was borne.

Her life had been so singularly empty—just a fight for bare existence. There had been no time for new friendships—old friendships had waned. And now this! O God, now this!

She did not try to answer him. His kisses stayed all speech. His arms encompassed her—lifted her. He sat down on the little horse-hair sofa in the growing darkness, holding her. And she clung to him—clung to him—in the abandonment of love's first surrender.

CHAPTER VII
ROGER

It was like a dream—yet not a dream. Over and over again she marvelled afresh at the wonder of it, lying on the hard little bed in her room with the sloping roof, watching the misty stars through their long night march.

They had parted—somehow he had torn himself away, she could not remember how. She only remembered that after he had gone, he had returned to the window and said to her laughing, "Why not come up on to the moor and do sacrifice to the high gods with me?"

And she had answered, also laughing—tremulously, "Oh no, really I couldn't bear any more to-night. Besides, it is misty—we might be lost."

"I should like to be lost with you," he had answered, and had gone away laughing.

There had been something wild and Pan-like in his laugh. It was the laugh of the conqueror, and she tingled to the memory of it, thrilling like a delicate instrument to the hand of a skilled player. He had waked in her such music as none had ever waked in her before. She did not know herself any longer. This throbbing, eager creature was a being wholly different from the Frances Thorold of her knowledge, just as the man who had laughed and vanished like Pan into the mist had a personality wholly apart from that somewhat cynical but kindly gentleman who was Montague Rotherby.

What magic had wrought the change in them? What moorland spell was this, holding them as surely as a net about their feet? She was as one on the threshold of an enchanted world, afraid not so much of the unknown that lay before her as of the desert that lay behind—that desert which she had so miraculously quitted for this place of amazing gladness.

Once in the night she arose and went to the little cottage-window since sleep was impossible. It came to her there as she stood gazing up at those far dim stars to breathe a deep thanksgiving for this strange deliverance. But the words she sought to utter would not come. The vague mist, floating like smoke, seemed to cling about her soul. She stood speechless, and so standing she heard a voice, denunciatory, fanatical, speak suddenly within.

"I tell you to go, because I cannot stop your sinning until you have endured your hell and—if God is merciful—begun to work out your own salvation."

So clearly fell the words upon her consciousness that she felt as if they had been uttered by her side. She almost turned to see who spoke. Then, remembering, a sharp shudder went through her. She shrank and caught her breath as though she had been pierced.

Was this the magic that had caught her—the awful magic of temptation? Was there poison in the draught which she had drunk with such avidity? This enchanted land to which she had come after weary years of desert journeying, was this to prove—her hell?

As if stricken with blindness, she stumbled back into the room and lay down. All her former doubts swept over her afresh in a black cataract of misgiving. Love her—faded and tired and dull? How could he love her? What could a man of this sort, rich, popular, successful, see in a woman of hers save an easy prey? She lay and burned in the darkness. And she had given him all he asked in that amazing surrender. She had opened to him her very soul. Wherefore? Ah, indeed, wherefore? Because he had overwhelmed her with the audacity of his desire! For no other reason—no other reason! How could this thing be Love?

So she lay, chastising herself with the scorpions of shame and fear and desolation—because she had dared to dream that Love could ever come to her. At last—in that terrible vigil—she found words wherewith to pray, and in an agony of supplication she made her prayer: "O God, keep me from making a mistake! Let me die sooner! Let me die!"

And though no answer came to her then, tears came instead and washed the burning anguish away. Afterwards she slept. . . .

In the morning she awoke to see the sun drawing up the mist like a veil from the green earth. All the evils of the night were gone. She arose wondering at the emotions that had so torn her a few hours before. After all, if she kept her soul with steadfastness, what had she to fear? She viewed the strange event of the previous evening with a curious sense of detachment, almost as if it had happened to another person, very far removed from herself. She was calm now, calm and strong and no longer afraid. The habit of years had reasserted itself. She girt herself anew in the armour which till then had never failed her. Work was her safeguard as well as her necessity. She would waste no further time in idleness.

After breakfast she set forth on a three-mile tramp to the nearest town to buy a newspaper, promising herself to spend the afternoon answering advertisements. Her way lay by a track across the moor which she had never before followed. The purple heather was just coming into bloom and the gold of coronella was scattered every where about her path. The singing of larks filled the whole world with rejoicing. She thought that the distant tors had never been so blue.

About a mile from the village, on the edge of a deep combe through which flowed the babbling stream of her sketch, she came to the farm called Tetherstones, and here, somewhat to her surprise, she was joined by the dog, Roger. He bounded to her, his brown eyes beaming good fellowship through his shaggy hair, and at once and quite unmistakably announced his intention of accompanying her. No amount of reasoning or discouragement on her part had the smallest effect upon his resolution. Beaming and jolly he refused to pay any attention to either, having evidently decided to take a day off and spend it in what he regarded as congenial society. She found it impossible to hide from him the fact that she loved his kind, and he obviously considered her honest attempt to do so as a huge joke, laughing whenever she spoke in a fashion so disarming that she was very soon compelled to admit herself defeated.

They went on together, therefore, Roger with many eager excursions into the heather, till Tetherstones was left far behind. Then, at last, Frances, growing weary, sat down to rest, and Roger came, panting but still cheery, to lie beside her.

She fondled his beautiful shaggy head with an understanding touch. "What a funny fellow you are," she said, "to follow me like this."

Roger smiled at her, his tongue hanging between his pearly teeth, and laid a damp, podgy paw upon her lap. She understood him to express his warm appreciation of the company in which he found himself.

"They'll think I've run away with you," she said.

And he shook his ears with a nonchalance that said very plainly that it was no concern of his what they thought.

Then there came a tramp of hoofs along the white, sandy track, and she saw a man on horseback coming towards them through the glare. Roger sat up sharply and, gulping, ceased to pant.

She saw that his eyes were fixed upon the advancing horseman though he made no movement to leave her side. The thud of the approaching hoofs had a dull fateful sound to her ears. She experienced an odd desire to rise and plunge deep into the heather to avoid an encounter. But the tenseness of the dog by her side seemed to hold her also motionless. She waited with a strange expectancy.

The dazzling sunshine made it impossible for her to see what manner of man the rider was until he was abreast of her. Then she realised that he was broad and heavy of build. He wore a cap drawn down over his eyes.

The sudden checking of the horse made her start. "Roger!" a deep voice said, "What the devil are you doing here?"

Roger started also, and she felt a quiver as of guilt run through him. He got up with an apologetic air, and stood wagging his funny stump of a tail ingratiatingly.

It seemed to Frances that even the horse looked apologetic halted there at his master's behest.

"Roger!" the new comer said again. Roger's tail dipped and became invisible in the bushy hair of his hindquarters. He crept forward with a slinking air as if he yearned for a deep hole in which to bury himself.

The man on horseback waited quite motionless till the dog reached his foot, then suddenly he leaned down and struck him a stinging cut with his riding-whip.

The dog cried out, and fled to a distance, and Frances, her hands gripped in the heather on both sides of her, uttered an involuntary exclamation.

The horseman, preparing to go on, paused. "Did you speak, madam?" he asked, scowling at her from under the peak of his cap.

She collected herself and rose to the occasion. "No! There are no words for a thing of that sort," she said, icily contemptuous.

He put up a hand, ironically courteous, and saluted her. She saw the hard line of a very prominent jaw as he rode on.

The dog fell in behind and meekly followed him.

"What a bear!" said Frances. "I suppose that is the owner of Tetherstones. Or—no! Someone said that was an old man. Then this must be his son."

She arose and pursued her way, a grim sense of amusement succeeding her annoyance. How curious it was of people to go out of their way to be objectionable! They so seldom injured anyone except themselves in the process.

She had not thought that a walk across the moors would have tired her overmuch, but the day was hot and she very soon realised that she would need a considerable rest before returning. She had breakfasted early and none too bountifully, and she had brought no refreshment with her, counting on obtaining it when she reached her destination at Fordestown.

But Fordestown was a long way off, further than she had anticipated, and she began after a while to wonder if she had done wisely in attempting the walk. She felt lonely after Roger had left her. The great spaces of the moors had a bewildering effect upon her tired senses. The solitude weighed upon her.

Then, after what seemed an endless period of walking, she came to a cross-track with no indication as to whither the branching by-path led. There was no habitation in sight, no sign of life beyond that of the larks singing interminably in the blazing blue overhead, no possibility of knowing in which direction she ought to turn.

Her heart began to fail her a little, and she sat down again to consider the problem. The whirr of grasshoppers arose in a ceaseless hum around her. The distant hills swam before her aching vision. She sank deep into the scented heather and closed her eyes.

She had meant to give herself only the briefest rest, but she was in a place where Nature reigned supreme, and Nature proved too much for her. Her lids were sealed almost immediately. The hum of insects became a vague lullaby to her jaded nerves. She slipped deeper and deeper into a sea of slumber that took her and bore her with soft billowings into an ocean of oblivion. She slept as a child sleeps—as she had not slept for years—the soul as it were loosed from the body—her whole being perfectly at rest.

CHAPTER VIII
THE ROAD TO NOWHERE

Often she wondered afterwards how long that sleep would have lasted, if it had been left to Nature to awake her. It was so deep, so dreamless, so exquisite in its utter restfulness. She never slept thus in the open before. The magic of the moors had never so possessed her. And she had been so weary. All the weariness of the weary years seemed to go to the making of that amazing sleep of hers in the heather. She was just a child of Nature, too tired for further effort. She slept for hours, and she would have slept for hours longer, but for the interruption.

It came to her very suddenly, so suddenly that it seemed to her that the soul had scarcely time to gird itself anew in the relaxed body, before the amazing battle was upon her. She sprang upright in the heather, gasping, still trammelled in the meshes of sleep, defenceless, to find the day nearly spent and a curtain of mist surrounding her; and, within that curtain, most terribly alone with her, she also found Montague Rotherby.

Her recognition of him came with a choking cry. She realized that he had only just reached her, that his coming must have called her back from that deep oblivion in which she had been so steeped. But that first sight of him—alone with her—alone with her—within that strangely shifting yet impenetrable curtain—showed her something which to her waking vision—made keen by that long spell of rest—was appalling. She was terrified in that moment as she could not remember that she had ever been terrified before.

He bent over her. "Found!" he said and laughed with a triumph that seemed to stab her. "I've had a long hunt for you. Have you been hiding here all day?"

"No," she said, through lips that felt strangely stiff, compelling her voice with difficulty. "I lost my way. I fell asleep. I am just going to Fordestown."

"Going to Fordestown! Why, it's miles away! Why didn't you wait till I came to you? You knew I should come."

His voice had a caressing quality. It drew her against her judgment. Her wild, unreasoning fear subsided somewhat. She smiled at him, though still her lips felt stiff.

"I expected to be back by that time," she said. "I started quite early."

"But why did you start at all?" he said.

He was still bending over her. She gave him her hands with a slight gesture of appeal to help her up. He took them and drew her upwards into his arms.

Holding her so, in spite of her quick effort for freedom, he looked deeply into her eyes. "Tell me why you went!" he said.

She hesitated, trying to avert her face.

"No, that won't help you," he said, frustrating her. "Tell me!"

Unwillingly she answered him. "I had a bad night, and I decided—in the morning—that—I had better look for work."

"Why did you decide that?" he said.

She made a more determined stand against him. "I can't tell you. It's natural, isn't it? I have always been independent."

"Till you met me," he said.

She summoned her courage and faced him though she knew that she was crimson and quivering. "I shall go on being independent," she said, "until we are married."

She expected some subtle change of countenance, possibly some sign of discomfiture, as thus boldly she took her stand. But at once he defeated her expectations. He met her announcement with complete composure. He even smiled, drawing her closer.

"Oh, I think not," he said. "After what happened yesterday we won't talk nonsense of that kind to-day. What is the matter, sweetheart? Has someone been troubling you?"

She relaxed somewhat. It was impossible not to respond to the tenderness of his voice and touch. But he had not satisfied her; the misgiving remained.

"Only my own mind—my own reason," she confessed, still painfully seeking to avoid his look.

"After—yesterday!" he said.

The reproach of his tone pierced her. She hid her face against his breast. "I couldn't help it. You must make allowances. There has been no time for—love-making—in my life."

"There's time now," he said, and again she heard in his voice the note of triumph that had so deeply disquieted her. "It's not a bit of good trying to run away at this stage. You're caught before you start."

"Ah!" she said.

He held her fast. "Do you realize that?"

She was silent.

He held her faster still. "Frances! Put your arms round my neck and tell me—tell me you are mine!"

She shrank, hiding her face more deeply. He had lulled her distrust, but he had not gained her confidence.

"You won't?" he said.

"I can't," she whispered back.

He felt for her face and turned it upwards. "You will presently," he said, and bending, kissed her, holding her lips with his till she broke free with a mingled sense of shame and self-reproach.

"What is it?" he said, watching her, and she thought his face hardened. "You have changed since yesterday. Why?"

She laid a pleading hand upon his arm. Yes, she had changed; she could not deny it. But she could not tell him why.

"I think we have been—rather headlong," was all she found to say.

And at that he laughed, easily, cajoling her. "Well, we've gone too far to pull up now. Perhaps it will be a lesson to you next time, what? But no more of your will-o'-the-wisp performances on this occasion, O lady mine! We'll play the game, and as we have begun, so we will go on."

He kissed her again, and his kiss was almost a challenge.

"Don't you realize that I love you?" he said. "Do you think I am going to lie awake all night for you, and then not hold you in my arms when we meet?"

He laughed as he uttered the question, but it had a passionate ring. His lean, sunburnt face had a drawn look that oddly touched her pity. She was even moved to compunction.

"I am sorry," she said. "I thought—perhaps—it was just—a passing fancy."

"My fancies don't pass like that," said Montague.

He spoke almost moodily, as if she had hurt him, and again her heart smote her.

"I am beginning to understand," she said. "But—you must give me time. We hardly know each other yet."

"That is soon remedied," he said. "I warn you, I am not a very patient person. There is nothing to wait for that I can see."

"Oh, we must wait," she said. "We must wait."

He broke again into that odd laugh of his. "We won't wait. Life is too short." He stooped again to kiss her. "You amazing woman!" he said. "Do you really prefer stones to bread?"

She could not answer him. He had her defeated, powerless. She had no weapons with which to oppose him. But still deep in her heart, the doubt and the wonder remained. Was this indeed love that had come to her? If so, why was she thus afraid?

Yet she met his lips with her own, for somehow he made her feel that she owed it to him.

"That's better," he said, when he suffered her to go again. "Now, what are your plans? Are you still wanting to go to Fordestown?"

She hesitated. "You say it is a long way?"

"It's miles," he said. "You are right out of your way. What made you wander up here?"

"They told me it was a short cut across the moor," she said.

He laughed. "Ah! These short cuts! Well, what are you going to do?"

She looked at him, "Do you know—I haven't had anything to eat all day—not since breakfast?"

"Good heavens!" he said. "You've been wandering about the moor starving all this time?"

She smiled. His concern touched her. Not for years had anyone expressed any anxiety for her welfare.

"Not wandering about much," she said. "I got as far as this this morning, and then, while I was considering which way to go, I fell asleep." She glanced about her uneasily. "Do you think this fog is going to get any worse?"

"Oh no!" he said lightly. "It's nothing. They often come up like this in the evening. But look here! I can't have you starving. We had better make for Fordestown after all."

"But—is it far?" She still hesitated. "Do you know the way?"

"I know the direction. I can't say how far it is. But it is nearer than Brookside. There is a fairly decent inn there. I am staying there myself."

"Oh!" she said with relief. "Then if we can only get there, you can motor me back to Brookside."

"The point is to get there," said Montague.

"But you know the direction. Do let us start before it gets any worse! I am quite rested."

She spoke urgently, for he seemed inclined to linger. He turned at once.

"Yes. You must be famished. This is the way."

He drew her hand through his arm with decision and began to lead her up one of the sandy tracks.

The mist closed like smoke about them, and Frances felt it wet upon her face. "We seem to be in the clouds," she said.

"I think we are," said Montague.

"You are sure we are going right?" she said.

He laughed at her. "Of course we are going right. Don't you trust me?"

Trust him! The words sent a curious sensation through her. Did she trust him? Had she ever—save for that strange, delirious hour last night really trusted him? She murmured something unintelligible, for she could not answer him in the affirmative. And Montague laughed again.

Looking back upon that walk later, it seemed to her that they must have covered miles. It was not easy going. The track was rough, sometimes stony, sometimes overgrown. She stumbled often from weariness and exhaustion; and still they went on endlessly over the moor. Always they seemed to be going uphill, and always the mist grew thicker. Here and there they skirted marshy ground, splashing through puddles of black water, and hearing the sound of running streams close at hand but invisible in the ever-thickening mist.

It began to grow dark, and at last Frances became really anxious. They had not spoken for a long time, merely plodding on in silent discomfort, when abruptly she gave voice to her misgivings.

"I am sure we are wrong. This path leads to nowhere."

"It leads to Fordestown," he declared stubbornly, "if you keep on long enough."

"I don't think I can keep on much longer," she said.

"I told you it was miles," said Montague.

She heard the sullen note in his voice, and her heart sank. Progress was becoming increasingly difficult. Very soon they would not be able to see the path.

She stood still suddenly, obedient to an inner urging that would not be denied. "Oh, let us go back!" she said.

He pressed her arm to his side with sharp insistence and drew her on. "Don't be ridiculous! Do you want to spend the night in the open moor?"

"It is what I am afraid of," she said desperately. "If we go back we can at least find the way back eventually to Brookside. But this—oh, this is hopeless!"

"Don't be ridiculous!" he said again. "It is just possible that we have taken a wrong turn in this infernal fog, but it's bound to lead to somewhere. There are no roads in England that don't."

She yielded to him, feeling she had no choice. But her alarm was increasing with every step she took. It seemed to her that they were actually beginning to climb one of the tors! Now and again, they stumbled against boulders, dimly seen. And it was growing very cold. The drifting fog had turned to rain. Her feet had been wet for some time, and now her clothes were clinging about her, heavy with damp. She felt chilled to the bone, and powerless—quite powerless—to do anything but go whither she was led.

It was as if her will-power were temporarily in abeyance. This man was her master, and she had no choice but to obey his behests. She began to move as one in a dream, dimly counting her halting footsteps, vaguely wondering how many more she would accomplish.

And then quite suddenly she seemed as it were to reach a point where endurance snapped. She pitched forward, against his supporting arm.

"I can't go—" she cried out—"I can't go—any further."

He caught her as she fell. She was conscious of the brief physical comfort afforded by the warmth of his body as he held her. Then, oddly, over her head she heard him speak as if addressing someone beyond her. "That settles it," he said. "It's not my fault."

She knew that he lowered her to the ground, still holding her, and began to rub her numbed and powerless hands.

CHAPTER IX
THE LIONS' DEN

"From all evil and mischief, from sin, from the crafts and assaults of the devil" . . .

Someone was saying the words. Frances opened her eyes upon blank darkness, and knew that her own lips had uttered them. She was lying in some sort of shelter, though how she had come thither she had no notion. The rain was beating monotonously upon a roof of corrugated iron. She lay listening to it, feeling helpless as a prisoner clamped to the wall. And then another voice spoke in the darkness, and her heart stood still.

"That's right. You're better. Gad, what a fright you gave me! Now do stop raving! You're only tired and a bit faint."

"I am not—raving," she said. "I am only—I am only—" Again without her conscious volition she knew herself to be uttering those words she had heard: "From all evil, and mischief, from sin, from the crafts and assaults of the devil—" She paused a moment, groping as it were for more, then:—"Good

Lord, deliver us!" she said, and it was as if her soul were speaking in the darkness.

"Frances!" a voice cried sharply, and she stopped, stopped even her breathing, to listen. "Stop talking that absurd rot! Be sensible! Try to be sensible!"

"I am only—praying," she said.

"Well, don't! It isn't the time for saying prayers. I want you to attend to me. You know what has happened?"

His voice sounded curt and imperious. She peered into the darkness, wishing she could see his face.

"I don't know," she made answer wonderingly. "How should I know?"

"I brought you here," he said. "You fainted."

"How stupid of me!" she murmured apologetically.

"It was rather." His voice was grim. "But you've got back your senses, and for heaven's sake keep them! This is just an old cattleshed on the moors and it's all the shelter we shall get to-night."

"Oh!" said Frances, and in her voice dismay and relief were strangely mingled. "It was better than the open moor. But yet—but yet——"

He spoke again with a species of humorous ruefulness. "Here we are, and here we've got to stay! That damned fog has defeated us. We can't hope to move before morning."

"I wish we had a light," said Frances.

She was gradually getting a grasp of the situation, and though her body felt oddly heavy and her head strangely light, her wits were recovering their customary business-like balance.

"I have got a few matches," said Montague. "Also a few cigarettes. Afraid it's useless to attempt a fire. We should only smoke ourselves out—and possibly fire the shed as well. The only comfort we have got is a little hay, and you are lying on it."

"Where are you?" she said.

"Here!" A hand suddenly touched her, and she started with involuntary shrinking. A great shivering came over her, and for a space she struggled to control her chattering teeth.

"You are cold," he said.

"Yes,—dreadfully cold. But never mind! It—it's better than being out in the open, isn't it? You have no idea where we are?"

"I lost my way," he said moodily.

She reached out to him a trembling hand, and realized that he was standing propped against the wall beside her. He stooped quickly, grasping her cold fingers.

"Frances, we've got to face it. You may as well give in to circumstances. We're both of us helpless."

His voice had an odd urgency. It was as if he pleaded with her.

"Oh, I quite realize that," she said, and she strove to force a practical note into her reply. "We've been very unlucky, but what can't be cured must be endured. We shall come through it somehow."

She would have removed her hand, despite the physical reluctance to relinquish the warmth of his, but he held it fast.

"You don't want me to go?" he said.

"Oh no!" she returned briskly. "I am not so selfish and unreasonable as that. We must just make the best of it. We must just—just———"

She broke off. Her teeth were chattering again, and in the effort to check them, she forgot the words she was trying to utter.

She felt him bend lower, and found him kneeling by her side. "It's no good offering you my coat," he said. "There's no warmth in it. Besides, it's wet through. But I'm not going to let you die of cold for all that—just for the sake of an idiotic convention. Frances—sweetheart—I'm going to hold you in my arms."

Fear stabbed her—sharp and agonizing. "Oh no!" she said, and drew herself back from him. "Not here! Not now!"

Her hand remained locked in his, but he paused.

"Why not here—and now?" he said.

She gasped her quivering answer. "Because—because—I am not sure if I have done right in—in letting you make love to me. I have not been sure—all day."

"You don't love me?" he questioned.

"I don't know," she said. "I can't—possibly—know yet."

"But you knew yesterday," he said.

"Ah, yesterday!" The word came almost with a cry. "I was mad yesterday," she said.

"Why mad?" he reasoned. "My dear, listen to me! Here we are—far away from everywhere—miles away from civilized society. What does it matter—what can it matter—if we throw aside these idiotic conventions just for one night? You know in your heart that it doesn't matter one jot."

"It does matter," she gasped back painfully, still striving vainly to free the hand he held so closely. "It does matter."

"That means you don't trust me," he said.

"I would if I could," she made desperate answer. "But—but———"

"But—" he echoed grimly, and let her go.

She heard him get up from his knees, and breathed a sigh of thankfulness.

A moment later there came the rasp of a match and a sudden glare in the darkness. Her eyes turned instinctively, though dazzled, to the light. She saw his face, and again instinctively she shrank. For in the eyes that sought her own there burned a fire that seemed to consume her.

He was lighting a cigarette. He looked at her above it, and his look held a question she dared not answer. Again a terrible shivering caught her. The light went out, and she covered her face.

The man spoke no further word. He smoked his cigarette in the darkness till presently it was finished, and then he threw down the glowing end and ground it under his heel.

The silence between them, like the darkness, was such as could be felt. Only the drip, drip of the rain sounded—oddly metallic, like the tolling of a distant bell.

Frances sat huddled against the wall, not moving, not able to move. Her heart was beating with dull, irregular strokes, and her fear had died down. Perhaps she was too exhausted to be actively afraid. A sense of unreality had descended upon her. She had the feeling of one in a dream. Though from time to time violent shivers caught her, yet she was scarcely aware of them. Only now and then the cold seemed to pierce her like a knife that reached her very soul.

And when that happened she always found herself repeating in broken phrases the prayer which no conscious effort brought to her lips. "From all evil and mischief—from sin—from the crafts—and assaults—of the devil—" Sometimes she thought it was the Bishop reciting the words, but she always realized in the end that she was saying them herself, and wondered—and wondered—why she said them.

Her impressions grew blurred at last. She must have dozed, for suddenly—as one returning from a long distance—she started to the sound of her name, and realized Montague once more—Montague whom she had forgotten.

With a great start she awoke to find herself in his arms. She made an instinctive effort to free herself but he held her to his breast, and she was too numbed to resist.

"I can't stand it," he said. "I can't stand by and let you die. Frances, you are mine. Do you hear? You are mine. Whatever comes of it, I'm not going to let you go again!"

She heard the rising passion in his voice. It was like a goad, pricking her to action. For a few seconds she lay passive, waiting as it were for strength. All her life she was to remember the strange calm of those waiting moments. She was as one ship-wrecked and in appalling danger, yet in some fashion aware of rescue drawing near.

And then quite suddenly deliverance came; she knew not how nor stayed to question whence. She realized only the presence of a power beyond her own, uplifting her, succouring her. She put away the arms that sought to hold her, and even as she did so, there came a sound beyond the dripping of the rain—the sound of a child's voice singing a little tuneless song to itself out in the darkness.

Frances gasped and uttered a cry. "Is that you, child? Is that you?"

The song ceased. A child's voice made reply. "Is that the pretty lady who gives me flowers?"

They could not see her, but she was close to them. She had entered the shed and stood before them.

"I dreamt I would find you here," she said. "It was Daniel in the lions' den at first, then it was you. Why are you in here?"

Frances was on her feet. The man behind her never stirred.

"I have lost my way, little darling," she said. "How did you get here in the dark?"

"I don't know the dark," said the child. "What is dark?"

Frances groping, touched and held a small figure standing before her. "Can you take me back, Rosebud?" she said.

A tiny hand, full of confidence, found and clasped her own. "I will take you to Tetherstones," said the child.

They went out together, hand in hand, into the dripping darkness.

PART II

CHAPTER I
THE STRANGERS

How long she wandered with the child, stumbling through the darkness, Frances never knew. All that she realized and that with a deep thankfulness, was that her guide was quite sure of the way.

They spoke but little during the journey, only now and then the child's voice, sweet and confident, broke the silence with words of encouragement.

"I'm so glad I found you. . . . We're nearly there. . . . Granny has a big fire that you can get dry by. . . . And you can come and sleep in my bed. I can sleep with Aunt Maggie. . . . Are you very tired? We shall soon be there."

And then at last there shone a glare of light in the darkness, and Frances roused herself to speech.

"What is that light?"

"That is Tetherstones," said the child. "That is home."

Ah, home! Somehow the words brought the hot tears to Frances' eyes. She was weak with the long struggle, with the mingled fear and pain and exhaustion of the day. She longed—very desperately she longed—for some safe shelter where she could sink down, and this child spoke to her of home. She could not check her tears.

"Never mind!" said the voice at her side. "Don't cry! We are just there. Here is the gate!"

Frances fumbled at it, but the child opened it. They went through together and trod the smooth stones that led to the house.

The glare dazzled Frances. She went as she was led, making no effort to guide herself. They came to the porch. She heard the rustle of falling rain upon thatch, and there came to her nostrils the aromatic scent of burning wood. A great quiver went through her. This was Tetherstones—this was home.

The door opened before her. "Come in!" said the child. "We'll find Granny."

They entered, and then it seemed to Frances that the light became so intense that she could bear it no longer. She uttered a gasping sound, and fell against the wall. There seemed to be a great many people in front of her, a confusion of voices, and out of the indistinguishable medley she heard a man utter a terrible oath. Then there came a crash, whether within the room or within her brain she knew not. She only knew that she fell, and falling was caught by strong arms that held her up, that lifted her, that sustained her, in all the dreadful tumult in which her senses swam. She turned as one drowning, and clung to that staunch support.

"Bring her to the fire, poor thing!" said a woman's voice, soft with pity. "Mind how you lift her, Arthur! That's right, Oliver. You lend a hand!"

Helpless in every limb, she felt herself borne forward, and was aware of a great glow from an open fire. They laid her down before it, and she knew that she was safe. But still, as one who fears to drown, she clung to one of those strong arms that had lifted her.

"Look at that!" said another voice compassionately. "Just like a frightened child! Where did you find her, Ruthie?"

"Up in the old shed near the Stones," said the child. "I expect she was frightened too. She was lost."

"Let's give her some hot milk!" said the motherly voice that had first spoken. "Move a bit, Arthur! I can't get near her."

"I can't move." It was another voice speaking—a man's voice, short, decided. "Give me the cup! I'll see what I can do."

And then Frances felt the rim of a cup against her lips.

She drank—at first submissively, then hungrily. Her free hand came up to support the cup, and her eyes opened. She looked into a man's eyes—the hard, steady eyes of Roger's master.

"Oh!" she said weakly. "It is you!"

"There now! She knows you, does she?" It was not Roger's master who spoke, but another man beyond her range of vision. "That's funny, eh, Arthur? You who never look at——"

"Shut up!" said Roger's master, briefly and rather brutally. "Get out of it, Oliver! Look after the old man!"

He held the cup again to Frances' lips, and she drank until she drained it. Her eyes remained wide open, fixed upon those other eyes, black-browed and dominant, that had surveyed her so insolently that morning.

A quivering sigh went through her. "I shouldn't—have come here," she said.

He handed the cup with an imperious gesture to someone she could not see. "You're quite safe anyhow," he said. "There's nothing to frighten you."

His voice was deep and very resolute. It had the stern ring of a man accustomed to hard fighting in the arena of life. She wondered a little even in that moment of doubt and uncertainty. Somehow he did not seem to fit his surroundings. He made her think of a gladiator of ancient Rome rather than a farmer in the depths of peaceful Devon.

"I shouldn't—have come," she said again, speaking with difficulty. "I am sorry."

But still her fingers clung to the rough cloth of his coat like the numbed fingers of one who fears to drown.

"There's nothing for you to be sorry for," he said. "You're welcome to shelter here as long as you will." He spoke abruptly over his shoulder. "Speak to her, Mother! She's scared out of her life."

"Poor child!" said the woman's voice. "And no wonder—out there alone in the fog! Who is she, I wonder? Perhaps she will tell us presently."

The voice was refined. It had a kindly ring, but it sounded tired—too tired for any very poignant feeling. Yet it comforted Frances. It was a homely voice. With a great effort she braced herself for coherent speech.

"I am so sorry," she said, "to intrude on you like this. I am a visitor here—lodging with Mrs. Trehearn at Brookside. My name is Frances Thorold."

She heard the child's voice in the background. "Aunt Maggie, you know the lady. She paints pictures, and she watched you milk the cows. Don't you remember?"

"Why, yes, of course!" The fresh tones of the rough-haired girl took up the tale. "Of course I remember! We'll have to get her undressed and to bed, Mother. She'll die of cold in those wet things."

They came about her in a crowd, as it seemed to Frances' confused senses, but Roger's master kept them back.

"Wait!" he said. "Get a bed ready first! Get hot blankets and brandy! She's chilled to the bone. Make up the fire, Milly! You, Dolly, light a fire upstairs! Elsie, get the warming-pan! Lucy and Nell, go and draw some water!"

He issued his orders with a parade-like brevity that took instantaneous effect. The crowd melted magically. And still Frances clung to that solid supporting arm as if she could never bear to let go.

Suddenly, it seemed to her that she was alone with him. He bent over her and spoke.

"Tell me! What has frightened you so on the moor?"

His look compelled an answer. Even against her will she would have made it, but a violent shivering fit took her and speech became impossible. He grasped an arm of the old settle on which she lay and dragged it nearer to the fire.

"Don't be afraid!" he said. "You're safe enough here. Ruth!"

He raised his voice slightly. The child came and stood beside him—a small child, beautifully made, her sweet face upturned like the face of a flower that seeks the sun. Her eyes were always closed, sealed buds that no sun would ever open.

The man did not look at her. He was closely watching Frances.

"Why did you go to the Stones to-night?" he said.

"I had a dream," said the child.

"Go on! What did you dream?" The words were peremptory but the voice was gentle. Even in that moment Frances noted the difference of tone.

There was a momentary pause, then the child spoke, her face uplifted like the face of a dreamer.

"I dreamt first about Daniel in the lions' den, and then it turned into someone up by the Stones—someone who was lost and frightened—and praying for help. So I went to see."

"Weren't you afraid?" the man said.

"I? Oh no! There was nothing to frighten me. I knew the way. Besides, God was there," the child said simply. "It was quite safe. Is the lady better now?"

"She is getting better." The man reached out and grasped the slender shoulder nearest to him. "Come and hold her hand!" he said.

"May I? Won't she mind?" The small fingers clasped Frances' trembling ones. "You are not lost now," she said softly. "You are found."

Somehow Frances found her hold transferred. The man rose from his knees. The child nestled down by her side. A sense of peace stole upon her. She knew that she was safe. She closed her eyes to the glare of the fire and lay still. . . .

What happened to her afterwards she never clearly recalled. She was in the hands of strangers who yet in some inexplicable way were friends. They waited upon her, tended her, succoured her with every comfort, till at last the awful shivering passed. She drifted into sleep.

It was a strange sleep of inexplicable happenings—a fevered jumble of impressions, ideas curiously mingled. Daniel in a place of lions—or was it devils?—that was oddly called "The Stones"! Daniel, lost and very frightened, praying for help! And later the coming of an angel to his deliverance!

Yes, she remembered that part of it very clearly. "My God hath sent His angel. . . ." She heard again the voice of a little child singing in the darkness—a child who lived in utter darkness yet knew not the meaning of the word. She called to memory the closed eyes that no sun would ever open, and like a voice within her soul there came to her the words: "You are not lost now. You are found."

No, she was not lost any longer, but she was ill, terribly ill. There came a time when sleep no longer held her and pain took possession—dreadful intervals when breathing was agony and rest a thing impossible. It stretched out into days of suffering when her very soul seemed to be lacerated with the anguish that racked her body, days when she lay in the cruel grip of a torture such as she had never imagined in all the hardships of her life. Sometimes during those days, it seemed to her that death was very near. She stood on the brink of an abyss unfathomable and felt her soul preparing as it were for that great leap into the unknown. And it had ceased to appall her, as is the merciful way of nature when the body can endure no more. There was nought to fear in Death. It was only pain—earthly pain—that had any power to torment her.

And that power was lessening, hourly, hourly lessening. She was as a prisoner chained to a rock, yet waiting for a sure deliverance. Utter weariness possessed her, a weakness so complete that there were hours together when she would lie, conscious but too exhausted for thought or feeling, and with a dim wonder watch the strangers about her bed.

They were very constantly about her—those strangers. She came to know them by name though she hardly ever spoke to them except to whisper a word of thanks for some service rendered. They would not let her speak from the very outset. They always hushed her into silence whenever she attempted it. And—since speech was very difficult—she came at last to acquiesce dumbly in all that they did.

As the pain lessened and the weakness increased, she grew to lean upon them more and more. There was always someone with her, springing up at her slightest movement to help her. Maggie—the rosy, rough-haired girl who milked the cows—spent two hours each morning and evening after milking-time in ready service upon her, or sitting working by her side. They divided themselves, the six girls, into special watches of four hours each in the twenty-four, each girl serving two hours at a time by day or by night. Frances got to know the time by these watches, for they never varied. Milly, the second girl, used to come to her in the afternoon and in the very early hours of the morning. She liked Milly, who was sensitive and anxious to please, not very strong or very capable, but always full of sympathy and never-failing attention. Elsie, the third girl, was of the boisterous open-air type. She also had a night-watch and she kept it faithfully, though she did a man's labour on the farm and only rested for the two hours in the middle of the day that she spent in Frances' room.

"I'm used to broken nights," she used to say stoutly. "Maggie and I always come in for them in lambing-time."

Then there was Dolly—a girl of considerable character and decision—Nurse Dolly—Frances used to call her, for she was the one of them all whose touch was skilful and who had any real aptitude for nursing. Lucy and Nell were the youngest—girls of twenty and nineteen. Their watches came consecutively and they used to whisper a great deal in the sick-room when one of them relieved the other. It was mainly by their means that Frances learned how her condition went, and in a vague fashion it amused her to know. But somehow she never felt vitally interested.

When Nell—who always had hay-seed sown in her chestnut hair—told Lucy in hissing undertones that the doctor said she had no strength to make a stand and would probably go very suddenly in the end, Frances, still chained to her rock above the abyss, wondered what either of them would do if that amazing moment came while she was on guard. Lucy would certainly be frightened. She had a shy and gentle way with her. But Nell—Nell was extremely young and full of ideas. She would probably do something highly original before she quitted her post to find Dolly, as, Frances heard, had been arranged among them. Nell was a jolly girl, but she had a schoolboy's rudeness for all who came her way, and a funny boyish fashion of regarding life that appealed to Frances immensely.

There was someone on the farm, she learned from the girls' talk, for whom everyone had the profoundest contempt. Lucy and Nell always spoke of him as "the Beast." But who the Beast was and why he was always thus described did not transpire.

There was also Arthur, Roger's master, who, she gathered, knew how to assert his authority even over the sometimes mutinous Nell, and commanded her unbounded respect in consequence.

Then there was Oliver—"Oliver Twist" they called him. He was evidently a humorous person and his comic sayings often caused fits of suppressed giggles behind Frances' screen. Frances used to train her ears to catch the joke, but it always eluded her, the point smothered in laughter, after which Nell would come round to her, looking contrite, and beg her to try and get a little sleep, in the same breath dismissing Lucy brusquely from the room. Yes, Frances liked Nell. She was so delightfully and naïvely human.

But most of all she loved little Ruth of the blind eyes, and Ruth's granny—the patient, tired woman with the mother's voice who had pitied her on that first evening. They were curiously alike, these two, in their patience, their gentleness, their serenity. They brought an atmosphere of peace into her room—a sense of rest that none of the sisters possessed. They always came to her together, and Ruth's granny would speak tenderly in her tired voice, telling her she would be better soon.

She never stayed long, but Frances grew to look for her coming with a certain eagerness, so deep were the knowledge and the understanding in the grave kindly eyes. She had a feeling that this woman, with her white banded hair and sorrow-lined face was many years younger than she seemed. The blind child plainly worshipped her. "My dear Granny" was the fond term by which she always spoke of her, and it was evident to Frances that she filled the place of mother in the child's heart. She was the petted darling of all the sisters, but this elderly woman who petted her least of all was the beloved one of her heart.

Little Ruth brought her a flower every day, and she would stay on after her granny had gone, curling up beside her on the bed, very still and quiet, sometimes whispering a little, always holding her hand. Frances loved to have her there. The child's presence was as balm to her spirit. Even in her worst hours it comforted her to feel her near. She was the angel of her deliverance. Whenever that dreadful memory of evil assailed her, she wanted to clasp the little hand in hers, and always it brought her comfort. "My God hath sent His angel. . . ."

CHAPTER II
ROGER'S MASTER

The doctor—whose name was Square—was a bluff old countryman who was accustomed to ride miles over the moor every day on his old white mare, Jessie, in pursuit of his calling. A picturesque figure was Silas Square, immensely big and powerful, gruff and short of speech, but with a heart as soft as a woman's. He came every morning and evening during the worst period of Frances' illness, Nurse Dolly always accompanying him, and his strong kindly presence never failed to encourage, even at the time when Nell's whispered confidences told Frances that he believed the end to be near. He did not talk much in the sick-room. His remedies were old-fashioned and drastic, but he always in some fashion conveyed a sense of confidence to his patients. She generally managed to smile at him when he came.

"You've got some pluck," he said to her once, when he had watched the application of a poultice that caused her acute pain.

And she smiled at him again bravely, though she could not speak in answer, so tightly was her endurance stretched.

And then one day he looked at her with eyes that fairly beamed their congratulation. "You've done it!" he said. "You're through the worst, and, madam, you're the bravest woman it has ever been my lot to attend!"

She valued these words immensely. They were so spontaneous, and he was very obviously not a man given to flattery.

Thenceforward his visits dropped to once a day, but he always gave her a sympathy that amazed her with its intuition. His kindly concern for her welfare never failed, even when he had finally loosened her chain, and drawn her back from the abyss into safety.

But he would not hear of her being moved. "You've had a very stiff time," he said. "And you've got to rest. You're in excellent hands. The Dermots all love having you. So why worry?"

"Because they don't know me. Because I am a stranger," she made answer at last, when her strength had returned sufficiently for her to feel the difficulties of her position. "I can make no return to them for their kindness. I have got to make my living. I have no money."

"Is kindness ever repaid by money?" he said, with a smile in his shrewd eyes. "You can't go yet. I won't sanction it. That heart of yours has got to tick better than it does at present—a long way better—before you think of earning your living again."

"Then I must go to a hospital," said Frances desperately, "I can't go on in this way. I really can't."

"You'll do as you're told," said old Dr. Square with a frown. "And you'll take cream—plenty of it—every day."

Then he went away, and Frances was left to fume in solitude.

"You're fretting," said Nurse Dolly severely when she took her temperature a little later. "That's very wrong of you and quite unnecessary. Now you will have to take a sedative."

She did not want the sedative. She was approaching that stage of convalescence when fretting is almost a necessity, and she fought against any palliative. But Dolly would take no refusal, and in the end, with tears of weakness, she had to submit.

"There now!" said Dolly practically, when she had won the day. "What a pity to upset yourself like that! Now don't cry any more! Just go to sleep!"

She went to sleep, cried herself to sleep like a child that has been slapped, and slept deeply, exhausted, till late into the night. Then she awoke to find with great surprise the child Ruth curled up in the big bed beside her. The fair head was actually on her pillow, the flower-like face close to her own.

"Why, darling, little darling!" whispered Frances.

Ruth's hands, soft and loving, clasped hers. "I'm not asleep," she whispered back. "Do you mind me in bed with you?"

"Mind!" said Frances, gathering her close. "As if I could!"

Ruth gave a faint sigh. "I've been lying awake to ask you. I came because of a dream I had. Elsie wanted to send me away, but I wouldn't go. So she put me into bed with you while you were asleep. I'm glad you don't mind."

"Go to sleep, my Rosebud!" said Frances very tenderly. "I wouldn't part with you for all the world."

She found out later that little Ruth was accustomed to spend her nights promiscuously among her young aunts. She chose her own place of rest, like a wandering scrap of thistledown, disturbing none. They always welcomed her fondly wherever she went, but none ever coerced or persuaded her. She lived her own life; they had no time to spend upon her, and she was curiously independent of them all. She went in and out quite fearlessly, seeing her visions behind those sealed lids, a child of strange spirituality to whom grief was unknown.

She brought her simple comfort to Frances that night, and they slept together in absolute peace. It was the best night that Frances had had throughout her illness.

In the morning she felt better. She and the little girl lay murmuring together in the misty sunshine of the dawn.

"I am going to the Stones to-day," said Ruth. "I wish you could come."

"The Stones!" Memory pierced Frances, and she shrank a little involuntarily. But: "Tell me about the Stones!" she said.

"I go and play there," said Ruth. "Some people are afraid of them. I don't know why. The fairies play their pipes there, and I lie and listen. And sometimes, when they think I am asleep, the biggest stones talk. But I don't know what they say," she added quaintly. "It isn't our language at all. I daresay the fairies would understand, but they always run away and hide when the stones begin."

"What are the Stones?" said Frances.

"Oh, just stones, the same as God made when He made the earth. They stand in a big circle. I don't know why He put them like that, but they have been so ever since the world began. I expect He had a reason," said the child. "Don't you?"

"Yes, dear," said Frances gently. "And you like to go there?"

"Yes," said Ruth. She hesitated a moment as one to whom a subject is sacred; then: "My mother went to heaven from there," she said. "So of course God must come there sometimes. I hope He'll come there some day when I'm there."

"Wouldn't you be afraid?" said Frances.

"Afraid of God? Oh no! Why should anyone be afraid of God? He loves us," said the child.

Frances kissed the upturned face that could not see the sun. "Bless you, little darling!" she said. "Is there anyone who wouldn't love you, I wonder?"

Ruth left her soon after, and Nurse Dolly came in, brisk and efficient, to prepare her for the day.

"I am glad to see you better," she said. "But you mustn't sit up yet—not till you have had three days without a temperature. The doctor says so."

"I will be very good," Frances promised. "But do you think I might have my bed pushed near the window? I should so love to look out."

Dolly considered the request judicially for a moment or two. She was recognized commander-in-chief in the sick-room. "We'll see about it," she said. "But it's a heavy bed to move and has no castors. Still—we'll see."

She smiled upon Frances and proceeded with her toilet with her usual ready deftness.

Then she departed, and Frances heard her cheery voice calling for Oliver.

Through the window she heard a man's voice reply. "Oliver's gone to put the pigs in the cart for market. What do you want him for?"

"Oh, it's all right; you'll do," said Dolly, still brisk and cheery. "Just come along and help me to move Miss Thorold's bed! She has a fancy for lying in the sunshine."

There was no answer to that save a grunt, and a moment later the sound of a pipe being tapped against the side of the step. Frances felt a quick flush rising in her face. She wished with all her heart that she could have restrained Dolly's well-meaning arrangement as she heard the sound of a man's tread upon the stairs.

Dolly re-entered, looking well pleased with herself. "Here's Arthur come to move you," she said. "He's strong enough."

Arthur entered behind her. His great frame with its broad shoulders filled the narrow doorway. He looked straight at her, and she thought his look was oddly lowering, even challenging.

"Come in!" said Dolly.

Frances said nothing. She was tongue-tied.

He came forward into the room, moving with the careless strength of conscious power. He paused at her bedside.

"Are you feeling better?"

She recovered herself with an effort. "I am much better, thank you," she said, and held out her hand.

He paused an instant as if she had taken him by surprise. Then abruptly he gripped and held the outstretched hand. His face changed magically. He smiled at her, and his smile was good to see. It took years from his appearance, belying the iron-grey of hair that had once been as black as his brows.

"I'm glad of that," he said. "I hope they are doing all they can for you."

"They are doing far too much," Frances said. "I feel so ashamed lying here."

"Why ashamed?" he said.

She coloured again, painfully, under his eyes. "I have never been in anyone's debt before," she said. "And this—this is more than I can ever hope to repay."

His smile passed, and again his face was hard with the hardness of the fighter. "There is no debt that I can see," he said. "We are all at the mercy of circumstance. If it comes to that, we owed it to ourselves to do what we could for you."

It was brusquely spoken, but his look, grim though it was, seemed to her to hold a hint of friendliness. The dog Roger, who had entered behind him, came nosing up to the bedside and she slipped her hand free to fondle him. There was something in this man's personality that embarrassed her, wherefore she could not have said.

Roger acknowledged her attention with humble effusion, glancing apologetically towards his master the while.

"You are very kind to put it like that," she said at last, as he stood immovably beside her. "But I can't bear to be a burden upon anyone—especially—especially——"

"Especially what?" he said.

She answered with difficulty. "Especially people who have to work as hard as you do."

"People in our walk of life, do you mean?" he said, and she heard the echo of a sneer behind the words.

"Arthur, you are not to make her talk," said Dolly severely. "She had a temperature yesterday all through over-excitement and fretting, and it throws her back at once. Will you please move the bed and go?"

She spoke with her habitual decision, and Frances was aware of a strong resemblance between the brother and sister as Arthur turned to comply. She herself was near to tears, such was her weakness and distress of mind, and while her bed was being moved across to the window she could not look at either of them. But when the move was at length satisfactorily effected and she could gaze forth over the dewy sunlit fields, she commanded herself sufficiently to utter a low word of thanks.

He came back to her then, and stood beside her. "You are most welcome at Tetherstones," he said. "Please don't talk of debts and burdens! They don't come into the reckoning here."

His tone was restrained, but it held an unmistakable note of apology. She lifted her eyes in amazement, but he had already turned away. He went out of the room with the free, deliberate swing with which he had entered, and she heard him descending the stairs with Roger pattering behind.

"For goodness' sake, never take any notice of Arthur!" said sensible Dolly, as she whisked about the room setting it in order. "He always was a bear, and the circumstances he talks about haven't been such as to have a very taming effect on him."

Then she knew that by some means Dolly had obtained that semi-apology in order to keep her patient's temperature normal.

CHAPTER III
THE BEAST

From the day that her bed was moved to the window, Frances began to regain her strength.

It came back to her slowly, with intervals of pain and weariness, when she felt as if she were making no progress at all, but it returned, and her indefatigable nurses gradually relinquished their vigil.

"You can go downstairs and sit in the sun if you want to," said Dr. Square one morning.

And she thanked him and promised to make the effort. There was a corner of the old-fashioned garden that she could see from her window in which she had often longed to sit, but now that the time had come, all desire for change had left her. She lacked the energy for enthusiasm.

"That's because you are weak still," said Dolly. "Never mind! I'll arrange everything. We'll get the couch out of the parlour. I can make it very comfortable with some pillows and a rug. It's nice and cool under the cedar. Don't you fret now! Just leave it all to me!"

She went off briskly to make her arrangements, and Frances heard her from the garden calling Maggie to come and help her with the couch.

Maggie came, the hair as usual flying all around her sunny face. She was accompanied by the young man they called Oliver, who carried a stable-fork and had evidently just come from the farmyard. Maggie was looking unusually serious, Frances discovered, as the three of them paused at a corner of the old house for discussion.

Presently Maggie's clear tones reached her. "Don't you be a silly girl, Dolly! You've no right to risk it. You keep her where she is!"

Dolly for once seemed undecided, and Oliver, with a faintly rueful smile on his comical countenance, ranged himself on Maggie's side.

"Don't let's have a shindy for goodness' sake!" he said. "We've kept him quiet till now, but I won't answer for him much longer. The beast has got to break out some time. I told Arthur so this morning."

"Oh, but this is nonsense!" declared Dolly. "You can keep him in the farmyard surely. I know I could."

"Well, you'd better go and do it then, that's all," said Maggie. "For he's on the ramp this morning, and no mistake. I can't pacify him."

There followed some words in a lower tone which did not reach Frances at her window, and then the group dispersed, Maggie and Oliver departing in the direction of the farmyard, and Dolly entering the house.

Frances was left alone for some time, and presently coming to the not unwelcome conclusion that she was to remain in her room that day, she began to fall asleep. The day was sultry and very still. She heard vaguely the summer sounds that came through her window. The atmosphere was peaceful beyond words. The occasional lowing of a cow in the meadow beyond the garden where the chattering stream ran, the cooing of the pigeons on the roof of the old barn, and the cry of the wheeling swallows that nestled in the eaves, the singing of a thousand larks above the heather-covered moors, all came to her like a softly-coloured dream. She felt wonderfully soothed and at rest, too tired to speculate as to the meaning of that half-heard discussion below her window, content to drowse the time away as long as Nurse Dolly would permit.

The breeze, laden with the scent of heather, came in upon her like a benediction, playing lightly with her hair, closing her weary lids. She sank more and more deeply into repose.

Then, just when the spell seemed complete, there came a sudden and violent interruption, so startling that she sprang up in a wild alarm, not knowing whence it came.

It began like the bellow of a bull—a terrific sound that sent all the blood to her heart; then she realized that it came from somewhere in the house, not the farmyard, and sat there palpitating, asking herself what it could be.

It went on for many seconds. Sometimes it seemed to her strained senses like the shouting of an angry man, then its utter lack of articulation and intelligibility convinced her that it must be some animal gone mad and broken loose. In the midst of the din she thought she heard a woman's voice crying frantically for help, and then there came a frightful crash, and all sound ceased.

Frances sank back upon her pillows, completely unnerved. Something terrible had happened. Of that she was certain. But what? But what? Why was the house so deadly quiet after the uproar—that tumult that had made her think of devils fighting together? This mysterious Beast of whom the two girls whispered so freely—was it he who had broken loose, trampling wide destruction through that wonderland of peace? And had he escaped after that final crash, or was he dead? She longed to know, yet dreaded to find out.

Her limbs felt paralysed, and her heart was beating with slow, uneven strokes. A catastrophe of some kind had taken place. Of that she felt certain. Had one of the six sisters been hurt? That wild cry for help—she was sure now that she had heard it—which girl was it who had been in such sore distress? And had the help come in time?

Ah! A sound a last! A step upon the stair! The door opened with quiet decision and Dolly entered. She looked exactly as usual, her face perfectly calm and unclouded.

"I am sorry," she said, "but I am afraid it is a little too cold for you in the garden to-day. The wind has changed."

Frances gave a gasp, between relief and incredulity. For the moment words were beyond her.

"Is there anything the matter?" said Dolly.

With an effort Frances made reply. "I thought—something had happened—such a strange noise—it woke me."

Dolly looked at her with a kindly smile. "Ah, you've been dreaming," she said practically. "People often get nightmares after a bad illness. It's just weakness, you know."

She came and felt Frances' pulse. "Yes, I think you are well enough. I have got a letter for you here. Mrs. Trehearn sent it up this morning."

She gave an envelope into Frances' hand, but Frances only stared at her blankly.

"Well?" said Dolly after a moment. "Don't you want to read it?"

"Thank you," Frances said, recovering herself.

Dolly smiled again upon her and went to the door. "One of the girls will be in with your cocoa directly. I must go down and help Mother with the bread."

She went, still unruffled, serenely sure of herself. But Frances, who at first had been almost bewildered into imagining that she had actually dreamed the disturbance below, lay back again with a feeling akin to indignation. Did Dolly really think that she was to be deceived so easily?

She suddenly remembered the letter in her hand, and looked down at it. A man's writing sprawled across the envelope, and again her heart gave a jerk. What was this?

No word from Montague Rotherby had reached her since little Ruth had led her to Tetherstones on that night of darkness. She had been too ill to think of him till lately, and now in her convalescence she never voluntarily suffered her thoughts to wander in his direction. She had come to regard the whole episode of her acquaintance with him in the light of a curious illusion, such an illusion as she would always remember with a sense of shame. With all her heart she hoped that she would never see him again, for the bare memory of him had become abhorrent to her. Here in the wholesome security of Tetherstones she felt that she had come to her senses, and she would never again be led away by the glitter of that which was not gold.

And so, as she looked at the letter in her hand, there came upon her such a feeling of revolt as had never before possessed her. It was as though she grasped a serpent, and she yearned to destroy it, but dared not.

There came again to her as a sombre echo in her soul the memory of the Bishop's words: ". . . Until you have endured your hell, and—if God is merciful—begun to work out your own salvation."

But had she yet endured her hell? Of the hours spent with Rotherby on the moor before the coming of the child her memory was vague. A long wandering, coupled with a growing fear, and at the last an overwhelming sense of evil that she was powerless to combat were the only impressions that remained to her. But with a great vividness did she remember how she had surrendered herself to him the evening before, and burned with shame at the memory. No, she never wanted to see him again, and she longed to destroy his letter unread. The very touch of it was horrible to her.

But something stayed her hand. Something called within her—a mocking, elusive something that taunted her courage. What was there in a letter to frighten her? If she were sure of herself—if she were sure of herself—She tore open the envelope with a gesture of exasperation. Of course she was sure of herself!

"Circe, my beloved!" So the note began, and before her eyes there swam a mist. No man in the whole world had ever called her beloved before! She gripped herself firmly, nerving herself for the ordeal. This was not Love—this was not Love! This was an evil that must be firmly met and cast out. But ah, if it had been Love!

Resolutely she read the letter through. It was written from the inn at Fordestown. "I lost you on that night of fog, but I have found you again, and I have been waiting ever since. They tell me you are better, but I can't meet you among strangers. When will you come to me? Come soon, Circe beloved! Come soon!

"I am yours, M. R."

She looked up from the letter. So he was waiting for her still! Somehow she had thought that he would not have deemed it worth his while. A curious dazed feeling possessed her. He was waiting for her still! The ordeal was not over yet. How was she going to face it?

There came a knock at the door—Nell's boyish knock. She entered, carrying a tray with cocoa and cream upon it.

"I'm sorry I'm late," she said. "I hope you haven't been wanting it very badly."

Frances crumpled the letter in her hand. She looked at the girl and saw that Nell's usually rosy face was pale.

"Is anything the matter, Nell?" she said.

Nell's chin quivered at the question. "Oh, there's been a frightful row," she said. "But I mustn't tell you anything about it. Arthur would be furious if he knew."

"You needn't be afraid of that," said Frances. "He won't know."

"Thank you," the girl said, and dried her eyes. "But I can't tell you all the same. It wouldn't be fair. You don't know the beast's ways, and it's a good thing you don't. Please don't ask me anything—or I shall say too much! I know I shall."

"My dear, I don't want you to tell me anything against your will," Frances said kindly.

"No, it isn't that," Nell said. "But I don't want you to think you ought to go. We've been so glad to have you. We've loved looking after you. But there's never any peace—and never will be so long as Arthur—" She broke off abruptly. "Oh, I'd better go. I'm making a muddle of things, and there'll be a worse row if he finds out."

She left the room precipitately, and Frances was again alone. She closed her eyes to think. Something in Nell's confused words had given her a shock.

So they wanted her gone! That was what it amounted to. She had outstayed her welcome, and she must go. The thought of all the kindness they had showered upon her sent a pang to her heart. How good they had been to the unwelcome stranger within their gates! And all the while there had been no peace at Tetherstones because of the black-browed master who wanted her gone.

No peace at Tetherstones, and how nobly they had striven to keep it from her! Ah well, she knew now—she knew now!

Her hand clenched unconsciously, and she became aware of the letter she held. A great wave of feeling went through her. Her eyes were suddenly full of tears. Ah, if it had been Love that called her! If it had been Love!

CHAPTER IV
REBELS

Two days later, Frances went out into the garden. She leaned upon Dolly's arm, for she was very weak, and Lucy came behind, carrying rugs and cushions. They settled her on a couch under the great cedar-tree that spread its branches over the lawn, and there little Ruth came and nestled beside her while the two elder girls went away.

"When you are well enough," said Ruth, her sweet face upturned to the chequered sunlight, "I would like you to come to the Stones with me."

"When I am well enough, sweetheart," said Frances, "as soon as I can walk, that is, I am going away."

"Right away?" said the child.

"Yes, darling. Right away. I have stayed too long, much too long, as it is."

"I would like you always here," said Ruth.

Frances pressed her to her side in silence.

It was a perfect summer morning. From across the field that bordered the old garden there came the babble of the stream. There was a line of sunflowers along the red-brick wall, and below them the blue of delphiniums that brought to mind the Bishop's garden. The warm scent of sweet-peas filled the air. Some distance away, Nell's sunbonnet was visible, dipping among the green. She and Lucy were gathering peas, and their careless chatter came to Frances where she lay. The peace of the place rested upon it like a benediction.

"You will come with me to the Stones before you go, won't you?" said Ruth.

It was hard to refuse her. "Perhaps, darling," she said gently.

There came the tread of a horse's hoofs on the cobbles of the yard. "That is Uncle Arthur," said Ruth, and freed herself from Frances' encircling arm.

"Are you going?" Frances asked.

"I shall come back," she said.

With perfect confidence she left the shade of the cedar-tree and moved through the hot sunshine that bathed the lawn. Frances watched her wonderingly. She did not run, but she went quickly over the grass, and never faltered when her feet reached the gravel-path. Unerringly the little blue-frocked figure found the gate that led into the yard, and disappeared beyond the wall. Frances breathed a sigh. The place seemed empty without her. Some minutes passed, and the child did not return. She began to grow drowsy, and was actually on the verge of slumber when a rustling sound close at hand suddenly recalled her. She came to herself with a sharp start.

The rustling ceased immediately, but she had an acute sense of being watched that sent a strange uneasiness through her. She made an effort to raise herself.

Her heart was throbbing fast and hard, and she was conscious of intense weakness, but she managed to drag herself into a sitting position and to turn her head in the direction whence the sound had come.

At first she perceived nothing, for a screen of nut-trees that bounded an orchard beyond the garden effectually concealed everything else from sight. Then, as though drawn by some magnetism, her eyes became riveted. She saw two other eyes peering at her through the leaves, and vaguely discerned a figure crouched and motionless, a few yards from her.

The blood rushed to her heart in a great wave of apprehension. There was something ominous in its utter stillness. She felt like a defenceless traveller who has made his couch all unwittingly on the threshold of a wild beast's lair.

She lay very still, not moving, not daring to breathe.

Suddenly from across the lawn she heard the deep tones of a man's voice. She turned her eyes swiftly in the direction whence it came and, with a throb of mingled relief and embarrassment, saw Arthur Dermot crossing the grass towards her, little Ruth holding his hand. She glanced back swiftly again into the green of the nut-trees, but the space whence those eyes had glared so fixedly at her was empty. Without a sound the watcher had gone.

An acute wave of reaction went through her—an overwhelming sense of helplessness. She sank back upon her cushions, weakly gasping. The sunlight swam before her eyes.

"Miss Thorold!" said a voice.

She looked up with an effort, seeing him through a mist. "I am quite all right. Just—just a passing faintness! It is nothing—really nothing!"

She heard herself uttering the words, but she could not lift her voice above a whisper. At the touch of a quiet hand laid upon her own, she knew she started violently.

"It has been too much for you, coming out here," he said.

"I am quite all right," she assured him again tremulously. "I am only sorry—to have given—so much trouble."

"That's not the way to look at it," he said.

She felt his fingers close up on her wrist and wondered a little, for there was something very quieting in his touch.

"You mustn't attempt too much at a time," he said. "Square told me so only two days ago. You are not wanting to leave us yet, are you?"

The direct question, coming from him, took her by surprise. Her vision was steadying, but an odd flutter of agitation still possessed her. She did not know how to answer him for the moment; then the memory that he wanted her gone came upon her, and she braced herself to reply.

"I must go—yes. I have been here much too long as it is."

His fingers left her wrist, but he still stood above her motionless, looking straight down at her, yet not as if he watched her, but rather as if he debated something with himself.

"May I ask a question?" he said suddenly.

She felt herself colour. There was something unexpected about this man. She wondered why he embarrassed her so. She tried to smile in answer to his words though his expression was grave to sombreness. "If it isn't too hard a one," she said.

"It's only this," he said, in his quiet, rather ponderous fashion. "Have you anywhere to go to—if you leave us?"

"Oh, that!" said Frances, and knew she had betrayed herself before she could formulate her reply. "Why, yes,—of course I have."

"Why 'of course'?" he said.

She hesitated. "Because—well, every woman has somewhere to go to. I have—a brother."

"A brother?" he said.

She found herself explaining further as if under compulsion. "Yes, in the North,—a business man. He would take me in."

"Have you any intention of asking him to?" Somehow the question stung her. It was so direct, so unerring, like the flick of a whip-lash. She dropped her eyes before his look. "I can do so," she said with pride.

"Do you intend to?" he insisted.

She did not answer. Before that straight regard she could not lie.

He waited a moment or two, then to her surprise he sat down upon the grass by her side. "Ruth," he said to the blind child standing silently beside him. "Go to the house and find my tobacco-pouch! Maggie is in the dairy. She will know where it is."

Ruth went with instant obedience, and Arthur Dermot took off his cap and laid it on the grass.

"Now, Miss Thorold," he said, "I am going to ask you another question."

He spoke with the authority of a man not accustomed to be gainsaid, and again that odd quiver as of apprehension went through her. She lay in silence, waiting.

When he spoke again, she knew he was looking at her, but she did not meet his look.

"I want to know," he said, "what it was that scared you so up at the Stones the night you came to us."

"Ah!" She made a quick movement of protest. "I can't tell you that," she said.

"You don't want to tell me," he said.

"I can't tell you," she said again.

He was silent for a space, but she was conscious of his eyes still upon her, and she had an urgent desire to escape from their scrutiny. They were so intent, so unsparing, so full of resolution.

"Someone was up there with you," he said suddenly.

She clenched her hands to check the swift leap of her heart. "I don't think you have any right—to press me like this," she said, her voice very low.

"No right whatever," he agreed, and in his quiet rejoinder she caught an unexpected note of relief. "I knew you had had a fright, and the Stones have a bad name hereabouts. I wondered what bogey had frightened you. But apparently it wasn't a bogey this time."

He smiled a little with the words and she felt the tension relax. She lifted her eyes and met a gleam of friendliness in his.

"No," she said. "It wasn't a bogey."

"Perhaps you don't believe in them," said Arthur Dermot.

She hesitated, remembering the eyes that had glared at her through the nut-trees, and then wondering within herself if they had been a dream. He went on with scarcely a pause.

"Whether you do or not, I shouldn't go to the Stones again in the dark if I were you. It's not a healthy spot."

"But the child goes!" she said in surprise.

"The child!" He lifted his brows. "The child is different," he said briefly. "The child goes everywhere."

His tone did not invite comment. She wondered and held her peace.

After a moment he went on, his jaw set in the fighting fashion she had come to associate with him. "All this is beside the point, though you've satisfied me in one particular. Now, Miss Thorold, to return to the charge! Why must you go from here before you are fit?"

"I think you know why," she said.

"But if you have no one to go to—" he said.

"I am going to work," said Frances, with decision.

"What is your work?" he asked.

She answered him without reserve, for his manner had undergone a change. "I am a typist. I have been secretary to the Bishop of Burminster."

"Burminster!" he repeated the name sharply. "What is his name?"

"Dr. Rotherby."

"Ah!" She saw his face twist suddenly, as if at a spasm of pain. "That man!" He ground the words between his teeth.

"Yes, that man! Do you know him?"

She asked the question with a certain hesitation, but he answered it immediately. "I knew him once—before he came to Burminster. What is he like now? Did he treat you decently?"

"He never treats anyone decently," said Frances.

"You quarrelled with him?" He looked at her sharply.

"Yes. I quarrelled with him," she answered with simplicity. "I think he is the hardest man I have ever met."

Arthur Dermot was silent. He picked up his cap and began to turn it in his hands, moodily meditative.

"Well," Frances said, after a moment, "that is a closed chapter now. I am looking out for another post."

"They are not very easy to find, are they?" he said.

The indomitable courage that Montague Rotherby had admired in her sounded in her reply. "Of course they are not easy. That's just the best of life. We've got to work for everything worth having."

"Some of us have to work for what isn't," he said.

"Yes. I've done that too," she answered.

He lifted his eyes abruptly to hers, dark eyes that seemed to her to hold a curious protest. "And you've found it worth while?" he said.

She countered the question. "Have you?"

He shook his head. "I didn't say I'd done it."

"But you know what it feels like," she said.

He smiled at that. "You are very shrewd. Well, I have done it. But I don't see any results—any decent results. I never shall see any."

"Does one ever really get results before the work is done?" said Frances.

"I don't know." He dropped his eyes again moodily, and she found her own resting upon the silvery gleam of his bent head. "Life can be pretty damnable," he said, "most particularly to those who have a sense of duty."

"It is more damnable if we rebel," said Frances quietly.

"You speak as one who knows," he said.

"Yes. I do know." She uttered the words with conviction. "I have been a rebel. But that is over. I am going back now to work in the furrows—if a place can be found for me."

He frowned at her words. "Those infernal furrows! We plough our very souls into the soil! And to what end? Of what use?"

"So you are a rebel too!" said Frances, with the suspicion of a smile.

He threw her his sudden, challenging look, and she thought he was angry. But in a moment, sombrely, with eyes downcast, he made answer. "Yes, I am a rebel too."

There fell a silence between them that was curiously sympathetic. Frances reflected later that it was that silence that banished all her former embarrassment. She knew when he spoke again that it would not be as a stranger. Somehow they had ceased to be strangers.

He looked up at her again at length. "Miss Thorold, I want to ask you something, and I don't know how to put it. I've lived among clods too long to express myself with much delicacy. Will you make allowances for that?"

She met his look with frankness. "You do not need to ask me that," she said.

"Thank you." His eyes held hers with a certain mastery notwithstanding the humility of his address. "I have no intention of being offensive, I assure you. But I know—I can't help knowing—that you have come through a pretty bad passage lately. I don't want to ask anything about it. I only want to lend a hand to help you back to firm ground. Will you let me do this?"

"I have already accepted too much from you," she said.

His look hardened. "I know. So you think. But you only see one point of view. I want you to realize that there is another. And if you leave Tetherstones now, well, you won't have done all you might towards lessening what I believe you regard as an obligation."

"What do you mean?" she said. "I thought you wanted me to go."

"You thought wrong," he returned with finality. "There is room for you here, and no reason whatever why you should go back to old Mrs. Trehearn, who is utterly unfit to look after you. Square says it would be madness. I beg you will not contemplate such a thing for a moment."

He spoke with a force that he did not attempt to conceal, and she heard him with a strange mixture of surprise and doubt. She could not understand his insistence, but at the back of her mind she was oddly conscious of the fact that she lacked the strength to combat it.

Instinctively she sought to temporize. "It would be quite impossible for me to stay on here indefinitely. You have all been much too kind to me already, and I couldn't—I really couldn't."

"Wait!" he said. "I haven't suggested your doing that. I know you wouldn't. What I do suggest is that you should stay here to convalesce while you are looking about for another post. Can't you do that as easily here as with your brother in the North for instance?"

She smiled a little at his words, but she shook her head. "I can't go on living on your kindness, and I have so very little money left. You must understand how impossible it would be."

"I don't understand," he said doggedly. "You are a woman, and a woman has got to be protected when she is at the end of her resources. If you really want to make any return, you can do the farm accounts for Milly. She never had any aptitude for figures. But for heaven's sake don't talk of going until you are well! I won't hear of it."

There was little logic in the argument and more than a little dogmatism; but for some reason Frances found herself unable to combat the point further. He was evidently determined that she should stay, and she was too tired for further resistance.

"We will talk of this again," she said gently. "Meanwhile, I am very, very grateful to you, and—should like to help with the farm accounts if I may—while I am here."

"Thank you," he said.

He got to his feet with the words. She thought he was going to take her hand, then suddenly she saw him stiffen, and realized that they were no longer alone.

She raised herself to see the bent figure of an old man coming towards them over the grass.

CHAPTER V
MR. DERMOT

"My father!" said Arthur Dermot.

The old man had reached them. He stood, leaning on a knotted stick, looking at her. Again she marvelled, for it was the face of a scholar—a dreamer—that she beheld. It had the grey hue of one who seldom moves in the sunshine. The eyes were drawn as if they did not see very clearly or were continually looking for something beyond their range of vision. His hair was snowy white. She thought he must be very old.

"Is this our visitor from the moors?" he asked, in a feeble tenor voice that somehow stirred her compassion.

"Yes,—Miss Thorold." Arthur's reply was curt, almost as if he resented the old man's presence. His whole attitude was uncompromising.

"I am very pleased to meet you," said Mr. Dermot courteously addressing Frances. "I was so grieved to hear of the unfortunate result of your adventure. I trust you are now nearly restored to your normal health?"

"I am much better," Frances said. "I have been telling your son how very, very grateful I am for all the kindness that has been shown me here."

"Not at all—not at all," said Mr. Dermot. "It has been a great pleasure to us all to be of any service to you. You are a stranger in this part of this world, I hear?"

"Yes. I came here for a rest. It was foolish of me to get lost on the moor," said Frances, smiling ruefully. "I shall never do that again."

"Ah! It must have been a very unpleasant experience. It is strange that you should have been found at the Stones." The tired old face reflected her smile. "There is a tradition hereabouts that the devil walks there at night. You did not meet him by any chance?"

"No," Frances said. "I did not meet him. Curiously enough, I have never even seen the Stones. I did not know they were there. The night was so dark and misty."

"It is a very interesting spot," said Mr. Dermot. "A Druidical circle—according to some—though others believe it to be the result of a volcanic upheaval many thousands of years ago. I myself held the former theory. There are certain marks which in my opinion can only have been made by iron staples. This supports the current belief that Druidical victims were chained there previous to sacrifices. Hence the name of Tetherstones."

He uttered the word deliberately, with a smile towards his son, who stood on one side moodily fidgeting with the riding-whip he held.

"What a ghastly idea!" said Frances.

"It is somewhat gruesome certainly, but it holds considerable interest for the student. If you are at all attracted by this type of research I shall be very pleased to conduct you to the Stones one day and to point out all the features which in my opinion tend to support this theory. My son Arthur," again he smiled, "has no use for relics of any description. He is too busy tilling the ground to give his attention to the study of mere stones."

"Too busy grinding his bread from them!" put in Arthur with a cynical twist of the lips. "Miss Thorold will not be equal to a climb to the Stones for some time yet. And I doubt if they would interest her very greatly when she got there."

"Indeed they would interest me," Frances said. "I have always been attracted by the study of old things. I hope Mr. Dermot will one day be kind enough to show me what he has just been describing."

"With pleasure—with pleasure," said the old man, evidently gratified by her sympathy. "Sunset is a very favourite time for seeing them. The evening shadows are very beautiful up there."

"Little Ruth has been telling me about them," Frances said.

"Ah! The child! The little blind child who lives with us! Yes, yes, of course, the child!" The old man's voice was suddenly vague. He frowned a little as one who seeks to capture an elusive memory. "It is strange how little her infirmity hampers her," he said, after a moment. "I sometimes think she has an inner vision that serves her more effectually than physical sight. The brain of a blind person must be a very interesting study."

"She seems wonderfully happy," Frances said.

"Yes, yes, she is always happy—like—like—another child I used to know." Old Mr. Dermot's eyes took a sudden pathetic look. "I lost that child," he said. "There are a great many others—a great many others; but she was the darling of them all." He turned with sudden querulousness upon the younger man standing silently by. "Why are you waiting here? Why don't you go back to the grinding of your stones?"

"I am waiting for Ruth," his son made quiet rejoinder, without the movement of a muscle. "I have sent her to fetch something."

Mr. Dermot's fine mouth curved satirically. "My son likes to be waited upon," he observed to Frances. "When you are well enough, he will make use of you too. We all have to work for him. He is a hard taskmaster."

Frances smiled. "I shall be only too glad to be of use to any of you," she said. "I am very much in your debt at present."

"Oh, nonsense, nonsense!" he returned paternally. "We do not talk of debts at Tetherstones. Nor do we let our visitors work. Unless," he smiled back at her with a kindliness that won its way to her heart, "you would like to help me perhaps. I am writing a book on the Stones."

"Miss Thorold is not well enough to do anything at present," said Arthur with brief decision. "We must not worry her. Remember, she is an invalid, and she must be treated as such."

"Oh, but I am much stronger," Frances said quickly, for it hurt her to see the sudden animation fade from the grey old face. "I should love to help you if I could. Do you think I can?"

"I don't know," said Mr. Dermot, and she was surprised by an odd hopeless ring in his voice. "A great many have tried to help me, but it is a very difficult matter, and no one has succeeded yet."

"You must let me try," Frances said gently, with the feeling that she was comforting a child. "I should like to try."

She uttered the last words with a glance towards Arthur and was surprised by the sternness of his expression. He was not looking at her, but at the old man who stood leaning on his stick with his faded blue eyes gazing sadly before him.

"You may try if you like," said Mr. Dermot. "But my moments of inspiration are getting rare. Yet I should like to have finished that book when I come to die. It is good to leave something behind to mark where one fell."

The dreaminess of tone and words smote upon her senses like a knell. Again she tried to find some comforting words, but they were checked by the sight of Ruth coming across the grass in her light, confident fashion. They all watched her, as it were by common consent. She was singing to herself, her little tuneless song.

"Strange!" said the old man suddenly. "They say that blind birds always have the sweetest notes."

He moved to meet the child, and she put out her hand to him with a smile.

"Oh, Grandpa, are you back again? I am so glad you are back."

"Are you glad, little one?" He stooped to kiss the upturned face. "Have you missed the old man all this time?"

"I like it best when you are here," she answered. "We all do. Shall we go for a walk now, Grandpa? My dear Granny said I might go to the Stones. I want to gather some giant harebells for Miss Thorold."

"May I have my pouch?" said Arthur.

She had it in her hand. She turned and gave it to him. "And there is a letter for Miss Thorold Aunt Maggie told me to bring out. Old Mrs. Trehearn has just brought it."

"A letter!" said Frances, and felt her heart jerk upon the word.

Silently Arthur handed it to her. One glance at the address was enough. She could not control the swift tremor that went through her as she murmured her thanks.

"And Dr. Square is here," said Ruth. "He is drinking elder-flower wine in the kitchen. He told me to say he is just coming out to see Miss Thorold."

"Then we will go," said Mr. Dermot, turning towards the couch with a courteous gesture. "Miss Thorold, I hope I have not tired you. You are very pale. Give Dr. Square my compliments, Arthur! Tell him I am back again and feeling much better. Good-bye, Miss Thorold! When next I have the pleasure of seeing you, I shall be bringing you my book to read."

He went, Ruth treading lightly by his side, noiseless and dainty as a scrap of thistledown.

Arthur had not stirred from his post by the foot of the couch. He stood there, massively, filling his pipe. And Frances lay, breathing quickly, her letter unopened in her hand.

Suddenly the man's eyes looked across at her, straight and challenging. "Aren't you going to read it?" he said.

She quivered at the abrupt question. She knew that she could not open that letter in his presence.

He realized the fact instantly, and she saw an odd gleam of triumph in his eyes. He turned and picked up his cap.

"All right. I'm going. But don't forget—whatever he has to say—you've promised to stay here for the present!"

He was gone with the words, striding away towards the house, leaving her oddly disconcerted and unsure of herself.

Yes, she had promised to stay. At the bidding of this man whom she scarcely knew, she had yielded the point and she knew that he would keep her to it. His attitude was wholly incomprehensible to her, convinced as she was that he had wished her gone. But in his taciturn, ungracious fashion he had somehow made it impossible for her to go. She wondered, as she watched him depart, if he were pleased—or otherwise—with his morning's work. Even with his last words vibrating in her mind, she greatly doubted if he had acted in accordance with his own inclination. She knew he had meant to be kind, but was it under pressure perhaps from someone else—Dolly, his mother, or the old tired man his father, who had evidently but just returned to the farm after a prolonged absence? It was impossible to tell. She was bound to suspend judgment. And meantime—meantime that second letter from Montague Rotherby was yet unopened in her trembling hand.

CHAPTER VI
MAGGIE

It was still unopened when Dr. Square came out of the house with Dolly, and at his approach she pushed it behind a cushion.

Whether he noted any agitation on her part or not she could not say, but he was very emphatic in his orders to her to rest, and impressed upon Dolly the necessity for absolute quiet. Then he departed, and, before she could open her letter, Milly came out with her work and a chair and sat down beside her with the evident intention of remaining. Milly was the silent one of the family, a shy, diffident girl who shared Ruth's adoration for her mother, but had little in common with the rest. She was stitching at a flannel shirt for Arthur, and she worked steadily without lifting her eyes.

Frances did not attempt any conversation. She was very tired, and the thought of that letter which could only be read in solitude burdened her. She had not answered the first, and he had written again so soon! She had a bewildered feeling as of being driven against her will, but whither she could not have said. Only she knew that if she would save herself this letter must be answered. He was growing impatient, and perhaps it was not surprising. She had given him a certain right over her. He could at least with justice claim an explanation of her changed attitude. But the bare thought of such an explanation revolted her. She had a passionate desire to thrust him out of her life, never to see him, never to communicate with him again. Only she knew—too well—that he would not submit to such treatment. Sooner or later he would demand a reckoning. And—torturing thought!—after all, had he not a right?

Oliver's cheery voice across the lawn diverted her attention. He was leaning on the sill of the dairy window, talking jauntily to someone within. She liked Oliver—Oliver Twist as they called him, on account, she had discovered, of a slight limp, the result of a kick on the knee in his boyhood. He had a gay personality that appealed to her, and the comic flash of his daring blue eyes was a thing to remember. He was never depressed, whatever the weather.

He was plainly enjoying himself on this occasion, and presently a ringing laugh in unison with his told her who was the companion of his idle moments. There was only one person at Tetherstones who ever laughed like that.

Milly glanced up nervously from her work at the sound, but made no comment. Only, as the distant figure suddenly leapt the sill and disappeared into the dairy, she coloured very deeply as if ashamed. Frances, who had viewed the whole incident with amused interest, felt a little out of patience with her. She had noticed before that Maggie and Oliver were evidently kindred spirits.

She closed her eyes with the reflection that Milly must be something of a prude, when a sudden commotion rekindled her interest and she opened them again in time to see Oliver come hurtling through the window with amazing force to land on his back in a bed of mignonette. With amazement that seemed to choke her she saw Arthur, his head lowered like an infuriated bull, draw back from the window into the dairy.

"Good heavens!" she said aloud. "Did he do that?"

"Yes," said Milly under her breath. She added very nervously, "It—it—it was Oliver's fault."

"Good heavens!" said Frances again.

The glimpse of Arthur's face, dead-white, a mask of anger, had set her pulses wildly throbbing. She watched tensely to see what Oliver would do.

What he did do amazed her almost more than his first involuntary gymnastic. He got up from the mignonette laughing as if he had just come out of a football scrum, straightened his attire without the smallest hint of discomfiture, and coolly vaulted back through the window into the dairy.

"Ah!" whispered Milly, and held her breath.

She clearly expected some further act of violence, and trembled for the young man's safety. Frances also watched with keen anxiety. But at the end of many seconds she began to realize that the episode was over. No one approached the window again.

Milly drew a deep breath and resumed her work in silence.

It was clear that she did not wish to discuss what had just taken place, and Frances was far too considerate to trouble her with questions or comments. But the incident had very successfully diverted her own thoughts. She actually forgot that disturbing letter which lay hidden under her cushion.

Her thoughts dwelt persistently upon Arthur Dermot. The man puzzled her. There was something tragic about him, something fierce, untamed and solitary, with which she found herself strangely in sympathy. She realized that the life he led was a singlehanded fight against odds. He was like a swimmer battling to make headway against an overwhelming current, succeeding only in keeping afloat; and she who for so long had also fought alone was aware of a quick sense of comradeship urging her to a readier comprehension than it seemed anyone else at Tetherstones possessed. She was beginning to understand what had made her first visualize him as a gladiator standing alone in the arena of life.

The rest of the morning passed uneventfully, save that Oliver presently appeared, unabashed and cheery of mien, armed with a hoe, and proceeded, whistling, to restore order in the bed of crushed mignonette. Then Dolly came out with her midday meal, after which the sisters took her back to her room to rest. She slept deeply during the afternoon, only awakening when the shadows were beginning to grow long. Then, looking forth from her window, there came to her the sudden memory of the letter she had forgotten. A gleam of something white under the cedar-tree where her couch had been caught her eye, and she realized immediately that it must have fallen there when they gathered up her rugs. The house was very still and seemed deserted. She guessed that those of the family who were not occupied in farm-work were gathering apples for cider in the orchard on the other side of the building.

There was no one to send for her letter, and that sense of shame with which the bare thought of Rotherby now inspired her urged her strongly not to leave it for any chance comer to discover. She was stronger far than she had been, and she made swift decision to use her strength. She got up from her bed and slipped on her shoes. She was already dressed, and she only paused to throw around her a shawl that Dolly had left handy. Then, with an odd feeling of guilt, she opened her door and went out into the dark oak passage.

The stairs were steep and winding. She knew that they would try her endurance and prepared to descend with caution. The dizziness of weakness came upon her as she reached them. And she hung upon the rail of the banisters to gather her forces.

In those moments of semi-helplessness there came to her the sound of voices talking in the kitchen below, but having embarked upon the expedition she was in no mood to draw back on account of a little physical weakness and it did not even cross her mind to call for help. Resolutely she summoned her strength, and, conquering her giddiness, began to descend.

It seemed to her that the stairs had become inexplicably steeper, and her hold upon the rail had developed into a desperate clinging with both hands before she rounded the final curve which brought her in sight of the bottom. Her heart was thumping uncontrollably, and her legs were almost refusing to support her by the time she reached the last stair. It was necessity rather than expediency that induced her to sit down there at the foot to gather her forces afresh.

So sitting, with her throbbing head in her hands, there came to her words at first dimly, then with a growing meaning which, too late she realized, were never intended for her ear to hear.

"I'd do it in a minute—you know I would,—" it was Maggie's voice, but strangely devoid of its customary cheery lilt—"if it weren't for Mother. But—I believe it would kill her if another of us went wrong."

"I'm not asking you to go wrong!" Swift and decided came the answer in Oliver's voice. "I wouldn't do such a thing. I love you too much for that. Good heavens! Don't you think your honour is as dear to me as it is to your mother—or Arthur?"

"Yes, but—" Unmistakable distress sounded in Maggie's rejoinder. She gave a little sob and left it at that.

"Well, then!" said Oliver, in the tone of one who scores a triumph.

There was a brief pause, then a sudden movement, followed by a muffled whisper from Maggie that was half protest and half appeal. "I don't know what Arthur would say. He'd half kill you."

"Oh, damn Arthur!" came the cheery response. "Why can't he get a girl of his own? P'raps he'd be more human then."

"He wouldn't—he wouldn't! Nothing would make him that, so long as—" Again the words broke off in half-hearted remonstrance.

"Rot!" said Oliver. "Once you were married to me, he'd have to come into line."

"No—no, he wouldn't! You don't understand." Maggie's answer came with a sound of tears. "You don't know him if you think that. He would simply kick you out of the place. And Mother—Mother would break her heart if I went too."

"Don't cry!" said Oliver softly.

Maggie was plainly sobbing against his shoulder. "I can't help it. Oh, Oliver, we'll have to be patient. We'll have to wait."

"But what are we going to wait for?" There was a hint of exasperation in Oliver's query. "I don't see what we gain by waiting. You're twenty-eight. I'm thirty-two. We've both of us waited five years as it is."

"Yes—yes! But let's go on waiting—there's a darling. Something'll happen some day. Something's sure to happen. And then we'll get married." Urgent entreaty backed the words. "It's no good getting married if we can't live together. And we—we—we are—very happy—as we are."

More tears followed the assurance. Maggie was evidently aware of pleading a lost cause.

"Oh, we're awfully happy, aren't we?" said Oliver, grimly humorous. "Don't cry, darling! I want to think. There's no law against our getting married—even if we don't live together—that I can see, is there? It would make things more sure anyway, and I guess we'd be a lot happier."

"Oh, Oliver! Deceiving everyone! I couldn't do it! Why, I'd be miserable every time I went to church!"

"No, you wouldn't. There'd be no harm done to anyone. You're old enough to manage your own life, and no one has any right to know how you do it." Oliver spoke with blunt decision. "You love me and I love you, and if we choose to marry—well, it doesn't matter a damn to anyone else. I may not be good enough for you, but that's your business, not Arthur's. If I'm good enough to love, I'm good enough to marry."

"Yes." Dubiously came Maggie's answer. "But then, Oliver darling, what's the use? We couldn't be together any more than we are. And we——"

"That's rot, isn't it?" Vigorously Oliver overruled her argument. "Well, anyway, you marry me and see!"

"Ah, but I'm afraid. The beast—the beast might do you a mischief!"

There was almost a wail in Maggie's words, but Oliver's hearty laugh drowned it. "Bless the girl! What next? Seems I'd better carry a pitchfork about with me. No, now listen! I'll fix it all up, and I won't even tell you till it's all cut and dried. Then one day you and I'll go into Fordestown to market, and when we come back we'll—" Inarticulate whispering ended the sentence. "There now! Will you do that?"

"I don't know, Oliver. I'm frightened. I'm sure it isn't right, and yet I don't know why."

Maggie's answer sounded piteous, yet somehow Frances knew that her arms were clinging about her lover's neck.

There came a pause, then Oliver's cheery voice. "There now! Don't you fret yourself! You may take it from me, it is right. And I'm going in to Fordestown to-morrow to get it settled. Mind, I shan't say another word to you till everything is ready. You won't back out? Promise!"

"Back out! Oh, darling—darling!"

Broken sounds came from Maggie that brought Frances to an abrupt realization of her position. She straightened herself and got up. Her knees were still trembling, but she forced them into action. She tottered down the passage to the nearest door and out on to the brick path that led to the garden.

The sun was going down. She passed between tall hollyhocks and sunflowers into the kitchen-garden. The lawn lay beyond. It was further than she had thought, and her strength was failing her. She came upon a rough bench set against the wall out of sight of the house and dropped down upon it with a feeling that she could go no further.

How long she had sat there she could not have said, for she was very near to fainting, when there came the sound of a man's feet on the path beside her, and, looking up, she saw Arthur in his shirt-sleeves, a spade on his shoulder.

He stopped beside her, and drove his spade into the ground.

"Miss Thorold!" he said. "What are they all thinking of? How did you come here?"

She tried to smile in answer, but her lips felt very cold and numb. "Oh, I just—walked," she said.

"You—walked!" Amazement and displeasure sounded in his voice. "Where is everyone?" he said. "Where is Maggie?"

He swung on his heel as if he would go in search of her, but Frances put forth an urgent hand to detain him.

"Don't go! It—really doesn't matter. Maggie is busy—getting the tea. I—I didn't like to interrupt her. I give too much trouble as it is."

Arthur growled something very deeply into his chest, but he checked his first impulse at her behest.

"Well, but what are you doing here? Why did you come out?" he asked, after a moment.

She hesitated to answer him. Then: "I dropped a letter," she said. "It is under the cedar-tree. I just thought I would fetch it."

"You must be mad," he said. "Stay here while I fetch it!"

He strode away, and she sat and waited for his return, shivering against the wall, wondering if Maggie and Oliver had separated, wishing with all her heart that she had not overheard their talk.

She heard the tramp of his heavy boots returning. He came back to her.

"The letter is not here," he said briefly. "Does it matter?"

She started. "Not there! But—I thought I saw it from my window. I thought——"

"It is not there," he repeated. "It has probably blown away. Is it of any great importance?"

His tone seemed to challenge her. She looked up and met his eyes watching her with a certain hardness.

"No," she said, and wondered what impulse moved her to utter the word.

"You are sure?" he said.

She smiled a little at his insistence. "Yes, quite sure. Please don't trouble about it! It will probably turn up later."

He dropped the subject without further discussion. "I had better carry you back now," he remarked, and stooped to lift her.

She drew back sharply. "Oh, don't, please! I can walk quite well."

"You're not going to walk," he said, and in a moment the strong brown arms encompassed her.

She abandoned protest. Somehow he made her feel like a child, and she knew that resistance was useless. It was not a dignified situation, but it appealed to her sense of humour, and as he bore her solidly back along the paths between the hollyhocks she uttered a breathless little laugh.

"What a giant you are!" she said.

"So you're not angry?" he said.

"Why, no! I am obliged to you. To be quite honest, I rather doubt if I could have walked back without some help."

"Then it is just as well I am here to carry you," he rejoined.

There was no sound of voices as he entered the house, and Frances breathed a sigh of thankfulness.

He carried her straight through and up to her room. "I hope you will not attempt that again before you are fit for it," he said, as he deposited her upon the bed.

"Thank you very much. I hope I shall soon be fit," said Frances.

He lingered in the doorway, his rugged face in shadow. "I hope you won't," he said suddenly and unexpectedly, and in a moment flung away down the passage awkwardly, precipitately, as if he feared he had stayed too long.

"Good gracious!" whispered Frances to the lengthening shadows. "What—on earth—did he mean by that?"

But there was only the queer uneven beating of her heart to answer her in the silence.

CHAPTER VII
THE PATH THROUGH THE WILDERNESS

Frances slept badly that night. There were a good many things to trouble her and keep her brain at work. The thought of Maggie's clandestine love affair worried her most, though why this should have been so she could not have said. There seemed to be a league among the sisters against their brother's authority, and she felt that against her will she had been drawn into it. She would have given anything not to have overheard that talk in the kitchen, but she found it impossible to forget it. And yet to interfere in any way seemed to her impossible. Maggie was of an age to direct her own affair, as surely Arthur ought to recognize. Her love for young Oliver was evidently of long standing, and, however unsuitable it might appear, no third person had the right to attempt to frustrate it. To Frances, who had guarded her own independence so jealously for so long, such a course was inexcusable. But the secret worried her. There seemed to be forces at work at Tetherstones of which she had no knowledge—sinister forces with which Maggie obviously felt unable to cope. And Arthur was so strange, so headlong, so impossible to manage.

Arthur! The thought of Arthur held her in a kind of breathless wonder. The man amazed her at every turn, but he never awaked in her that palpitating doubt with which she had always regarded Rotherby. He might possess violent impulses, but he was upright, he was honourable. What he said, he meant. There was even something terrible in his simplicity. He was a man who would suffer the utmost torture sooner than betray a friend. He was also a man who might inflict it without scruple upon an enemy who had incurred his vengeance.

His attitude towards herself had a curious effect upon her. She was aware of a strong bond of sympathy between them. They were rebels together. They had eaten stones for bread. They could not remain as strangers. There was that about him that made her wonder if he had ever had a friend before. He stood out above and beyond the rest with a kind of solitary grandeur that strangely moved her—a man who should have made his mark in the world of men, but condemned to till the soil to give them bread—a slave who had been fashioned for a conqueror. The irony of it stirred her strangely. She wondered if anyone else saw in him aught but a tiller of the ground. The old man, his father, perhaps? But no! He had spoken of him with contempt. She had been aware of a hostility scarcely veiled between them. The old man evidently despised him for the very servitude that so plainly galled his soul. Did no one understand him, she wondered? And then the memory of the mother, white-haired and patient, came to her, and by a flash of intuition she realized that here lay the explanation of many things. He had harnessed himself to the plough for her sake. She could not doubt it. Though she had never seen them together, she knew that she had discovered the truth, and she was conscious, poignantly conscious, of a feeling akin to indignation. How could any woman accept such a sacrifice?

Of her own affairs, of Montague Rotherby, she thought but little that night. The inner voice that had so urgently warned her no longer spoke within her soul. The need was past. Inexplicably, the attraction of the man had gone with it. The loss of her letter had vexed her temporarily, but now she had almost forgotten it. By her silence she would sever all connection with him. She judged him as not ardent enough to follow up the quest. The madness was over and would never return. Once again, and this time with a sense of comfort, she reflected that she was not the type of woman to appeal to such a man for long. That last letter of his had probably been one of farewell. On the whole she was not sorry that she had not read it. She wanted to forget him as soon as possible and with him the bitter humiliation he had made her suffer. It was better to forget than to hate. No; decidedly it was not on his account that Frances passed a restless night.

With the early morning came sleep that lasted till the sun was high, and Ruth came in to perch on her bed while she breakfasted. She had been out in the cornfields, she said. They were cutting the corn in the field below the Stones. Next week, when Frances was strong enough, they would go and sit among the sheaves. Or perhaps they might go to-day if Uncle Arthur would take them in the dog-cart. The idea attracted Frances though she only smiled. The day was hot, and she was feeling better. She had a desire to go out into the sunshine, away from the old grey house and its secrets, of which already she felt she knew too much.

She did not know that the child had read acquiescence in her silence till later, when Dolly suddenly announced that the cart would be round in half-an-hour, and they must hurry.

"It would do you good to spend the whole day out to-day," said the practical Dolly, whom Frances suspected of being secretly a little tired of a job that had ceased to be interesting. "Elsie and Lucy and Nell will all be to and fro if you should want anything. And no one could possibly catch cold on a day like this. Milly and I are going to Wearmouth to do some shopping, but I shall be back in good time to get you to bed. Dr. Square said he might not come to-day. If he does, it won't hurt him to ride as far as the cornfield to see you."

It had evidently been all talked over and arranged beforehand, and Frances had no objection to raise. In fact, the prospect delighted her.

"I should like to take my sketching-block," she said. "And I shall be quite happy."

So, armed with her beloved box of paints and brushes, she presently descended to find Arthur waiting somewhat moodily at the door with a pie-bald cob harnessed to a light dog-cart. His dark face brightened at the sight of her. He took the pipe from between his teeth and knocked out its contents on the heel of his boot.

"Better this morning?" he asked, as she came out.

She smiled at him, panting from her descent of the stairs, but resolutely ignoring her weakness. "Yes, I am much better. I am as strong as a horse to-day. Are you really going to drive me to the cornfields? How kind of you!"

"Jump up!" said Arthur. "You go to his head, Dolly! I'll help Miss Thorold."

He issued his orders with characteristic decision, and they were obeyed. Almost before she knew it, Frances found herself lifted on to the high seat where he wrapped a rug about her knees and pushed a cushion behind her.

The next moment he mounted beside her and took the reins. Dolly stepped back. The horse leaped forward.

"Hold on!" said Arthur.

They were out in the winding lane before Frances found breath to ask for Ruth. "Won't she come with us? Have you forgotten her?"

"We never trouble about Ruth," he replied. "She finds her own way everywhere. She will probably go across the stepping stones and get there first."

"Are you never afraid of her coming to harm?" she asked.

"She never does," said Arthur. He spoke briefly, and immediately turned from the subject. "Do you mind if we go for a stretch first? The horse is fresh."

"Mind!" said Frances. "I'd love it!"

He laughed, and she knew in a moment that the plan was by no means an impromptu one. "It will do you good," he said, and turned the horse's head towards the moors.

They came out upon an open road and went like the wind. The day was glorious, the distant tors all blue and purple in the sunshine. They followed a direction she had never explored, and presently turned off up a wide track that seemed to wind into the very heart of the hills.

"Afraid it's rather bumpy," said Arthur. "Do you mind?"

"I mind nothing," she answered simply.

He glanced at her. "You are not disliking it?"

She drew a long breath. "I don't believe I ever knew what life could be before to-day."

He said no more. The guiding of the horse took up all his attention. They came presently to a track crossing the one they were following.

He reined in as if he had reached his destination. Frances looked about her. The place was lonely beyond description. Here and there vast boulders pushed through the short grass, surrounded by tufts of heather that seemed to be trying to hide their nakedness. They were closely surrounded by hills, and the gurgle of an invisible stream filled the air with music.

"Have you ever been here before?" said Arthur.

"Never," she said.

"Yes, you have," he returned bluntly.

She started a little, and looked about her more attentively. Was the place familiar?

He pointed suddenly with his whip along the track they faced. "You and Roger!" he said. "Don't you remember?"

She uttered a gasp of surprise. "Why—yes! But was it here?"

"It was round the curve of that hill," he said. "Afterwards, you came on here alone, and lost your way, took the wrong turning. Remember?"

"I wanted to get to Fordestown," she said. "But I was tired. I fell asleep."

He nodded. "And then you wandered up to the Stones."

She felt herself colour. With an effort she answered him. "It wasn't quite like that. I met—a friend, or rather—he found me here. We got lost in the fog. That was how it happened."

"Yes," said Arthur.

He turned the horse up the wild track to the left without further words, and they went on in silence at a walk.

A great stillness brooded about their path. A certain awe had taken possession of Frances. The ruggedness of the place, its austerity, held her like a spell. The high hills shut them in, and the music of many streams was the only sound.

"You are taking me to the Stones?" she said at length, and unconsciously her voice was sunk almost to a whisper.

"Yes," he said.

They went on up the lonely track. She tried to picture her walk with Montague through the blinding fog. Here she had slipped into bog, there she had stumbled among stones. Then as now, the vague sounds of running water had filled the desolation as with eerie, chanting voices. The smell of bog-myrtle came to her suddenly, and in a moment very vividly the terror of that night was back upon her. The thud of the horse's hoofs on the wet track fell with a fateful, remorseless beat. She experienced a swift, almost overwhelming desire to turn back.

It must have communicated itself to the man beside her, for he checked the animal with a curt word and brought the swaying cart to a standstill.

"Miss Thorold, what is it? Have I brought you too far?"

The concern in his voice reassured her. She met his look with a smile. "No! I am quite all right. It is only my foolish imagination—playing tricks with me. Shall we go on?"

"Do you wish to go on?" he said.

"Yes. I am longing to see the Stones. I think this is rather a dreadful place, don't you? It makes one think of"—she stumbled a little—"of human sacrifice. Do you hold your father's theory about the Stones?"

"I seldom agree with my father about anything," he returned sombrely. "Yes, you are right. This is a dreadful place. It has a bad name, as I told you before."

They went on up the grassy track, mounting steadily. The rocky nature of the ground became more and more pronounced as they proceeded. The grass grew more sparsely though the tufts of heather continued.

"Are you frightened?" Arthur asked abruptly.

"No," said Frances.

He looked at her. "You are sure?"

"What is there to frighten me?" she said.

"You were frightened the last time you came," he said.

"Oh, that was different. It was foggy. I was lost." She spoke quickly, with a touch of confusion, aware of the old embarrassment stirring within her.

He turned his eyes deliberately away and stared at the horse's ears. "Would you be frightened now," he said, "if a fog came up and you didn't know the way?"

"Not with you to guide me," she said.

"Thank you," he said quietly.

The hills closed gradually in upon the track till it was little more than a narrow passage, winding among boulders. The horse's feet clattered upon stones. Quite suddenly the path mounted steeply between two large rocks and disappeared.

"Can we possibly get up there?" said Frances.

The man beside her made no reply. He merely struck the animal with the whip, so that he plunged at the steep ascent, and in a few moments was clambering up it with desperate effort. The cart rocked and jolted, and Frances clung to the rail. They reached the two grey rocks at the summit and passed between them on to a flat open space that shone green in the sunshine.

"This is the place," said Arthur.

Frances looked all about her and drew a long, deep breath. "Ah! How—wonderful!" she said. "What a wilderness!"

CHAPTER VIII
THE STONES

They stood up all around, forming a great amphitheatre—the great, grey stones that had weathered so many centuries. Stark and grim, sentinels of the ages, they stood in their changeless circle, as they had stood in the early days of the world ere men had learned to subdue the earth.

Frances sat and gazed and gazed with a curious feeling of reverence upon that forgotten place of sacrifice.

"Isn't it strange?" she whispered to herself. "Isn't it wonderful?"

And then she turned to the man by her side. "It reminds me of the days when you were a Roman gladiator and I was one of the slaves who sprinkled the saw-dust in the arena."

He looked at her with his brooding eyes. "So you were a slave?" he said.

"I have always been one," she answered, with a quizzical lifting of the brows.

"You were not intended for a slave," he said.

She smiled a little. "May I get down? I should like to walk here."

"Are you strong enough?" he said.

"Of course I am strong enough. When I am tired, I will curl up and sleep in the sunshine."

"You're not afraid?" he said.

She faced him. "Of course I am not afraid. Why should I be?"

He lifted his shoulders slightly. "You were—or I imagined you were—a little while ago."

"Oh, that was different," she said. "Anyway, I am not so foolish now. I could sit here for hours and sketch."

"It has been called the devil's paradise," he said rather harshly.

She snapped her fingers and laughed. "I am never afraid of the devil when the sun is out. Are you?"

"Sometimes," he said.

He jumped to the ground and turned to help her, the reins over his arm.

She slipped down into his hold. "But there is nothing to frighten anyone here," she said.

Even as she spoke, her heart misgave her a little. The Stones looked more imposing from the ground. Some of them had an almost threatening aspect. They seemed to crouch like gigantic monsters about to spring.

"It is certainly a wonderful place," she said. "And the farm is close by?"

"Just down the hill on the other side," he said. "It takes its name from them. Some bygone race probably used the place for sacrifice. The actual Tetherstones to which the victims were said to have been fastened are over there, close to the cattle-shed in which Ruth found you. The shed is just out of sight below the brow of the hill."

"It is a wonderful place," Frances said again.

She relinquished his arm, and began to walk a few steps over the grass. The man stood motionless, watching her. His brows were drawn. He had a waiting look.

Suddenly she turned and came back to him. She was smiling, but her face was pale. "Mr. Dermot, I am not sure that I do want to stay here after all," she said. "There's something I can't quite describe—something uncanny in the atmosphere."

"You want to go?" he said.

She shivered sharply, standing in the full sunshine. "I don't want to be left alone here."

"No," he said, in his brief way. "And I don't mean you to be here alone." He put out a hand and pointed to a curiously shaped stone so poised that it seemed to be on the point of rolling towards them. "Do you see that? That is one of the great tetherstones. It is called the stone of sacrifice. It is so balanced that a child could make it rock, but no one could move it from its place. There are marks on that stone that scientists declare have been made by human hands, places where staples have been driven in, and so cunningly devised that prisoners chained to those staples were unharmed so long as they remained passive. But the moment they strained for freedom, the stone rocked slowly to and fro and they were crushed—gradually ground to death."

"Oh, don't!" Frances cried. "How gruesome—how horrible!"

"A devil's paradise!" he said.

"But why did you bring me here?" she protested. "Why do you tell me these dreadful things?"

He shrugged his shoulders again. "I brought you here to satisfy your curiosity. My father will tell you much more horrible things than that. His book is full of them."

"Let us go!" she said, shuddering. "I won't come here again."

"As you wish," he said. "There are certainly pleasanter places."

He helped her back into the cart, and wrapped the rug about her knees. As he did so, with his face turned from her he spoke again in a tone that affected her very strangely.

"Miss Thorold, I haven't told you everything. There is a much more modern tragedy connected with this place which I haven't told you of. It isn't a subject that is ever mentioned among us, and I can't go into any details. But—you've probably discovered by this time that there is something that makes us different from the rest of the world. It is—that."

He spoke with an effort, and for the first time in all her knowledge of men there came to Frances that tender, motherly feeling that comes to every woman when she is face to face with a man's suffering.

She sat for a moment or two without moving or speaking; then she put out a hesitating hand and touched his shoulder. "I am sorry," she said very gently.

He drew in his breath sharply, but still he did not look at her. "I have never spoken of it to anyone outside before. But you are somewhat different. You have been through the mill, and you are capable of understanding?"

"I hope so," she said.

He jerked up his head with an odd movement of defiance. "There's one thing I would like you to know," he said. "Though I am no more than a country clod and grind my living out of the stones, I've made a success of it. There's not a single farmer hereabouts who can say that he has a better show than mine. In fact, they know quite well that Tetherstones beats them all."

"That was worth doing," said Frances.

"Yes. It was worth doing. But now that it's done, anyone could run it—anyone with any experience. Oliver could run it." He spoke contemptuously.

"Then why not let him," suggested Frances, "and take a holiday yourself?"

"Let him!" He turned upon her almost violently. "Leave Oliver to run this show! You don't know—" He pulled himself up. "Of course you don't know. How should you? Oliver is very useful, but he is only a labourer after all. I don't see myself putting him in my place. He thinks too much of himself as it is."

"Ah!" Frances said, with an unpleasant feeling of duplicity at her heart. "But you like him, don't you? He is a good sort?"

"I hope he is a good sort," Arthur said grimly. "He needs to be kept in his place. I know that much. And I'll see that it's done, too."

He looked at her hard with the words, as if challenging a reply. But Frances made none. Her years of rigorous work had taught her to maintain silence where she felt speech to be futile. She never wasted her words.

And in a moment Arthur relaxed. "I couldn't leave my post in any case," he said. "There are—other reasons."

"Yes," Frances said, glad of the change of topic. "I realize that."

"Do you? How?" Again that peremptory, challenging look met hers.

But she answered him with absolute simplicity. On this point at least she felt no qualms. "On account of your mother," she said. "I guessed that."

His face changed, softening magically. "Yes, my mother," he said. "But what made you guess it?"

"It just came to me," she said. "I knew you must be fond of someone."

He looked away from her to a gap of blue distance in front of them, and for a few seconds there was silence between them. Then: "Thank you for saying that," he said, "and for thinking it. You have an extraordinary insight. Do you read everyone's motives in this way? Or is it only mine?"

There was a hint of melancholy in the question, as though he invited ridicule to cover an unacknowledged pathos. But Frances did not answer it, for she had no answer ready. She felt as if in his silence he had lifted the veil and given her a glimpse of his lonely soul. She saw him as it were surrounded by a great solitude which she could not cross. And so she turned away.

"I am not a great reader of character," she said. "Only I know that there is only one way of turning our stones into bread. And if we don't find it, we starve."

"Yes, starve!" He repeated the word with his eyes still upon the blue distance. "I'm used to starving," he said slowly. "It's a sort of chronic state with me."

The sound of the reaping-machine came whirring through the sunlit silence, and the man pulled himself together with a gesture of impatience. "Well, I suppose we must go. You have seen the Stones, and I hope you are satisfied."

"I am glad you brought me," she said. "But I don't think I shall come again."

He looked at her, and she thought there was a hint of relief on his face. "You have seen all there is to see," he said. "I think you are wise."

He mounted into the cart beside her and walked the horse forward over the grass.

"There is little Ruth," said Frances.

The child had come suddenly into view from behind one of the great stones, moving as was her wont lightly and fearlessly, her face upturned. She was carrying a small bunch of harebells, and as she came towards them she stooped and felt among the grass for more. Her soft, chirruping song rose up like the humming of a fairy. Finding some of the wiry stalks she sought, she knelt down in the sunshine to gather them.

"How happy she is!" whispered Frances.

The man said nothing. He walked the horse straight up to the little kneeling figure and reined in beside it.

"Is that you, Uncle Arthur?" said little Ruth.

"Yes," he said. "Come here to me and I will take you back to the corn-field!"

She got up and came to him. He stooped and grasped her shoulder, guiding her to the step.

"Is Miss Thorold there?" said the child.

"Yes, darling. I am here," Frances answered, and made room for her in the seat.

Ruth mounted the step, and in a moment nestled in beside her. "I gathered these flowers for you," she said.

"Thank you, darling." Frances took the flowers and stooped to kiss her.

"I've been waiting for you a long, long time," Ruth said. "Have you liked your drive?"

"I have loved it," Frances said with simplicity.

"Thank you," said Arthur quietly, on the other side.

They passed on through the great circle and out between the stones on to a narrow track that led steeply downwards to a lane.

The buzz of a car rose from below them as they approached it, and Arthur drew in his horse. The car went by unseen, but to Frances in the high cart there came a sudden, sharp sense of insecurity that was almost panic, and for a moment she ceased to breathe. She knew that car.

Her agitation subsided gradually. They went on down the lane and turned into the corn-field.

"I must leave you here," Arthur said.

He helped them both down and settled them comfortably with a rug and cushions in the shade of the hedge.

"Will you be all right here?" he asked Frances. "I will tell Elsie to look after you."

"I shall be quite all right," she assured him. "Please don't let anyone waste any time over me!"

He smiled and turned away. She watched him go with an answering smile upon her lips.

Roger came up and lay down beside them. The peace of a perfect day descended upon the harvest-field. The fragrance of the cut corn was like an oblation.

"Are we alone?" said Ruth.

"Yes, darling. Why?"

The little girl came pressing close to her side. "Because I've got something to tell you, and it's a secret. I met a man to-day in the lane, who said he was a friend of yours. He didn't tell me who he was, but it was the friend who wrote that letter to you. And he said—would I tell you that he will be at the Stones again to-night at ten."

CHAPTER IX
THE LETTER

"At the Stones again to-night." All through that morning in the corn-field the words were running in Frances' brain. She tried to sketch, but her hand seemed to have lost its cunning, and there were times when a great trembling seized her. His letter she had thrust out of her mind. She had not read it, nor had she greatly desired to know what it contained. But his message was different, and again with the words she seemed to hear that rushing of an unseen car, and recalled the man, his bearing half-insolent, half-cynical, the curious persistence with which he had pursued her, the nameless attraction of his personality. She did not want to answer his message. She did not want to meet him. But yet—but yet—deep in the very heart of her she knew that a meeting was inevitable. A reckoning must come, and she was bound to face it. She might, if she so chose, avoid him now, but she could not avoid him always. Sooner or later she would have to endure her ordeal, and tell him—plainly tell him—that the madness was over and her eyes were open. She was not, and never had been, the type of woman which apparently he had taken her to be. And if he could not learn this by her silence she must summon strength to put the matter baldly into words. She shrank from the thought, but brought herself back to it again and again. The idea of writing to him presented itself, but she discarded it with an even greater distaste. When the ordeal was over, she desired—earnestly desired—that no trace of it should be left behind. No written word from her was in his possession now, nor should it ever be. She wanted to thrust away this unclean thing that had come into her life so that no vestige of it remained. And not until she had done this would she feel free.

So she argued with herself all through the long sunny morning, while the bundles of corn fell in ever-increasing numbers, and little Ruth flitted to and fro playing with the long golden strands that she drew from them.

After a while Oliver came up with a smile on his merry face to talk to her, but he had scarcely reached her when there came the sound of a horse's feet in the lane, and Dr. Square appeared at the gate.

"They told me I should find you here," he said, and came in and sat down beside her, while Oliver saluted and went away.

She told the doctor of her drive in the dog-cart to the Stones, and he expressed some surprise that Arthur had taken her there.

"He usually avoids the place like the plague," he said.

Her curiosity awakened. "Do you know why?" she said.

"Yes, I know," said Dr. Square.

She looked at him. "Is it a secret?"

She thought his red, wholesome face had a dubious look, but he answered her without actual hesitation. "Not that I know of. Naturally they don't talk about it here at Tetherstones. It was the scene of a very unhappy tragedy some six years ago." His eyes rested upon Ruth busy among the corn-sheaves at a little distance. "It was one of the sisters," he said, "the child's mother,—a lovely girl—a lovely girl. She died up there in a blizzard one winter night. She was out of her mind at the time. She took the little one with her. When we found them, she was frozen stiff, but the child still lived. Poor mite—poor little girl! She'd better have gone with her mother."

"Oh, why do you say that?" Frances said. "She is happy. There are plenty to love her."

The doctor's eyes dwelt very tenderly upon the little figure. "I say it because it is true," he said. "She is not like other children, Miss Thorold. She never will be. She is just—'a little bit of heaven' strayed down to earth. She is one of those the gods love."

"Oh, do you mean that?" Frances said.

He nodded. "I mean it—yes. I told them long ago—the child won't live to grow up. They all know it."

"But they take so little care of her!" said Frances.

"It is far better she should lead a natural life," he said. "She is just like a flower of the field. She will have her day—her little day, Miss Thorold. They are wise to leave her alone. Cooped up within four walls she would never have lived so long. Freedom is life to her."

"I often wonder that they dare to let her wander as she does," Frances said.

"It is far better," said Dr. Square. He turned to her with a smile. "Has it never occurred to you that she is under special protection? I have often thought it. They are all too busy to look after her, yet she is safe and happy. I think she is one of the happiest little souls I have ever met. I have never seen her cry. We need not pity her too much. In fact, I sometimes think she is hardly to be pitied at all."

"Perhaps you are right," Frances said.

The doctor's philosophy appealed to her. She liked the simple fashion with which he regarded life. She would not question him further concerning the Dermot family, for some sense of loyalty restrained her. But when he was gone, she pondered over the matter. Why did they stay in a place that contained such painful associations for them? She had Arthur's word for it that he had made a success of the farm, and every indication pointed to the fact. But it had been an uphill fight. Why had he chosen to make it there?

Midday came, and with it Lucy and Nell to take her back to the house. It was no great distance across the field to the garden, but it taxed her powers somewhat, for the ground was rough. She was glad when they reached the shade of the cedar-tree and she could sit down on the bench beneath it to rest.

"You had better not go to the corn-field again," said Nell.

And she acquiesced. She would not do anything strenuous for the rest of the day. The thought of her letter recurred to her, and she looked about but saw nothing of it. Evidently it had blown away.

After a brief interval she continued her journey to the house where Maggie joined them with kindly concern on her rosy face.

"You do look tired," she said. "Come and sit down in the kitchen for a little and see Mother scalding the cream!"

The kitchen was oak-raftered and possessed an immense open fire-place with a brick oven at the side. Frances went in and was welcomed by Mrs. Dermot in her gentle, tired fashion, and made to sit down in a high-backed, wooden arm-chair.

The girls buzzed around her, and she had almost begun to forget her own pressing problem in the homely atmosphere when a sudden angry shout rang through the house, and in a moment every voice in the kitchen was hushed.

Frances, who was speaking to Mrs. Dermot at the moment saw her put her hand to her heart. Maggie came to her quickly and put an arm about her. But she spoke no word, and the silence was terrible.

Then from the stone passage outside came a voice, Arthur's voice, short and peremptory.

"I'll stand no more of this, and you know it. Let me pass!"

There was a brief pause, then an answering voice—the broken, quavering voice of an old man. "I have no wish to keep you here. You come into my room, tamper with my belongings, threaten me. I only ask you to go. What have I done that I should be treated like this?"

"What have you done?" A sound that was inexpressibly bitter followed the words. "Well, not much on this occasion perhaps. But I warn you, it had better not happen again. I will have no more of it. You understand?"

"No." Sudden dignity dispelled all agitation in the rejoinder. "I do not understand how my son who, if he is not a gentleman, has at least had the upbringing of one, as well as the advantage of good birth, can bring himself to treat his father with a brutality that he would not display towards the dog in the stable. I protest against your behaviour, though I am as fully aware as you are that I have no remedy."

"None, sir, none." Again that horrible jarring note was in Arthur's voice. "It would be as well if you always bore that in mind. I am the master here, as I have told you before."

"You are a damned blackguard," said the old man in a voice that was deadly cold. "Now leave my room!"

There came the instant closing of a door, a step outside, and Arthur entered. The veins stood out on his forehead; his face was terrible. He looked round the kitchen, paused for a moment with his eyes upon Frances as if he would speak; then, without a word, took a glass from the dresser, and went out to a pump in the yard.

Mrs. Dermot drew a deep breath and gently released herself from Maggie's arm. She turned as if to follow her son, but in a moment checked the impulse and busied herself over the fire.

He entered again almost immediately, the tumbler half full in his hand. He went straight to his mother and murmured something in a low voice. She shook her head in silence. He drained the glass and set it down. Again his look went to Frances, and again he seemed on the verge of speech. Then a faint sob came from Lucy, and he swung round upon her with a scowl.

She recoiled from him, and instantly Nell the valiant sprang into the breach. "Oh, for goodness' sake, Arthur, stop ramping!" she said. "Go away if you can't control yourself, and come back when you feel better! We'll have dinner ready in twenty minutes."

"Then you can send mine out to the farm-yard," he rejoined curtly. "I'll wait for it there."

He was gone with the words, and there went up a breath of relief from the kitchen at his exit.

"Hadn't we better get to work?" said Mrs. Dermot in her weary, subdued voice. "Father will be wanting his dinner too."

Frances stood up. "I will go up to my room," she said.

"Shall I come?" said Elsie.

"No, please don't! I can manage quite well alone." She passed the girl with a smile, intent upon removing herself before they should discover her presence to be an embarrassment. As she left the kitchen she heard a buzz of talk arise among the girls, and one very audible remark from Nell pursued her as she went. "Oh, we'll get his dinner for him. It's a pity he doesn't always feed among the pigs."

Frances passed on, feeling oddly shaken. As she rounded the corner of the stairs, Oliver came clattering in from the back premises and overtook her. He stopped her without ceremony.

"I just want a word with you, Miss Thorold. Do you mind? Don't think it's cheek on my part. It's too urgent for that."

She stood and faced him. "Oliver, what's the matter?"

"Oh, don't worry!" he said. "Don't be scared! It's just this. A friend of yours was just outside here to-day, asking for you. That is to say, he asked Ruth about you, for I asked her what he wanted and she said he gave her a message for you."

"Yes; that is so," Frances said. "But what—what——"

"What business is it of mine?" he said. "It isn't my business, that's straight. But you just listen a minute! I'm not rotting. You get that friend of yours out of the way—quick! Understand? There's no time to be lost. If he stays in the neighbourhood there'll be trouble. You tell him to go, Miss Thorold! It's a friend's advice, and for heaven's sake, take it!"

He spoke with great earnestness, and she saw that there were beads of perspiration on his forehead.

"It's true as gospel," he said. "He's in danger. I can't tell you what it is. But I'll take my dying oath it's true. It's up to you to warn him, and if you don't—well, you'll regret it all your life, that's all."

He paused and wiped his forehead on his shirt-sleeve. She stood and looked at him, conscious of a feeling of dread that made her physically cold. What was the meaning of these tumults and warnings, these mysterious under-currents that seemed to be perpetually drawing her towards tragedy? What was the direful secret of this sinister house?

Oliver saw her distress, and dismissed his own with a jerk. "Don't be upset!" he said. "There's no harm done yet—not so far as I know. But don't let him hang round any longer! If Arthur were to get a sight of him—" He broke off. "That's all. Hope we shall see you in the field again to-morrow. It's good weather for harvesting. We ought to be carrying by the end of the week if it lasts."

She knew from his tone that he was speaking for the benefit of a third person, but she did not turn her head to look. She knew without that that Arthur was standing at the end of the passage, and she began to ascend the stairs with a distinct feeling that escape was imperative. Oliver went away into the kitchen, and she rounded the curve of the old staircase and began to quicken her pace. But her knees were so weak and her breathing so short that she thought she would never reach the top. Then, with a sudden start of consternation, she heard the tread of Arthur's feet below, and knew that he was coming up behind her.

She mustered all her strength then in desperation, for she felt she could not face him at that moment; and gasping, stumbling, unnerved, she practically fled before him.

The door of her room stood open, but she lacked the power to close it as she entered. She could only stagger to the nearest chair and fall into it, panting.

He came on up the stairs. She heard his feet upon the bare oak. He reached the open door and stopped.

"Miss Thorold!" he said.

Then he must have seen her condition, for he came in without further ceremony.

"You've been frightened," he said.

She could not answer him because of the wild palpitation of her heart. He bent over her; then suddenly knelt beside her, and she felt the strong grip of his hand on hers.

"There's nothing to frighten you," he said, in his deep voice, and she knew that for some reason he was moved.

She leaned her head against the back of the chair, battling with her weakness. "I am not very strong yet," she managed to say.

"I know—I know! You'll be better presently. Don't take any notice of these trifles!"

The gentleness of his voice amazed her; it had the sound of a half-suppressed appeal, and something within her stirred in answer.

"You are very good to me," she said.

"Good! To you!" There was almost a passionate note in his reply. His grip upon her hand tightened, and then in a moment he seemed to control himself, and very slowly he set her free and rose. "What I wanted to say to you," he said, "is just that I am sorry that you should have been upset in any way by any unfortunate family disagreements. I don't know what Oliver was saying to you on the subject; he probably told you that they are by no means unusual. But please take my word for it that it shall not happen again if I can possibly prevent it, and make allowances where you can!"

The appeal was unmistakable this time, and again that sense of comradeship possessed her in spite of all misgiving. She smiled at him without speaking, and somehow his answering smile sent a quick thrill to her heart.

He turned to go, then abruptly wheeled back to her. "One thing more! I've found your letter—the one you lost in the garden. Do you want it back, or may I destroy it?"

She gave a gasp of surprise. "You have found it? Where—where was it?"

"In the garden," he repeated, with a certain doggedness.

She looked up at him. "Where is it now?"

"In my pocket," he said. "Do you want it?"

"I think I had better have it," she said.

"You are sure?" His eyes met hers with the old challenging look, and her own fell beneath them.

Nevertheless she held out her hand. "Please!" she said.

The next moment she found the missing letter thrust into her fingers, but she did not even look at it. She was staring at his retreating figure as he went out and closed the door sharply behind him.

CHAPTER X
REVELATION

She had it in her hand at last—that letter which had caused her so much doubt and anxiety. She sat there holding it after the closing of the door, wondering, puzzled, troubled. He had found it—he must have found it—under the cedar-tree the night before. Why had he kept it back? Or, having kept it, why did he give it to her now? Suspicion stabbed her, and she turned the envelope over. Had it been opened? It was impossible to say. It had obviously been rubbed from having been carried in a pocket; but there was no sign of weather-stain upon it. She was instantly convinced that it had not lain out all night. Yet why had he kept it?

An odd thought came to her, born of that strange new note of appeal that she had begun to hear in his voice—a thought which sent the blood to her face in a great wave and for a moment almost dazed her. Was it jealousy that had prompted him? He had known that her letter had caused her agitation, that it was from another man. He had almost openly done his best to counteract that other man's influence upon her. He had taken her to the Stones only that morning in the hope of inducing her to be frank with him regarding her adventure there. It was not curiosity—it could not be mere curiosity—that had actuated him. She recalled his behaviour of the night before when he had carried her in, how he had bluntly given her to understand that his own desire was to keep her there as long as possible. And then Oliver's warning flashed upon her, illuminating all the rest. With a gasp she faced the situation, suspicion merging into certainty, amazing but irrefutable. He cared for her, this extraordinary man who ruled at Tetherstones with so heavy a hand. For some reason wholly inexplicable to her, his fancy had lighted upon her—just as had

Montague Rotherby's in an idle hour. But with what a difference! It was at this point that Frances arose and went unsteadily to her dressing-table to lean upon it and stare in stupefaction at her own reflection. Had all the world gone mad? What on earth did they see in her—the faded, the drab, the tired? She gazed for a long, breathless space, and slowly her eyes widened. What did she see in herself? Was there not something present here that she had never seen before? What was it? What was it? A sudden tremor went through her, and she drew back.

What were those words he had said to her that morning? Vividly the memory rushed upon her, and his eyes—the look in his eyes—as they had rested upon her. . . . "You were not intended for a slave."

Was it this that they saw in her—a slave who had broken free—her shackles in the dust? Was it this that she had suddenly seen in herself?

She was quivering from head to foot. A feeling of giddiness came upon her, and she dropped down upon the edge of the bed. Something had frightened her, badly frightened her,—something wholly apart from the gloomy secrets of Tetherstones, the undercurrent of rebellion that existed there, the muttered warnings, the element of violence barely masked—something that had looked at her out of her own eyes—something that throbbed very deeply in her own heart—a thing so widely different from anything she had ever know before that she was amazed, that she was actually terrified, beyond thought or speech.

It was this that had stirred within her in answer to that unspoken appeal for understanding. It was this that had inspired that sense of comradeship within her. She had called it intuition, sympathy. But now—she knew now that it had another name. And what was she going to do? How was she going to treat this amazing thing? Was she prepared to let it grow and become great? Was she prepared to yield herself to it, her cherished independence, her very life, and become a slave again? Was she going to stake all she had—all that the unknown future might hold for her—upon one fatal throw? To be absorbed into this tragic atmosphere, to feel the ground unstable beneath her feet, to hear the grim clash of antagonisms shattering the peace, to be in bondage to this man of harsh judgments and unrestrained passions,—to be a slave again, perhaps to cower as Lucy had cowered from his ungoverned fury! But no! She would never do that! Sheer pride came to her aid, and she straightened herself with a little smile of self-ridicule. Why was she permitting this panic? She knew herself well enough to be quite sure she would never do that.

"I believe I could manage him alone," she reflected. "But in this atmosphere of servitude and oppression—well, of course—" she laughed a faint laugh and felt the better for it—"any man would be bound to become a tyrant—like the Bishop—only worse." Her letter slipped from her grasp, and she stooped to recover it. Something of the old official attitude was hers as she sat up again and prepared to open it. "Well, we will put a stop to this anyhow," she said with decision. "And then we must consider the best and safest way of leaving Tetherstones without giving rise to foolish conjecture."

Again that odd little smile of hers tilted her lips. The feeling of dismay had gone.

"I shall get over it all right," she said. "It's a pity of course, but it isn't big enough yet to hurt me much. If I had been younger—" she lifted her head suddenly—"but dash it, I'm not so old as that. If he wants me he must get rid of his retinue of slaves and take the trouble to win me. But to add me to the number—make me the chief one at that—no, no, no!" She shook her head in humorous negation. "It isn't good enough, my dear man. Love doesn't thrive in that soil."

But even as she said it, a little gibing voice rose up in her soul and mocked her. Who was she to say from what small beginnings Love the Immortal might spring? Like the wonderful, purple flower on the grey stone arch in the Palace garden that no human hand had ever planted!

She opened her letter almost absent-mindedly, and began to read it with an interest as impersonal as she would have bestowed upon the letter of an employer.

"Circe—beloved enchantress," so the letter ran. "Am I to have no word from you? It is getting urgent, and I have news for you. First, let me make a confession! When I left you that evening at the cottage, I stole one of your sketches—the one of the stepping-stones. I sent it to a friend of mine in town, and have to-day received it back. He speaks very highly of it, and declares you have a living in your talent, if not a fortune. How does that appeal to you? The old woman tells me you are better, but that you are staying on at Tetherstones. I must see you somewhere where we can talk undisturbed. Will you come to the Stones to-night at ten? I will wait for you there.

"Yours with all my love as ever. M. R."

So that was why he had written a second time! He had news for her. Such news as she had little expected—news that made her heart leap wildly. This was freedom. This was deliverance. Strange that they should have come to her by his hand!

No further doubt existed in her mind with regard to meeting him. She would certainly meet him. She put her letter away with a business-like precision that wholly banished her agitation. It was the best tonic that she could possibly have received. She wondered what had made him take the trouble, and the thought of being under an obligation to him oppressed her for a time, but she thrust it away from her. She could not afford to be too scrupulous in this particular. To make her own living successfully seemed to her at that moment the goal of all desire.

The arrival of Nell with her tray diverted her thoughts. Nell's face was flushed, her eyes round and indignant.

"A nice family of wild beasts you must think us!" she said, as she dumped the tray on a corner of the dressing-table. "I suppose you're making plans to leave us by the next train. It's enough to make you."

Frances looked at her, and saw that she was near to angry tears. "My dear child," she said gently, "please put that idea quite out of your mind! When I go—and it will probably be soon now that I am so much better—it won't be with any feelings of that sort. It will only be with the very warmest gratitude to you all for your goodness to me."

"Do you mean that?" said Nell.

"Of course I mean it," Frances said.

"Well, I'm glad—awfully glad." The girl spoke with honest feeling. "We're all so fond of you, Miss Thorold, and we do do our best to make you happy. It isn't our fault that—that—" She checked herself. "I expect you understand that," she ended more calmly.

"I know you are all much too kind to me," Frances said.

"We're not!" said Nell stoutly. "We'd do anything for you. And we hate you to think us rough and ill-mannered. It's Arthur's fault if you do, but even he means well."

"But, my dear, I don't," Frances protested.

"Sure?" said Nell.

"Yes, quite sure." Frances laid a friendly hand on her arm. "I couldn't think anything horrid of you if I tried," she said.

"Thank you," said Nell somewhat pathetically. "It's rather hard to be judged by one's men-folk, I sometimes think. They can be such beasts."

"I expect it depends how you take them," said Frances practically.

Nell looked at her with a hint of envy. "It's all right for you," she said. "You're not under any man's heel."

"I have been," said Frances, with a sudden memory of the Bishop. "But I never shall be again."

"You will be if you marry," said Nell.

"Oh, I don't think so," smiled Frances. "But as I am not going to marry, that is beside the point."

"How nice to be sure you don't want to!" said the girl with a sigh.

Whereat Frances laughed with a curious lightheartedness. "I didn't say that, did I? But women of my age think twice before they sign away their liberty."

"Your age!" Nell stared. "Why, I thought you were quite young!" she said, then blushed violently and turned to go. "Oh, I suppose I oughtn't to have said that—but it's true!"

The door closed behind her upon the words, and Frances was left still laughing. "What can have come to them all?" she said. "Me—young! If I am, it's something in the air that has made me so. I never used to be!"

And then a fantastic thought came to her, checking her laughter. She had never been young before. She had never had time to be young. Could it be possible that for her, here at Tetherstones, life had but just begun? If so—if so—was she right to turn away from aught that life might have to offer?

CHAPTER XI
FAILURE

Well as she knew the way to the Stones from the farm, she had never trodden it save on that one occasion in the fog when Ruth had been her guide. They were approached by a steep and winding lane that led up between high banks to the still steeper track on the open moor that ran directly to them. The whole distance could not be more than half-a-mile, she reflected, as she sat in her room that evening, considering the task that lay before her.

She hoped to accomplish it unobserved, for she knew that the entire household retired by nine, and some of its members even before that hour in view of the early rising that the farm work entailed; and since she had no intention of allowing her interview with Rotherby to be unduly prolonged, she anticipated that the whole adventure need not take more than half-an-hour or at the most three-quarters. She intended to assume an attitude so prosaically business-like that he would find it impossible to return, or even to attempt to return, to their former relations. In fact, she felt herself to be armed at every point and ready for him. For she felt neither attraction nor repulsion for him now, merely a sort of cold-blooded, wholly impersonal, interest in him as a stepping-stone to that independence which was the dream of her life. It seemed he could help her; therefore she was not in a position to throw him aside. But as a man she scarcely regarded him at all. He had become no more than the medium for the attainment of her ambition—the stepping-stone to ambition—no more than that. How often in life do we thus deceive ourselves, imagining ourselves free and not discerning the bonds of our slavery?

The coming of Dolly at nine o'clock was usually the signal of the general retirement of the rest of the family, but Dolly was a little late that night. She and Milly had been absent for the whole day and they evidently had a good deal to talk about. When Dolly came to her eventually, it was nearly half-an-hour later than usual. Frances was sitting by her open window, watching the moon rise.

"So you're not in bed yet!" said Dolly. "I was afraid you would be tired of waiting."

"Oh, no," Frances said. "I can quite easily put myself to bed, thank you. Have you had a good day? Has all gone well?"

"Oh, yes, on the whole. We were rather surprised to come upon Oliver in Fordestown on our way back. It isn't like him to absent himself without permission, especially at such a time as harvest. Of course we thought Arthur had given him leave. Did you know he was going?"

"I?" said Frances, and stared for a moment in amazement; then suddenly remembered the reason of his going and felt the unwelcome knowledge burn her. "What makes you ask?" she said, after a moment.

"Oh, nothing." Dolly came to her to take down her hair. "Ruth said he was talking to you just before he went, that was all. I wondered if possibly he might have mentioned what he was going to do and why. It doesn't matter in the least.

There will probably be a row when he comes back, that's all. He generally manages to get round Arthur, but I don't think he will this time."

"I should like to do my hair myself to-night," said Frances. "Thank you very much. I am really strong enough now, and I am sure you must be very tired after your long day."

"Just as you like," said Dolly. "I am not tired at all. In fact, if it weren't for getting up in the morning, I should feel inclined to sit up and see what happens."

"But what can happen?" questioned Frances quickly.

Dolly laughed briefly. "Well, he can find himself locked out for the night, that's all—unless Arthur sits up for him. But I should hardly think he'll do that. He has got to be up early himself."

"What will he do if he is locked out?" asked Frances.

"Probably one of the girls—Maggie—would let him in if the coast were clear. If not, he would have to sleep out somewhere. That wouldn't kill him," said Dolly cheerfully. "Well, if you are sure you can manage all right—Have you had a good day?"

"Quite, thank you," said Frances. "Good night! I am feeling much stronger than I was and quite able to put myself to bed."

"That's all right," said Dolly. "It's much pleasanter to do for oneself, isn't it?"

She went, and Frances was once more alone. She blew out the candle that Dolly had lighted and settled down again to wait.

Dolly's news was disquieting. She had hoped that all the household would have been wrapped in slumber before the time arrived for her own expedition, but it seemed that this was not to be. She wondered how she would manage to elude observation. She hated the thought of creeping out by stealth, but there seemed to be no help for it. Time was getting short, and if Arthur proposed to sit up for the defaulter she would have no choice but to risk it.

Slowly the harvest moon mounted in the sky. The boughs of the cedar-tree stood out black against the radiance. She rose at last and wrapped her shawl about her. The night was warm, and she would not be long. She had not heard Arthur pass her door, so she concluded that he was still in the kitchen. She had thought the whole matter out and decided upon her plan of action. There was a casement window in the parlour, easily opened and near the ground. She would not need to pass the kitchen to reach this room, and only the window of the old man's study overlooked that corner of the garden. She felt sure that he would have retired long since, and even if he had not, he was the last person in the world to act the spy.

She smiled to herself as cautiously she opened her door. A certain spirit of adventure had entered into her; her brain was cool, her nerves steady. She was even conscious of a mischievous feeling of elation. It seemed so long since she had taken any step on her own initiative. She realized that the general sense of bondage had begun to oppress her also.

The passage was in darkness, but a light was dimly burning at the foot of the stairs. Arthur was sitting up, then. She wondered what would happen when Oliver returned, if there would be high words between the two men, if Oliver would manage to vindicate himself, or carry the situation with a high hand as on the previous occasion which she had witnessed. Then Oliver's warning came back upon her, his urgent words, his barely disguised agitation. He had been very much in earnest when he had counselled her to dismiss Rotherby. What did it all mean, she wondered? Perhaps Rotherby himself might be able to throw light upon the mystery.

She crept to the head of the stairs and paused. As she did so, she heard the soft opening of a door a few yards behind her, and a chink of light gleamed along the passage. It was impossible to return to her room unobserved, but she was dressed in grey and the shawl she wore was a dark one. She knew herself to be invisible against the wall in the gloom, and she stood up against it and waited.

In a second or two a white-clad figure stole out, came bare-footed almost as far as her hiding-place, but stopped just short of it and hung over the banisters to listen. Frances stood rigid, not daring to breathe. In a moment there came a faint sob from the bending figure so close to her, and a sharp dart of compassion went through Frances. She was actually on the verge of betraying herself when there came another sound from along the passage, the creak of footsteps, a piercing whisper—Elsie's:—"Maggie, what are you doing there? Maggie, come back to bed! We'll never wake in time to get the cows milked if you don't."

Another figure came sturdily into view with the words, and Maggie turned sharply back to meet it.

"Oh, Elsie, I thought you were asleep!" she said.

"I was," said Elsie. "And then I found you weren't there. For goodness' sake, be sensible and come to bed! What is the good of hanging about out here?"

"I'm worried about Oliver," Maggie said rather piteously. "Will there be a row, do you think?"

"Good gracious, I don't know," said Elsie. "Don't care either. Oliver's quite capable of taking care of himself. If he isn't—well, I've no use for him. Come along to bed, do, and don't make a fuss about nothing!"

"Arthur was in a bad mood this evening," protested Maggie. "I expect that's why Oliver went without asking. He knew it wouldn't be any good. Oh, I wish he hadn't done it. I'm so afraid——"

She left the sentence unfinished, for suddenly there sounded a movement from below, followed by the tread of a man's feet on the stairs.

"Come on!" said Elsie, and the two girls fled back to their room.

The impulse to follow their example seized upon Frances, but in a moment she restrained it. The chances were very much against his seeing her, and she had fled from him once that day. Pride came to the aid of her courage, and she remained where she was.

He came up the stairs heavily, as if weary. He carried no light, but he had not extinguished the glimmer below. Presumably he had left this for Oliver's benefit. Further along the passage, the moonlight filtered in through a latticed window, but the stairs themselves were in almost complete darkness.

Slowly he ascended them. He was close to her now, and involuntarily she shrank from him, pressing harder against the wall. She felt her heart begin to beat fast and loud, and wondered if he would hear it in the silence. But he came on and passed her without a sign. Then, as she still stood there palpitating against the wall, she heard him go deliberately along the passage to the door through which the two girls had just retreated, and open it without ceremony.

His voice come to her where she stood. "If either of you comes out again to-night, there'll be trouble, so take warning and stay where you are!"

He shut the door again without waiting for any reply and turned aside into his own room.

It was her opportunity and she seized it. Swiftly she gathered herself together, stood a second poised and listening, then, hearing nothing, began to descend the stairs.

They creaked beneath her feet notwithstanding her utmost caution, but no sound came to her from above, and she went on with increasing rapidity.

Reaching the foot, she discovered that the glimmer of light came from the half-open kitchen door. Evidently a lamp was burning within, and that seemed to indicate that Arthur meant to return. But her way lay in the opposite direction, and she slipped into the dark passage that led to the parlour.

She thought she knew the place by heart, but there was one thing she had forgotten. Half-way to the parlour, in an angle of the wall, there stood an old oak settle, and into this she suddenly ran headlong. The settle scraped on the stone floor with the force of the impact, and she herself fell over it with arms outstretched, bruised and half-stunned with the violence of the collision. It all took place so rapidly, and her dismay was such, that she scarcely knew what had happened to her ere the sound of feet on the stairs told her that she was discovered. She sank down in a quivering heap on the floor, gasping and helpless, no longer attempting any concealment. And in another moment Arthur had reached her, was bending over her, feeling for her, lifting her.

She gave herself into his hold with a curious sense of fatalism.

CHAPTER XII
THE FIRES OF HELL

She had never before so fully realized the grim, uncompromising strength of the man as at that moment. The day before he had lifted and borne her as though she had been a child. To-night she was a pigmy in the grasp of a giant.

He carried her without words to the kitchen and set her down there in the leathern arm-chair. She had a glimpse of his face as he did so, and it was as it had been earlier in the day—a mask of anger.

He did not speak to her, but went to a cupboard in the wall and took therefrom a bottle and a glass. Weak and trembling from her fall, she watched him pour out a small dose of spirit and add thereto water from a jug on the dresser. Then he came back to her, stooped and put it to her lips. His arm was behind her head as she drank. She felt the strong support of it, the compulsion of the hand that held the glass. But she could not raise her eyes to his. She drank in mute submission.

The dose steadied her, and she sat up. His silence oppressed her like a crushing weight. She felt it must be broken at all costs.

"I am so sorry to have given you this trouble," she said. "You will think me very strange, but I am afraid I can't explain anything. I will go back to my room."

He set down the glass with decision and spoke. "I am sorry to appear unreasonable—or anything else unpleasant. But I am afraid I can't let you go back to your room at present."

She turned and gazed at him. "What on earth do you mean?"

His look came to her, and his anger seemed to smite her as with physical force. "My reasons—like yours—won't bear explanation," he said.

She gripped the arms of her chair. Had she heard him aright? The thing was unbelievable. "Are you mad?" she said.

He was standing squarely in front of her. He smiled—a smile that turned her cold. "That I can't tell you. What is madness? I know I have got you here—in my power. And I know I mean to keep you. If that is madness, well—" he lifted his shoulders slightly, the old characteristic movement—"then I am mad."

She stared at him in growing apprehension. Was the man sober? The doubt flashed through her mind and vanished. He was so deadly calm in his anger. He had locked away his fury as if it were a flaming furnace behind iron doors. But his strength was terrible, unsparing. It menaced her, whichever way she turned.

But her spirit was reviving. It was not her way to submit meekly to the mastery of any man. Very suddenly she rose and faced him. "This is more than I will endure," she said, speaking briefly and clearly. "Nothing on earth shall keep me in this room against my will!"

She needed to pass him to reach the door into the passage. He stood squarely in her path. She heard him draw a hard breath.

"There is such a thing as brute force," he said.

She looked him straight in the eyes. "You wouldn't dare!"

His eyes leaped to flame, holding hers. "Don't tempt me!" he said, between his teeth.

That checked her for a moment. Something seemed to clutch at her heart. Then pride leaped up full-armed, and she flung it from her. She laughed in his face.

"Do you think you are going to treat me as one of your slaves?" she said contemptuously, and made to pass him.

He flung out an arm before her. His voice came, low and passionate. It was as if the locked doors were opening. She felt the scorching heat behind.

"If you attempt to pass me—you do it at your own risk," he said.

She stopped. His eyes seemed to be consuming her. In spite of herself, she shrank, averting her own.

"At your own risk," he said again, and very slowly his arm fell.

There followed a silence that was somehow appalling. She stood as one paralysed. She would have returned to her chair, but lacked the strength. So he was in earnest, this extraordinary man. He actually meant to hold her against her will. And wherefore? She almost challenged him with the question, but something held her back—perhaps it was the consciousness of that intolerable heat of which she had been aware with the utterance of his last words.

She spoke at length. "I don't understand you. What is the matter?"

He made a harsh sound in his throat; it was as though he choked a laugh. "Do you really wish me to be more explicit? If so, by all means let us drop all subterfuge and come down to bare facts! Why are you trying to creep out of the house by stealth? Answer me!"

It was he then who meant to force a battle. The sudden knowledge gave her back her courage, but she knew it for the courage of desperation.

She lifted her head and faced him. "What is that to you? Does the fact that I have been your guest—your helpless and involuntary guest—entitle you to control my movements or to demand an account of them? I resent your attitude, and I absolutely repudiate your authority. You may keep me here against my will—if you are coward enough. But you will never—however long you wait—induce me to confide my affairs to you. And let me tell you this! When I leave this house, I shall never—no, never—enter it again!"

Fiercely she flung the words, answering challenge with challenge, realizing that it was only by launching herself on the torrent of her anger that she could hope to make any headway against him. For he stood in her path like an opposing force, waiting to hurl her back.

Panting, she ceased to speak. The effort of her defiance was beginning to cost her dear. Almost by instinct she groped for the table and supported herself against it, conscious of a whirling tumult in her brain that she was powerless to still. Too late she realized that the power to which she had entrusted herself had betrayed her.

She saw it in his face—the sudden mockery that gleamed in his eyes. He spoke, and his words cut with a stabbing accuracy straight through the armour of her indignation. "Had I known—what I now know," he said, "What I might have known from the beginning from the manner of your coming, I certainly would not have entertained you in this house. I have my sisters to think of."

"Ah!" she said, and no more; for words failed her. The horror of it overwhelmed her utterly and completely. It seemed to her that she had never known the meaning of pain until that moment—pain that bereft her of all normal self-control—pain that made her gasp in sheer agony.

The walls of the room seemed to be closing in upon her. She felt her feet slip away from under her. Desperately she tried to recover her balance, failed, sought to cling to the table but felt her hands could find no hold upon the hard wood.

And then there came the consciousness of his arms surrounding her. He lifted her, he held her to him, and she felt again the awful flame of his look, consuming her.

"And I loved you!" he said. "I—loved you!"

She fought against him breathlessly, feeling that if his lips touched hers life would never be endurable again. But he mastered her without apparent effort. He conquered her slowly, with a fiendish precision that was as iron to her soul. With that dreadful smile upon his face he overcame her spasmodic struggles for freedom. He kissed her, and by his kiss he quelled her resistance; for she felt the fires of hell, and fainted in his hold.

CHAPTER XIII
ESCAPE

Was it a dream—a nightmare of her fevered brain? Was she back again in the tortures of her long illness, with Lucy and Nell whispering behind the screen, wondering how soon the end would come? Had she imagined that dreadful struggle against overwhelming odds? If so, why was she lying here, gazing at the fitful firelight on the oak rafters of the kitchen instead of on her bed upstairs? Or was this too a dream—a strange, illogical fantasy of her diseased imaginings?

She was very tired—that much she knew—sick with long delirium or too great exertion. Her limbs were as lead. And at the back of her mind there hovered that dreadful shadow—was it memory? Was it illusion?—that filled her with a sense of terror indescribable.

But consciousness was returning. Her brain was groping for the truth, and the truth was coming to her gradually, inevitably, inexorably. She remembered her flight down the stairs, her headlong fall in the passage. She remembered the coming of Arthur, the brief interview in the kitchen, his terrible unspoken accusation. She remembered his kiss. . . .

Again the anguish burned her soul; she thrust it from her with a sick shudder. It was more than she could bear.

Then she awoke to the fact that she was lying on the stones before the fire with a man's coat spread under her. Trembling, she raised herself and found she was alone.

The moonlight filtered in through the bars of the unshuttered window, mingling with the firelight. The lamp that had burned on the dresser was gone. She found the table within her reach and dragged herself up by it, but it was many seconds before she mustered strength to stand alone.

At last with difficulty she made her way to the door that led into the passage, turned the handle and found it locked. Her heart stirred oddly within her like a stricken thing too weak for violent emotion. She crept round the room to the door into the yard. This also was locked and the key gone. The window was barred. She was a prisoner.

She went to the window and stood before it. It looked on to thick laurel bushes that successfully screened the farm-yard from view. Standing thus, there came to her a sudden sound across the stillness of the night, a sound that seemed to galvanize her to a more vivid consciousness of tragedy—the report of a gun. It was followed immediately by another, and then the silence fell again—a silence that could be felt. Tensely, with every nerve stretched, she listened, but though her ears sang with the effort she heard no more. The moonlight and the silence possessed the world.

She began to think of the Stones, of Rotherby and his fruitless vigil, of Oliver. And then—a thing of terror leaping out of the darkness—another thought seized upon her. Oliver's warning—Rotherby's danger—the gun-shot she had just heard. Following that, came the memory of her letter, delayed and at length delivered. That brought illumination. The letter had been opened and read. It was from that letter that Arthur had framed his conclusions. Recalling it, she realized that it had been couched in the terms of a lover. But what vile impulse had induced him to open it? And by what means had Oliver become aware of the danger? Her brain was alert now and leaping from point to point with amazing rapidity. Oliver's knowledge had come from Ruth. Then there was some reason apart from that letter to herself for which Montague Rotherby was accounted an enemy. Remembering Oliver's very obvious anxiety, she marvelled, seeking for an explanation. Was he aware of Arthur's passion for herself? Had he really feared that jealousy might drive him to extremes? She found herself shivering again. What had actually happened? Had Rotherby been surprised at the Stones, waiting for her? Had Arthur——

A feeling of physical sickness came upon her so overwhelmingly that she had to sit down to combat it.

Slowly the minutes crawled away, and again through her fainting soul there beat the old, throbbing prayer: "From all evil and mischief, from sin, from the crafts and assaults of the devil, Good Lord deliver us."

Her lips were still repeating the words mechanically when through the dreadful stillness there came at length a sound—the soft trying of the handle and then the turning of the key.

Frances raised her head. In that night of dreadful happenings she had not expected deliverance. The coming of it was like a dream. A small white figure stood on the threshold, barefooted, with face upraised, listening.

"Are you here?" whispered a childish voice.

"My dear!" Frances said.

The little figure came forward. The moonlight fell upon the upturned, flower-like face. "Please will you take me to sleep with you to-night?" she said.

Strength came back to Frances. The instinct to protect awoke within her, reviving her. She got up and went to the child.

"What made you come to me here, Rosebud?" she said.

"I thought you called me," Ruth answered. "But perhaps it was a dream. I thought you were frightened, as you were that night at the Stones. You are very cold. Are you frightened?"

"I have been," Frances said.

Ruth pressed close to her. "Has someone been unkind to you? Is it—is it Uncle Arthur?"

But Frances could not answer her. She was conscious of a weight of tears at her heart to which she dared not give vent.

"Shall we go upstairs?" said Ruth, with soft fingers entwined in hers. "And perhaps you will be able to sleep."

She yielded to the child's guidance as she had yielded before without hesitation or misgiving. They went out into the passage. But here a sudden sound made her pause—it was the opening of the door that led into the garden.

Ruth pulled at her hand. "It is only Grandpa. He is always late to bed."

But Frances drew back sharply. "You run up, darling!" she whispered. "I can't come yet."

"Oh, please come!" said little Ruth.

But though she heard a piteous note in the child's voice, she could not. She freed her hand from Ruth's clasp. "Run up!" she repeated. "I will come afterwards—if I can."

What impulse it was that urged her she could not have said, but it was too strong to be resisted. She saw Ruth start obediently but somewhat forlornly up the stairs, and she drew herself back into a deep recess under the staircase and crouched there, not breathing.

Ruth was right. It was the old man who had entered. She discerned him dimly as he came up the passage, moving with the weary gait of age. He paused at the kitchen-door as though he were listening, and she shrank more closely into her hiding-place, dreading discovery. But in a moment he pushed open the door and entered, closing it behind him.

Then the impulse to escape came to her, or perhaps it had been there, dormant against her breathless heart, the whole time. She saw the place as a monstrous prison, stone-walled and terrible, herself a captive guarded on all sides, helpless, beaten by circumstances, broken by Fate. And then this chance—this solitary chance of freedom.

Swiftly upon the closing of that door, she left her retreat, stole along the passage to the door, lifted the latch and was out upon the brick path in the moonlight.

The hollyhocks looked tall and ghostly; the garden lay before her as if asleep. She caught her shawl about her, and fled along the narrow path. She reached the door in the wall, and opening it peered forth. There was no weakness about her now. She was inspired by the strength that is borne of utter need.

She saw no one, and so slipped out on to the lawn by the bed of mignonette in front of the dairy-window. The scent of it rose up in the night like incense. As a thief she crept along in the shadow of the house to the gate that led into the farmyard.

And here Roger greeted her with loud yells of delight from his kennel. She cowered back against the wall, but he continued to cheer and make merry over her unexpected appearance for many seconds, till the conviction that his enthusiasm had failed to elicit any response from her suddenly dawned upon him, and he broke into howls of disappointment, punctuated with urgent whines of encouragement and persuasion.

Discovery seemed inevitable, and the courage of despair entered into Frances. Later she marvelled at herself, but at the time she was scarcely aware of making any effort, either mental or physical. Quite suddenly, as if propelled by a force outside her, she found herself calmly walking forward to the gate. It opened at her touch so easily that it might have been opened for her, and she walked through, hearing it swing creaking behind her between the renewed shouts of jubilation from Roger.

She passed him by, looking neither to right nor left, neither hastening nor lingering, hearing his wails of grief again behind her as she went. She reached the further gate and found it stood open to the lane. Very steadily she passed through and began to walk down the hill between the steep banks. The scent of honeysuckle came to her here, so overpoweringly that she caught her breath with an odd feeling of hurt.

Then—and it seemed to her later that this was the very thing she had been expecting—the one thing for which she had come—there sounded on the hill behind her the whirr of an engine, the slipping of wheels in the mud. Quite calmly still she turned and faced the lights of a small car coming rapidly down upon her. She did not know how it happened, or how near she was to death,—at that moment it would not have interested her to know—but she heard a shout and the sharp grinding of a brake applied to the utmost, followed by the ominous sound of locked wheels that grated to a standstill within a yard of her. Afterwards she remembered thinking that that hot, protesting engine was like a dragon baulked of its prey.

"Who is it?" cried a man's voice. "What the devil do you want? I'm in a hurry."

The voice was agitated; it had a desperate sound. This also she noticed, but her own was clear and calm.

"Will you take me with you?" she said. "I am going your way."

"Frances!" he said in amazement.

"Will you take me?" she repeated.

"Of course I will take you! Get in! Get in!"

She moved along the side of the car. His hand came out to her, the door swung open.

The next moment they were rushing down the lane into a gulf of blackness, and she knew that the prison-walls would menace her no more.

PART III

CHAPTER I
THE VICTIM

Of that wild rush through the night Frances never recalled any very clear detail afterwards. She only knew a strange dazzle of moonlight that filled the world, making all things seem unreal, and once she fancied she caught a glimpse of the Stones grimly outlined upon a distant hill.

Her companion never spoke to her, his whole attention apparently being occupied in forcing the utmost speed from his car, despite the extreme unevenness of the moorland road they travelled. In the end they ran into a little town and straight up the one broad street in an inn, Frances always remembered the sign-board of that inn, for it was the first thing that made a definite impression upon her after her flight. The inn was called *The Man in the Moon*, and the sign-board portrayed the same, being an enormous yellow face with the most quizzing expression possible to imagine—a face that would have provoked a smile from the least humorous. Somehow that face served to jolt Frances back to the ordinary and the commonplace. It enabled her to put the overwhelming sense of tragedy away from her and assume something of her old brisk and business-like attitude.

"Is this where you are staying?" she said.

"Yes," said Rotherby. "It's comfortable enough in a homely way. Will you get out?"

She turned in the seat and faced him. By the light of the moon he looked ghastly pale, but he managed to call up a smile.

"If there is another inn in the place I'll go to it," said Frances.

"I'm afraid there isn't," said Rotherby. "And you probably wouldn't get in if there were. But you needn't be anxious on that account. I'll call you my sister if you like."

His manner reassured her. Moreover, he had the look of a man at the end of his strength. She wondered what had happened to affect him so.

She got out of the car without further discussion and waited while he ran it under an archway into the stableyard. It seemed a long while before he joined her again, and then she noticed that he moved with a curiously halting gait, almost as if he were feeling his way.

"It's all right," he said, as he reached her. "The door's open. Come inside!"

He extended a hand to push it back for her, but very strangely the intention was frustrated. It was as if he had found some obstacle in his path. And as she turned towards him in surprise he suddenly uttered an inarticulate exclamation and grabbed at her arm. She was aware of his whole weight flung abruptly upon her, and she caught at him, supporting him as best she could.

He staggered against the door-post, breathing heavily. "I shall be all right in a minute—in a minute," he gasped out. "Just hold me up—if you can! I won't faint."

She held him up, exerting all her strength.

Several dreadful seconds passed, then he made a determined effort and straightened himself. As he did so, she felt the sleeve of his coat at the elbow and found it wet through. A ghastly doubt assailed her.

"What has happened?" she said through trembling lips. "Your arm! Is it—is it——"

"Blood? Yes. I got it in the shoulder. Don't be frightened! I shall get over it. Can you open the door?"

He spoke jerkily, but with more assurance. Frances opened the door with a sick wonder if the horrors of that night would ever pass.

Rotherby staggered in, and she followed him closely, half expecting him to fall headlong. But he had mastered himself to a certain extent, and she heard him speak with some authority to the shock-headed landlord who came sleepily out of the bar-parlour to meet them.

"This lady is my sister. Can you give her a comfortable room for the night?"

"There's the room you told me to prepare, sir," said the man, with a loutish grin.

"That'll do. Take her to it! See that she has everything she wants! Good night, Frances! You follow him! I shall see you in the morning."

Rotherby spoke calmly, but it was through clenched teeth.

Frances stood hesitating. The landlord waited at the foot of a steep, ill-lighted staircase.

"That's all," said Rotherby. "I'm sorry I can't do more to-night."

He was obviously putting strong restraint upon himself. Frances waited a moment longer, then spoke.

"I can't—possibly—leave you like this. You have been hurt. You must let me do what I can to help you."

Again for an instant she saw his smile, and she saw the clenched teeth behind it.

"I shall be all right," he said again. "I don't think there is anything to be done. It isn't serious. I'll see a doctor in the morning if necessary."

But Frances was too practical to be thus reassured. "You must let me help you," she said. "You must."

He yielded the point abruptly. "Very well—if you wish it. Get some hot water, Jarvis! I've had a bit of an accident."

He moved forward to the stairs, and Frances went with him, feeling herself once more the victim of an inexorable Fate.

They went up together, Rotherby stumbling until she gave him her arm to steady him. Reaching a small landing on which a gas-jet burned low, he directed her into a room with an open door, and they entered, he leaning upon her.

The moonlight flooded in through the uncovered window, and she saw that it was a bedroom with an old four-poster bed. She helped Rotherby to it, and he sank down upon the foot with a sigh of relief.

"Have you got any matches?" she said.

"In my pocket—on the right," he said. "Can you get them?"

She felt for and found them. As she stood up again he surprised her by catching her hand to his lips. She drew it quickly away, and he said nothing.

She lighted the gas, that flared starkly in the shabby, old-fashioned room, and turned round to him again, forcing herself to a calm and matter-of-fact attitude.

"Shall I help you off with your coat?" she said.

He turned to her suddenly, and she was conscious of an unwilling admiration of the man's courage when she saw the effort of his smile.

"I say, don't dislike me so!" he said. "I'll make Jarvis help me. Don't you stay! There's a room for you next-door—my room as a matter of fact, but I'll stay in here for to-night."

Against her will she was softened. Something about him—something which he neither uttered nor betrayed by look or gesture—appealed to her very strongly. She found herself unable to comply with his suggestion and abandon him to the mercy of the landlord who was even now lumbering heavily up the stairs. She realized clearly that whatever came of this night's happenings, she was bound in common humanity to stand by Rotherby now. No other course of action was open to her.

"I shall not leave you," she said, "till I have done all I can to help you—unless you make that impossible for me."

"Heaven forbid!" said Rotherby, still smiling his twisted smile.

"Well, I am in earnest," she said, as she bent to help him.

"I like you best that way," said Rotherby.

She felt that in some fashion he had worsted her, but she put the matter resolutely away from her. It was not the moment for close analysis of the situation. She could only go as she was driven.

With the utmost care she helped him remove his coat, and was shocked to find that the shirt-sleeve was soaked with blood from shoulder to elbow.

"Don't let Jarvis see!" said Rotherby sharply, and she covered it while the man was in the room.

Jarvis was too sleepy or too fuddled to be curious. He merely set down the can, wished them good night and stumped away.

Then Frances bent to her work. She found a jagged wound in the shoulder, from which the blood was still oozing, and she proceeded to bathe it with a strip of linen torn from the shirt-sleeve. The means at her disposal were wholly elementary, but she performed her task with a deftness that was characteristic of her, finding with infinite relief that the wound was not vitally deep. Rotherby endured her ministrations with a stoicism that again stirred her to admiration. He seemed bent upon making the business as easy for her as possible.

"Don't mind me!" he said once. "Just go ahead! I'll tell you if I can't stand it."

And then when she had finished at last, he told her where to find some handkerchiefs for bandaging purposes in the room that he occupied.

"You will go to a doctor in the morning, won't you?" she said, pausing. "I have only cleansed it. There is bound to be some shot in the wound."

"Some what?" said Rotherby, and looked at her with one of his most quizzical glances though his face was still drawn with pain. "Oh, didn't I tell you that I tore it on some barbed wire?"

She felt herself colour deeply, but she did not take up the challenge. "I should go to a doctor all the same," she said quietly.

He laughed at her with a touch of impudence that she could not resent. "Very good, Sister Superior, I will. Now if you don't mind tying me up, I shall be grateful. Where would you like me to sleep—in this room, or my own?"

"In your own," she said firmly.

He sobered suddenly at her tone. "Look here, you won't run away in the night, will you? I promise you—I swear to you—I'll play the game."

What game, she wondered? But she did not put the wonder into words.

"I have nowhere to run to," she said, and turned away from him that he might not see the bitterness on her face.

When she returned with the handkerchiefs she was a practical self once more. But she was beginning to be conscious of intense physical weariness, and she felt a sense of gratitude to him for noticing it.

"I say, you are tired! You've been ill, haven't you?"

"I am well again," she said.

He swept the assurance aside. "You don't look it. Don't bother about me any more! Oh, well, just tie a wet pad over it and then leave me to my fate!"

He became urgent in his solicitude and the knowledge that he was suffering considerably himself made her respond far more graciously than would otherwise have been the case.

But when it was over at last, when she was alone in the strange room and realized how completely that night's happenings had changed the whole course of her life, a blackness of despair came down upon her, more overwhelming than any she had ever known. She cast herself down just as she was and wept out her agony till sheer exhaustion came upon her and she drifted at last into the merciful oblivion of dreamless sleep.

CHAPTER II
THE BARGAIN

It was late in the morning when she awoke in response to a persistent knocking at the door, on the opening of which she found a bare-armed country-girl who informed her without preamble that the gentleman was waiting breakfast for her downstairs. Having delivered this message, she retired, and Frances was left to perform what toilet she could with the very limited means at her command.

Her long sleep had refreshed her and she reflected with relief that her strength was certainly returning. The thought of meeting Montague Rotherby gave her no dismay. Very strangely he had ceased to possess any very great importance in her eyes, her only determination being to break off all connection with him as soon as possible.

Somehow, as she entered the room where he awaited her, she had a feeling that he had never really mattered very greatly in her life. It was only what he had stood for—the realization of that part of her being which had lain dormant for so long, the throbbing certainty that for her also even the stones of the wilderness might be turned into bread.

She came forward to him, faintly smiling. "Are you better to-day?" she said.

She did not offer her hand, but he took it. His face twitched a little at her matter-of-fact greeting. She saw at a glance that he looked ill.

"I've had a foul night," he said. "But it's not serious. I'm going up to town. Will you come with me?"

She looked at him, startled. "Oh, no!" she said.

He bit his lip. "Are you still disliking me?" he said.

It was a difficult question to answer, so little did he seem to matter now. She replied after a moment without any conscious feeling of any sort.

"No. But I am not coming up to town with you. Is there any particular reason why I should? You are quite able to go alone, I suppose?"

He stared at her for a few seconds, at first frowningly, then with a growing cynicism. At length: "What have they done to you at Tetherstones?" he said. "Since you accepted my protection last night—more, asked for it—I should have thought there was quite a good reason why you should be willing to come to town with me to-day."

"Then you are quite wrong," she replied very clearly. "I am not prepared to do anything of the kind."

His frown deepened for a moment, then passed. "Shall we have breakfast?" he said. "Then you can tell me what your plans are. I am quite willing to fall in with them, whatever they may be."

Her plans! What were her plans? The old pitiless problem presented itself. Had he meant, she asked herself, thus to bring home to her the fact of her dependence upon his good offices? What were her plans?

"I have got to think," she said.

He nodded. "Perhaps I can be of use. I believe I can be. I'll tell you—when we've finished breakfast—what I meant by suggesting that you should come up to London with me."

She wondered if he were referring to the old plan of giving her secretary work. Or perhaps—though she hardly dared to think it—he was going to talk about her sketches and the possibilities therein contained. Against her will, that thought remained with her throughout the brief meal that they ate together. Upon one point only was she fully decided. She could live on charity no longer. She was resolutely determined to work for her living now, whatever that work might be.

She noticed that her companion ate very little, but he seemed fully master of himself, and she put away the feeling of uneasiness that tried to take possession of her. She would very thankfully have avoided any discussion of the events of the previous night, but she knew this to be inevitable. There were certain things that must be faced.

He pushed back his chair at length and spoke. "There's only one way out of this tangle," he said. "You must realize that as I do. But perhaps I have not made myself very clear. What I want you to do is to come up to town and—marry me. Will you do that?" He smiled at her with the words. "I'm sorry my courtship has hung fire for so long. But you will admit I am hardly responsible for that. And I am quite ready to make up for lost time now. What do you say to it?"

Frances was on her feet. He had roused her to feeling at last, but it was not such feeling as would have moved her a few weeks earlier. She had to stifle an almost overwhelming sense of indignation before she could speak.

"It is quite impossible," she said then, with the utmost emphasis. "It is quite, quite impossible!"

"Impossible!" He stared at her. "But why? I understood it was what you wanted. I have a distinct recollection of your telling me so."

She gasped at the recollection. It stung like a scorpion. "But that was long ago—long ago," she said. "I don't want it now! I couldn't—possibly—contemplate such a thing now."

"But why?" Rotherby insisted in astonishment. Then: "Perhaps you think I don't love you. Is that it?"

"Oh, no!" She had begun to tremble. "That wouldn't make any difference. At least, it is not that that has made me change my mind."

"Ah!" he said with a sudden grimness. "Something else has done that."

She was aware of a sharp pain at her heart that was almost unendurable. It took all her courage to meet his eyes. But she forced her voice to steadiness. "Perhaps it would be nearer the truth to say that I have come to know my own mind rather than that I have changed it. I thought I loved you, but it was a mistake. As to whether you ever loved me, I have no illusions at all. You never did."

He got up. She saw his face twist as if he were in pain, but she knew that it was nothing physical that brought that look to his eyes, banishing the cynicism. "You seem very sure of that," he said, and turned from her to light a cigarette.

"So I am struck off the list, am I? Do you think you are altogether wise to do that—after what happened last night?"

The question surprised her, but it was wholly without malice. She could not take offence.

She answered him in a low voice, for the first time conscious of the dread of giving pain. "I have really no choice. I couldn't do anything else."

"What do you propose to do?" he said.

The old maddening question that she had had to answer so often. She tried to summon the old battling spirit, but it did not respond to her call. Her pride had been flung in the dust. What did she propose to do? Was there anything left that could ever restore her self-respect?

With a gesture that was quite unconsciously pathetic, she turned and went to the window in silence.

Rotherby smoked without speaking for a few seconds. If he felt the appeal of her hopelessness, he did not show it.

It was she who spoke first at length, without turning, and it was as though she uttered the words to herself with the dreary persistence of despair.

"I have got to begin again."

"What are you going to do?" said Rotherby.

There was a quality of ruthlessness in his voice that pierced her despair. She swung round abruptly and faced him. There was majesty in her bearing, though with it was mingled the desperation of the hunted animal at bay.

"I will work," she said. "I am not afraid of work. And I don't care what I do."

He came and joined her at the window. "Yes, it sounds all right," he said. "But you haven't the strength, and you know it."

She shrank at the blunt words, for they struck her hard. She knew—it was useless to dispute it—that she lacked the strength.

"What is the use of saying that?" she said, protesting almost in spite of herself.

"Because I want you to see reason," he rejoined, and she knew that he recognized his advantage, and would press it to the utmost. "Why don't you want to marry me, Circe? You might do very much worse."

She drew back from him. "Oh, don't you see that it is out of the question?" she said. "I couldn't marry you. I don't love you."

She saw his face harden. "That is plain speaking," he said. "But I want to know why. What have I done to forfeit your love?"

"But I never loved you," she said.

"Are you sure of that?" He spoke insistently. "You kissed me. You let me hold you in my arms."

She flinched at the recollection, but she compelled herself to face him. "That was a mistake," she said.

"You are sure of that?" said Rotherby.

"Quite sure," she answered with simplicity.

He shifted his ground. "Are you also sure you know what love is?"

She clenched her hands as though in self-defence. "Every woman knows that," she said.

"Then how did you come to make a mistake?" he countered.

Again she drew back as from the thrust of a dagger. "Oh, I suppose any woman might do that, but when once she has found it out—she doesn't do it again."

"How did you come to find out?" said Rotherby.

The inquisition was becoming intolerable, but still she faced him with resolution. "I have had a good many hours for thought," she said. "And I have thought a good deal."

"At Tetherstones?" he said.

"Yes."

She saw a gleam of something she did not understand in his look. He seemed to be watching narrowly for something. He spoke abruptly.

"What I don't understand—what I want to understand—is why you came with me last night."

She answered him with an effort. "I had to get away."

"Ah!" he said. "It wasn't on my account then? You weren't coming to meet me after all—in spite of my message? Did you get my message?"

She bent her head. "Yes. I had your message. Ruth told me. I was coming—I was coming—to meet you."

"Yes?" he said. "Why were you so late?"

She hesitated. She could not tell him of that awful interview in the farm-kitchen. She could not bring herself so much as to mention Arthur's name.

"I was coming to meet you," she said again. "I didn't mean to be late. But they are a strange family. I didn't want them to know."

"A very strange family!" said Rotherby. "Why should they know? Your affairs are your own."

"Yes. But they have been very kind to me. They might think they had a right——"

"A right to shoot anyone from outside who wanted to speak to you?" he said.

"Oh, no—no!" she protested, feeling the hot colour rise overwhelmingly under his look. "That was a piece of madness."

"You knew it was going to happen?" he questioned.

"No. I knew you were in some sort of danger. I didn't know what. I was coming to warn you."

Reluctantly she uttered the brief sentences. It was like the betrayal of her friends.

He seized upon the unwilling admission. "You knew? How did you know?"

She had to answer him. "One of the men on the farm told me. He didn't say why—merely that you were in danger—that I had better warn you to go."

"And then you decided to come with me?" said Rotherby.

"I decided that I couldn't stay any longer," she told him steadily. "You came up at the right moment, that was all."

"What?" His eyes searched her again, his expression slowly changing. "You were running away too, were you?"

She wondered that he did not press the point of the mysterious attack upon him further, but was thankful that he refrained. She turned from the subject with relief. "I had to get away," she said again.

"You're not going back?" he questioned.

Something rose in her throat. Again she was conscious of that intolerable pain. She forced her utterance. "Never, no, never!" she said.

He made no comment, but turned away from her and paced the length of the room before he spoke again. Then, with his back to her, he paused.

"And yet you would sooner work yourself to death than marry me!"

She answered him immediately with feverish insistence. "Yes, I must work. I must work. I can't go on being dependent. I can't endure it."

He turned round. "Perhaps—if you were independent—you might regard me differently," he said.

She was silent.

He came slowly back to her. "Circe! May I hope for that?"

She looked at him helplessly.

He stood before her. "I swear to you," he said forcibly, "that no one on this earth wants you as I do."

A curious tremor of feeling went through her. She was stirred in spite of herself.

He put out his hand to her. "Circe!" His voice came oddly uncontrolled. "Won't you—can't you——"

She did not know what moved her—his obvious earnestness or her own utter friendlessness. But somehow her mood answered his. Her hand went into his grasp.

"But I must be independent first," she said. It was the last effort of her pride. "You'll help me to be that?"

"I'll help you," he said.

CHAPTER III
THE TURN OF THE TIDE

The days that succeeded her flight from Tetherstones left an ineradicable impression upon Frances. She maintained her steady refusal to accompany Rotherby to London, but she did not remain at *The Man in the Moon.* She found a bedroom over the little Post Office at Fordestown, and here she established herself, after collecting her few belongings from her former lodging at Brookside. She had very little money left, but she built on the hope that her sketches might find a market. Rotherby had undertaken to do his best to dispose of the one which he had taken with him, and she had plans for making more while the golden weather lasted.

On the second day of her sojourn at Fordestown she wrote to Dolly at Tetherstones. She found it impossible to give any adequate reason for her abrupt departure, so she barely touched upon it beyond begging her to believe that in spite of everything she was and would ever be deeply grateful for all the kindness that they had shown her. She ended the letter with a request that the next time Oliver had to come to Fordestown he might bring her sketching materials to her. She posted her letter and went out on to the moor for the rest of the day.

The solitude of the great heather-clad space that she loved brought soothing to her tired spirit. She was at last able to review the situation deliberately and dispassionately; but the more she meditated upon it, the more did she feel that the disposition of the future was no longer in her own control.

Very curiously, and now it seemed inextricably, had her life been bound up with Montague Rotherby's. Neither attraction nor repulsion were factors that counted any more. He had laid claim to her so persistently that she had almost begun to feel at last that he had a claim. In any case she was too tired, too dazed by the blows of Fate, to battle any further. She who had fought so hard for her freedom was compelled to own herself vanquished at last. Like a stormy dawn romance had come to her, and by its light she had seen the golden vision of love. But the light had swiftly faded and the vision fled. And she was left—a slave.

"I will never have any more dreams," she said to herself, as she gazed through tears at the dim blue tors. "None but a fool could ever imagine that the stones could be made bread."

And then she sought to brace herself with the thought that she had not greatly suffered.

"It can't have gone very deep," she told herself very resolutely, "in so short a time."

But yet she knew—as we all know—that it is not by time or any other circumstance that Love the Immeasurable can be measured, and that no power on earth can ever obliterate the memory of Love.

Of Montague personally she thought but little during those days. Of Arthur Dermot she thought ceaselessly. Against her will the individuality of the man imposed itself upon her. Night and day she thought of him, puzzled, distressed, humiliated, seeking vainly for a solution to the mystery in which all his actions were wrapped. Why had he misjudged her thus? What madness had driven him to attempt the other man's life? Was he actually mad, she asked herself? It might have accounted for much, and yet somehow she did not believe it. The man's melancholy philosophy was the philosophy of reason, his cynical acceptance of life the deliberate and trained conclusion of a balanced mind. His love for herself she found harder to understand, but it moved her to the depths, appealing to her as nothing had ever appealed before. His violence, his brutality, had shocked her unspeakably, so that she prayed passionately that she might never see him again. But yet, strangely, the appeal still held. By that alone, he

115

had entered the inner shrine of her heart, and, strive as she might, she could not cast him out. His love for her might be dead. Never for a moment did she imagine that it could have survived that awful night. But the memory of it—ah, the memory of it—it would go with her all through her life, just as she would remember the purple flower upon the coping in the Palace garden, a thing of beauty beloved for a while and then lost—the gift that the gods had offered only to snatch away ere she had grasped it.

Those days of waiting were as the days spent by a prisoner awaiting trial, only there was no hope on the horizon. Like one of the prisoners of old of whom Arthur had told her, she was tethered to her stone and the first effort she made for freedom would crush her. Though to a great extent she had regained her strength, she knew that she was not equal to hard work—such work as she had done for the Bishop. There were times of faintness and inertia when she felt that the very heart within her must be worn out, times of overwhelming depression also, when for hours the tears would well up and fall and she lacked the power to restrain them.

No one knew what she was enduring. There was no one at hand to help her. Chained to her stone, she waited day by day, not for deliverance but for the coming of her fate.

And then one day there came a letter from Rotherby, and in that letter was an enclosure that sent the blood tingling through her veins. He had sold her sketch for five guineas, and he could dispose of more if she cared to send them. "Couldn't you do a companion picture to the stepping-stones?" he said in conclusion.

His letter held no endearments. It was the most business-like epistle she had ever received from him, and her gratitude was intense. She sent him all the sketches she had by the next post, and with them a note expressing her earnest thanks and asking how he fared.

Then she sat down to think. It seemed to her in the first flush of excitement that this was the most wonderful thing that had ever happened to her. It was like a tonic to her drooping spirits. Surely it was the turning-point at last!

The bleatings and patterings of a flock of sheep passing up the street brought to her mind the fact that it was market-day. She went to the window with an eagerness she had not known for long with the thought that Oliver might be coming at any time with her sketching materials. She longed to take up her beloved pastime again. If indeed it were to give her back her cherished independence, with what gladness would she spend her utmost effort to achieve her best. But it seemed too good to be true.

She looked in vain for Oliver or for any face she knew, and at length, disappointed, she turned away. But Rotherby's letter was close to her hand, and she sat down to read it afresh.

It was while she was thus employed that she heard the trampling of a horse's hoofs outside, and looked forth once more in time to see Dr. Square just rolling off his old white horse.

Her heart gave a leap at the sight, but the next moment she told herself that he had patients in Fordestown and it was not likely that he had come thither to seek her.

Nevertheless she listened anxiously, and presently heard the sound of his heavy step upon the stairs. She went to her door then and opened it, meeting him on the narrow landing outside.

She saw in a moment that his big face lacked its usual cheeriness though he greeted her with outstretched hand. "Ah, here you are, Miss Thorold! Dolly told me where to look for you, and they sent me up from downstairs. May I come in?"

"Please do!" she said, and led the way back into her room. Her first instinctive feeling of pleasure at sight of him had given way to one of misgiving. She turned very quickly and faced him. "Please tell me what is the matter! Something is wrong."

He did not attempt to deny it. "They're in bad trouble at Tetherstones," he said. "And when Dolly told me you were here, I said I'd come over and see you."

"Oh, what is the matter?" she said.

His kindly eyes looked into hers with a hint of concern. "Don't you upset yourself, Miss Thorold!" he said. "You're not too strong, remember. It's the little girl—little Ruth. She's had an accident, and she's very ill."

"Oh, poor mite!" said Frances. "How did it happen?"

"It's difficult to say. The child was lost for some hours the day after you left. Then they found her up at the Stones. She had been looking for you, she said. And that was all they could get out of her. She had had a bad fall off the Rocking Stone, and couldn't move."

"Oh, poor little girl!" Frances' voice was quick with anxiety. "Is she much hurt?"

Dr. Square nodded slowly once or twice. "She has no strength—and I'm afraid—very much afraid—there is some mischief to the spine. She keeps on asking for you, Miss Thorold. I said I'd come and tell you."

"Ah!" Frances said.

It came upon her like a blow—the cudgel-stroke of Fate. So there was to be no escape after all! A sense of suffocation came upon her, and she turned sharply to the window, instinctively seeking air. Blind for a moment, she leaned there, gathering her strength.

Behind her she heard the doctor's voice. "Now take it quietly! Don't let yourself be overcome! There's no need. The little one isn't suffering, and—please God—she won't suffer. It's only her anxiety about you that's worrying her. She's not used to worry, you know. She's only a baby." His voice shook a little. "But if you could just go to her—set her mind at rest—you'd never be sorry. You've had a hard life, Miss Thorold, but you've got a soft heart. And sometimes, you know, when we are throwing a line to others, the tide turns in our favour and we find we're drifting in to our own desired haven as well."

His words reached her through a great chaos of emotions. She leaned against the window-frame with closed eyes, seeing herself as driftwood upon the tide of which he spoke. To go back to Tetherstones, to face again the torment from which she had barely escaped, to feel the grey walls enclosing her once more and all the sinister influences that had, as it were, stretched out and around her to draw her down! She lifted her face to the soft grey sky with an inarticulate prayer for help.

She heard again the doctor's voice behind her, and realized that he was pleading for something very near his heart. Was not little Ruth near to the hearts of all who knew her?

"It won't be for very long," he was saying. "She's fretting her heart out for you because she had got hold of the idea that you are in danger—frightened—unhappy. No one can set her mind at rest except you, and it would be a kindness to them all at Tetherstones to go and do it. You would like to do them a kindness, Miss Thorold?"

That moved her. Very suddenly all her doubt and hesitation were swept away. To do them a kindness—these people who had brought her back from the gates of death, who had sheltered her, cared for her, comforted her in her extremity! What mattered anything besides? What was her pride compared with this? What though her very heart were pierced by the ordeal? She could not shirk it now. It was as though an answer had come to that half-formed prayer of hers. Whatever the outcome, she had no choice but to go back.

With a sharp, catching breath, she turned. "I will go—of course," she said. "How can I get there?"

He smiled at her with instant relief, and she realized that he had hardly expected to gain his point. She wondered how much he knew regarding her sudden departure. It was evident that he understood that she had a very strong reason for not wishing to return.

He got up. "Well, as I said, you'll never regret it," he said. "As to getting there, Oliver's in the town now with the cart. Do you mind going back with him? It may be for a few days, you know. You're prepared for that?"

"I will stay as long as little Ruth wants me," she said.

"That's right. That's like you." He held out his hand to her, "Good-bye, Miss Thorold! You're looking better. I believe the tide has turned already."

She tried to smile in answer, but she found no words. Driftwood! Driftwood! And even if the tide turned, whither could it land her now?

CHAPTER IV
RUTH

"Pleased to see you, Miss Thorold," Oliver touched his hat with his whip and gave her his friendly smile of welcome. "A bad business this about the little girl. They're all very upset at Tetherstones."

"I am sure they must be," Frances said. "What a terribly sad business, Oliver! Who was it found her?"

"I found her," said Oliver. "But we thought she was with you and no one missed her at first. She'd been lying there all night and a good part of the day before she was missed. We'd been busy, you see——" he jerked the reins——"busy with other things. Then Maggie came out to me and said you were gone and the little one couldn't be found, and I went straight away to the Stones to look for her. She was lying just under the Rocking Stone unconscious, and I carried her back. She's come to herself since, but they say she's somehow different—that she'll never be the same again—that she——" He broke off to cough and flicked the horse's ears with his whip. They clattered over the rough stones of the street for some distance in silence. After a while he spoke again. "She's only a child—a bit of a baby—but she isn't like others I've ever seen. Maggie is just breaking her heart over her."

"Poor Maggie!" said Frances gently.

"Yes." He nodded acquiescence. "Maggie and Nan—Ruth's mother—were always the pals, you see. There was only a year between them. Nan was Arthur's favourite sister too. He's feeling it pretty badly—though he'd sooner die than let anyone know."

Frances felt her heart contract. She said nothing.

They were out upon the open moor road before Oliver volunteered anything further. Then, somewhat abruptly, with a sidelong glance at her, he said, "It's decent of you to come back to us after the fright you had."

"I am only coming for little Ruth's sake," Frances said.

"Yes, I know. The doctor told me. I didn't think he'd get you to come," said Oliver frankly. "You'd had a pretty bad scare. But it might have been worse, I suppose. The fellow wasn't much damaged, was he?"

There was curiosity in his tone tempered with a reticence that she was quick to detect. A sharp sense of anger surged within her.

"It was no thanks to—to—the man who shot him that he wasn't killed," she said.

"No. I know," said Oliver. He added after a moment, "Anyway I did my best to prevent it. It wasn't my fault that it happened."

She turned upon him. "But—surely you didn't know it was going to happen?" she said.

He lifted his shoulders. "No, I didn't know, Miss Thorold. But I did know the chap was in danger. I told you so, didn't I?"

"But why—why?" said Frances.

He gave her again that sidelong glance. "Can't always account for things," he said. "We're a good long way from towns and civilization here."

"But he might have been killed!" she said.

He nodded. "So he might. But he wasn't. That's all that matters. Where is he now?"

"He has gone to town," she said.

"Then, if he's a wise man, he'll stop there," said Oliver with finality, and whipped up his horse.

The day was soft and cloudy, the tors wrapped in mist. There was a feeling of rain in the air and the sweetness of rain-filled streams. She heard the rushing of unseen water as they trotted over the winding moorland road. It filled her with a great sadness, a longing indescribable to which she could give no name.

She asked no more questions of Oliver, for she knew instinctively that she would receive no actual enlightenment from him. Moreover, something within her shrank from discussing Arthur Dermot and Arthur Dermot's motives with a third person. Any explanation, she felt, must come from the man himself.

They drove on up the stony road, drawing nearer and nearer to the great boulder-strewn tors, hearing the vague bleatings of sheep in the desolation but seeing no living thing upon their way. Again the eeriness of the place began to possess Frances. It was a relief to her when Oliver said abruptly, "We won't go by the Stones."

She believed it to be the quicker route, but it was rough, and she was thankful that he proposed to avoid it. Her dread of Tetherstones was growing with every yard they covered, but there was no turning back now. She could only go forward to whatever might be in store.

The mist gradually descended to meet them and turned to a small rain, drifting in their faces. The chill of the moor laid a clammy touch upon them. Frances shivered in spite of herself.

Oliver shot her his shrewd glance. "They'll be awfully pleased to see you," he said, and added, "We're nearly there."

Yes, they were nearly there. The atmosphere of Tetherstones seemed to be reaching out to receive them—the old grey place from which she had fled as from a prison.

They turned down the steep lane, and the scent of wet honeysuckle came to Frances mingling with the bog-myrtle of the moors. Something rose in her throat and she turned her face aside. She had fled from the place as from a prison, yet, returning, that exquisite scent came back to her as the breath of home.

They reached the white gate, standing wide to receive them, and drove through to the garden where Roger met them with extravagant antics of delight. His welcome sent a warmth to her heart that in some fashion eased the unacknowledged pain there. She approached the old stone doorway with more assurance.

Oliver saluted and turned the horse; she heard him driving round to the stables as she entered.

The door stood open according to custom. The passage was dark, but she heard someone moving in the kitchen and directed her steps thither, Roger bounding by her side. Then as she turned a corner there came the sudden tread of feet, and she drew back sharply. She was face to face with Arthur Dermot.

He also checked himself abruptly, and in a moment stood back against the wall to let her pass.

He did not attempt to address her, but she could not pass him so in his own house. She stood still.

But for a second or two her voice refused to serve her, and he made an odd movement as if to compel her to pass on. Then with a sharp effort she spoke.

"Little Ruth—I have come to see her. Is she—is she———"

"Dying—yes," he said. "It was—good of you to come. Nell and Lucy are in the kitchen. If you like, I will tell them you are here."

"Oh no," she said. "No. I will go to them."

She passed him quickly, thankful to escape, hearing his heavy tread as he went on, with that old fateful feeling at her heart. She wondered what he really thought of her for returning thus.

She found the two girls in the kitchen, very subdued and troubled though they gave her a ready welcome.

"We've missed you dreadfully," said Nell. "And little Ruth has hardly left off crying for you all these days." Her lip quivered. "Dr. Square said he should go and tell you after your letter came—but I didn't think you'd come."

"I had to come," Frances said.

"I thought you would if you really knew how badly you were wanted," said Lucy.

"I didn't," said Nell. "I knew you wouldn't stay that day of the row. I told you so, didn't I? And I never thought you'd come back. I told Arthur you wouldn't. Only you would have done it."

She looked at Frances with warm admiration in her eyes.

"You're a brick," she said. "And we'll none of us forget it. You might run and tell Dolly, Lucy. Now sit down, Miss Thorold, and I'll get you a glass of milk."

She bustled round the old raftered kitchen, and Frances, sitting in the horsehair arm-chair, tried to forget that awful night when she had awaked as from a nightmare to find herself lying before the great fireplace—a prisoner.

"Where are your mother and Maggie?" she asked, when Nell brought her the milk.

"Mother is in the study with the old man," said Nell. "Maggie is out somewhere. She and Elsie were getting hay down from the loft a few minutes ago. The work has got to go on, you know, whoever lives or dies." She checked a sob upon the words.

Frances leaned forward and held her hand. "Tell me about little Ruth!" she said.

"Oh, there isn't much to tell. She went to look for you the night you left. You had a fright, didn't you? So did we. There was a frightful row after you were gone, and we all of us forgot to wonder where she was till the morning. Then

Oliver found her—found her—" Nell choked and recovered herself. "It was up by the Stones. She'd been there heaps of times before and never come to any harm. But this time she must have gone right up on to the Rocking Stone and overbalanced. She was lying under it, and she'd been there for twelve hours or more, poor little darling. She was unconscious when Oliver found her, but she hadn't been all the time. She keeps on talking about it, about being a prisoner under that stone and begging God to set her free so that she can go to you. She has got a rooted idea that you are in trouble. You're not, are you? Everything's all right with you?" She looked down at Frances piteously, through tears.

"Don't you bother your head about me, my dear!" said Frances. "My affairs don't count now." She paused a moment, then, with some hesitation: "Will you tell me why there was such a disturbance after I went?" she asked.

"Oh, that!" said Nell, and also hesitated. "That's one of the things we're not supposed to talk about," she said, after a moment. "You don't mind, Miss Thorold? You'll try to understand?"

"My dear, don't you trouble!" said Frances very kindly. "I shall always try to understand."

But even as she spoke she felt again that cold misgiving at her heart. What species of monster was this whom they all combined to shield?

Lucy came running down again with an eager message. Dolly said would she go up at once? Little Ruth was in their mother's room. She would show her where it was.

Then, as they mounted the stairs together, she drew close to Frances and slipped a shy hand into her arm. "We have missed you so much," she said.

Frances patted the hand without speaking. The warmth of her welcome touched her very deeply.

They traversed two or three rambling passages before they reached Mrs. Dermot's room. It was over the kitchen, a low, oak-raftered apartment with an uneven floor. It contained two beds, and in one of these, close to a narrow, ivy-grown window, lay Ruth.

Her face was turned towards the door, and—it came upon Frances with a curious sense of shock—the eyes that had always till then been closed were open, wide open, and burning with a fire so spiritual, so unearthly, that for a moment she halted almost as one afraid. In that moment she realized very fully and beyond all possibility of doubt that little Ruth was dying.

Lucy's soft touch drew her forward. She was aware of Dolly, pale and restrained, somewhere in the background, but she did not actually see her. She went to the child's bedside as if she were entering a sanctuary.

Ruth greeted her instantly, but she lay like a waxen image with tiny hands folded on her breast.

"Have you come back at last, dear Miss Thorold?" she said, a thrill of gladness in her voice. "God told me you would in a dream last night."

Frances knelt down by the bed and closely clasped the little folded hands that never stirred to her touch. "My little darling!" she said softly. "Have you been wanting me?"

The burning eyes were fixed upon her. It was as though in them alone the living spirit lingered. She was sure that the spirit saw her in that hour.

"Yes, I have wanted you," the child said. "I have been calling you—crying for you—ever since that night. You said that you were coming then, but you never came."

"I couldn't," whispered Frances.

"No. You had to go," Ruth agreed, in her tired voice. "I knew that. But why didn't you go to the Stones? You meant to go there, didn't you?"

"I can't tell you now, darling," Frances said.

"It doesn't matter," said Ruth. "I think God didn't want you to go. But I didn't know that when I went to look for you. I thought you might be lost and frightened again—like you were that first night that I found you. And then—when you weren't there—I was afraid something had happened to you. Did anything happen, dear Miss Thorold?"

"Nothing dreadful, sweetheart," she answered softly.

"Then God took care of you," Ruth said, with conviction. "There was something dreadful very near you—very near you; but He sent it away."

Those blind eyes—the eyes of a visionary—kindled afresh with the words, and a sudden sense as of something vividly remembered smote Frances. She had seen those eyes before. Where? Where? Then it came to her—like a rending flash of lightning across a dark sky. The Bishop of Burminster had had that inner flame as of prophecy in his eyes on the night that he had denounced her. A great wave of feeling went through her. She had an overwhelming desire to shield herself, shrinking as one shrinks from the unsparing beam of a searchlight.

"We won't talk of it now, darling," she said almost pleadingly. "Try to go to sleep!"

"I don't want to sleep," said the child. "I want to give you a message, but it hasn't come yet. And if I go to sleep, I shall forget it."

"We will give her something to make her sleep presently," said Dolly gently. "She isn't in any pain—only a little tired. Take this chair, Miss Thorold! You must be tired too."

So Frances sat down beside the bed to wait, as all in that house were waiting, for the coming of the Angel of Death.

CHAPTER V
THE EXILE

Late in the afternoon Maggie came in, her plump, rosy face drawn and sad. She came and hung over the bed for a space in silence. Ruth was lying as she had lain throughout, with her eyes fixed upwards, as though waiting for a sign, and still they burned with that fire of inner sight which to Frances had been somehow terrible. Maggie straightened herself at last with a deep sigh. She looked across at Frances with the glimmer of a welcoming smile, but she did not speak. Softly she crept away.

The next to come was the white-haired mother, and to her Ruth spoke the moment she entered the room though her entrance made no sound.

"My dear Granny!" she said.

Frances rose quickly and proffered her chair; but Mrs. Dermot shook her head.

"No, no! I have only come for a moment." She bent over the child. "Are you happier now, my baby? Can you go to sleep?"

"Yes, I am quite happy," said little Ruth, "now that Miss Thorold is here. But I can't go to sleep till I get the message for her. I might die, dear Granny, and I shouldn't be able to give it her then. We can only send our love—after we are dead."

"But Miss Thorold can't stay here all the time, darling," said Mrs. Dermot, with a tender touch upon the child's brow. "She will get so tired sitting here. She has been ill, you know. She will want to rest."

"Someone will call her when the message comes," said Ruth. "I know she won't mind. She is always so good. Will you go and rest, please, Miss Thorold? It won't come yet."

"Please do!" said Mrs. Dermot. "My son asks me to say that he hopes you will regard Tetherstones as your home for as long as you care to stay in it. I think I need not speak for myself, or tell you how grateful we all are to you for coming back to set our little one's mind at rest."

There was infinite pathos to Frances in the quiet utterance. Mrs. Dermot was looking at her with eyes that seemed too tired for tears.

"How she has suffered!" was the thought that passed through Frances' mind, as she met them.

"You are much more than kind—as you always have been," she said very earnestly, as she rose to go. "Please remember that I am here to help, if there is anything whatever that I can do! Don't hesitate—ever—to make use of me!"

"Thank you," said Mrs. Dermot. "I should like you to rest now. Your room is quite ready for you. Perhaps—perhaps—in the night we may need you."

Frances knew what she meant. She stooped to kiss little Ruth and turned to go. "I shall be ready at any time," she said.

In the doorway she encountered Dolly entering with a cup of milk in her hand. Dolly stopped.

"Are you going downstairs for some tea? That's right. It's in the kitchen. Maggie is there. She will look after you. We are so glad you have come back."

She passed on into the room, and Frances went out alone.

The old house was full of shadows. She could hear the shrill cries of swallows wheeling about the eaves. The scent of honeysuckle was everywhere. How had she ever thought of it as a prison?

Slowly she went down the stairs, and turned towards the kitchen. As she did so, she heard a sudden sound in the recess in which she had hidden on the night of her flight, and started to see two figures emerge. They were very closely locked together, and she saw that in the dimness she was not observed. Involuntarily almost, she drew back.

"Don't fret, sweetheart!" It was Oliver's voice, pitched very low. "It'll be all right, you'll see."

"Oh dear, I do hope so," came back in a whisper from Maggie. "It doesn't feel right though I suppose it is."

"It is right," the man confidently asserted. "If we can't choose our circumstances we must adapt ourselves to them. It's the only way to live."

"Yes, I suppose so," said Maggie somewhat dubiously.

They passed down the passage to the kitchen, leaving Frances standing at the foot of the stairs.

So standing, down the passage to her left that led to the study, she heard a voice—an old man's voice, broken, pathetic, piteously pleading.

"I assure you—" it said—"I assure you—you are wrong. It is difficult to conceive how you can permit yourself to harbour these monstrous and terrible ideas. I sometimes think your brain is not normal. You are causing the greatest grief both to your mother whom you profess to love—and to myself, for whom I know but too well that all filial affection has long ceased to exist. I am an old man and helpless. Your behaviour is breaking my heart. I shall go down to my grave with the knowledge that my son—my only son—will rejoice to see me laid there."

There followed an agonized sound that pierced Frances like the cry of a child. Almost before she knew what she was doing, she had turned in the direction of the study. She went down the passage swiftly to the door that stood half-open and knocked upon it quickly and nervously.

"Can I come in?" she said.

It was the impulse to help, to protect, that moved her, and though she knew who was in the study with old Mr. Dermot, she did not hesitate. Only as she entered did he realize that her heart was thumping almost unendurably.

She paused just within the room. "Can I come in?" she said again, and felt her breath come sharply with the words. It needed all her resolution to control it.

A startled silence followed her appearance, and then very kindly and courteously the old man greeted her.

"Come in, Miss Thorold! Come in! I am delighted to see you!"

He was sitting in a leathern armchair in the failing light, and she was struck afresh by his frailty and the deathly whiteness of his face.

"Will you excuse my getting up?" he said. "I have had one of my bad attacks and they leave my heart very weak. Come and sit down, Miss Thorold, and give me the pleasure of a chat with you."

She went forward, keenly aware of Arthur standing motionless before the fireplace, but not glancing at him as she passed. She reached Mr. Dermot, and took the hand he extended. It was icy-cold and trembling, and it seemed to her that there was something almost appealing in the way it clung to hers.

"I am so sorry you have been ill," she said.

"Yes, we are a sad household—a sad household," he made answer. "I am told the little one is very ill—the little blind girl who lives with us. Can you tell me what is the matter with her? Some childish ailment, I suppose?"

As it were against her will, Frances glanced at Arthur. His eyes looked straight back at her from under frowning brows. He spoke briefly, coldly.

"I think you have been informed before, sir, that the child would not live to grow up. Perhaps under the circumstances it is hardly to be desired that she should."

"Under what circumstances?" said Mr. Dermot, and his voice was as cold as his son's, but with an edge of satire that was to Frances even more unbearable than the studied indifference of the younger man's utterance. "Since when, may I ask, have you been a qualified judge as to the relative values of life and death?"

Arthur made a very slight movement that might have denoted either protest or exasperation. "I referred to her infirmity," he said.

Mr. Dermot laughed, a soft, bitter laugh, and Frances shivered. She felt the tension between the two men to be so acute as to be near the snapping point, and wondered desperately what mistaken impulse had brought her thither and how she might escape. But in a moment the old man addressed her again, and there came to her a curious conviction that in some fashion she was needed.

"Will you not sit down, Miss Thorold," he said, "and take tea with me? I do not have my meals with my family as, on account of the weakness of my heart, quiet is essential to me. You were just going"; he turned very pointedly to his son; "will you be good enough to ask Elsie to bring tea for Miss Thorold as well as for myself?"

He spoke with frigid politeness as if addressing a menial, but there was a quaver in his voice that betrayed him. Frances realized very clearly in that instant which of the two men had the upper hand, and the realization was as a heavy weight laid upon her. She shook it off with conscious effort, telling herself that it mattered nothing to her at least since she had gained her freedom.

Arthur made no move of any sort in response to his father's request. He stood as before, grim as a gaoler, looking straight across at her.

Very steadily, with a certain stateliness that was hers upon occasion, she took the chair the old man had indicated. "That is very kind of you," she said to him. "I should like it very much."

His smile of pleasure warmed her heart. "I assure you it will be the greatest treat to me," he said. "It is hard to have to lead the life of a hermit. I have my books, and I am also writing—or I should say I have collected material to write—an exhaustive treatise upon the Stones. I think I told you of my intention the last time we met, and you very kindly offered to help me."

"I would gladly do anything in my power," said Frances, moved, as she had been moved before, by a certain forlornness in his attitude.

"Ah!" He nodded with obvious gratification. "That is kind of you. And I am sure you would be interested. There is so much that is strange and indeed almost uncanny about this subject." He turned again to his son with elaborate courtesy. "We need not detain you here. I am aware that this matter is one that holds no appeal for a brain like yours, and I have no desire to bore you with it."

"Very good, sir." Arthur made a sudden movement as one who has come to a decision. "I will go." He went to the door, and there paused, looking back, almost as if irresolute, then abruptly wheeled again. "I will send in tea," he said, and was gone.

They heard him tramp heavily down the passage, and it seemed to Frances that a shudder went through the frail old man lying back in the armchair. He made a weary movement with one hand as one who would dismiss a distasteful subject.

"Tell me a little more about your book!" she said gently.

He looked at her, and she saw his eyes kindle in the dimness.

"I am going to ask you to tell me something first," he said. "It all bears upon the same subject. This illness of the little blind girl which they say is so serious, is it in any way connected with the Stones—with any so-called accident that occurred there?"

He leaned slowly forward with the words, and though they were deliberately uttered there was an eagerness vibrating in them that made her wonder.

"Has no one told you about it?" she said.

"No one—no one. I am treated as a nonentity always." He spoke fretfully, querulously. "I believe it is on account of my health, but I often think my health would improve if I were allowed to lead a more normal life. My son has relegated to himself the rulership of this establishment, and everyone is made to bow down to him. I am told—nothing. I am consulted—never."

"He leads a hard life," Frances said. "Perhaps it has made him hard."

"No, no! It isn't that. It is just the passion for ruling. Let me warn you against him, Miss Thorold! Never allow him to attain any sort of influence over you, for he is a difficult man to thwart. You would not like to be bound to him for life. It would break your heart." He paused a moment and made again that gesture as of dismissing an unpleasant topic. "But now," he said, "about the little girl—you were going to tell me. Something happened to her up at the Stones. What was it? Do you know what it was?"

Frances looked at him. His voice was tremulous, and yet she had a curious conviction that it was not solely anxiety for little Ruth that made it so. She considered for a moment before replying.

"She had a fall," she said then.

"Ah! Was it near the Rocking Stone?" Mr. Dermot sat slowly forward. "You will tell me," he said. "I am sure you will tell me."

Again Frances hesitated. If the details of Ruth's accident had purposely been kept from him, was she justified in enlightening him?

"I only know what I have been told since," she said. "They found her lying unconscious, and it was evident that she had had a fall."

"And that is all you know? You cannot tell me who found her or why she went?" Suppressed excitement sounded in the words. Mr. Dermot was gripping the arm of his chair, and the bones of his knuckles stood out sharply. "I am very anxious to know all," he said. "They try to keep it from me, but it is wrong—it is wrong. She had a fall, you say? Was she—was she—alone when she fell?"

"I believe so," Frances said. "In fact, I am sure of it, for they say she was not found for some hours after."

"Ah!" The old man relaxed so suddenly that he almost fell back into his chair. "That is what I wanted to know. She was alone. They say so." He broke off, panting a little; but in a moment or two recovered himself sufficiently to smile at her. "Now that," he said, "gives colour, does it not, to the local rumour that the powers of evil are in some mysterious way permitted to haunt the Stones. This is a very interesting point, Miss Thorold. Can her fall have been due to something of this nature? Are you a believer in the occult?"

"Not to that extent," said Frances, suppressing a chill shiver. "I think it was perfectly easy for the poor mite to fall, considering her blindness."

"Ah, yes. They should not have let her wander so far. There is always the danger of a false step. But she is young. She may recover—she may recover. While there is life, there is hope; and if not,—there is the life beyond."

He spoke gently, a faint smile on his grey features, and again Frances was touched in a fashion she could hardly have explained. He was so old, so tired, so near to the life beyond of which he spoke.

She said nothing, and in a few moments Elsie came in with a tea-tray. She looked at Frances, round-eyed, as she sat it down, but somewhat to her surprise she gave her no word of greeting.

"Arthur said you would like your tea in here," she said. "Is that right?"

"Yes, Miss Thorold is my guest to-night," said the old man. "Will you pour out, Miss Thorold?"

Frances complied. Elsie hovered about the room as if uncertain whether to go or to remain.

Mr. Dermot paid no attention to her for some seconds, then very suddenly he seemed to awake to the fact of her presence. He turned in his chair.

"Pray return to your work in the farmyard!" he said. "I am sure you have no time to spare for the ordinary civilities of life."

His tone was quite quiet, but the words amazed Frances. The girl to whom they were addressed merely nodded and turned to the door. She went out in silence, leaving it open behind her.

"They always do that," said Mr. Dermot, with a sort of weary patience. "I wonder, might I trouble you to shut it?"

Frances rose to do so, her mind still full of wonder at the curious attitude he had adopted towards his daughter.

"You think it strange," he said, as she sat down again, "that there should be so great a lack of sympathy between certain members of my family and myself. But I assure you it did not originate with me. I am a student, Miss Thorold, and perhaps it is not surprising that those who devote the whole of themselves to manual labour on a farm should find it difficult to keep in touch with me. It is said that if you associate with the animals you will in time assimilate their characteristics. This has already happened to Arthur, and some of the girls are following in his footsteps. Milly is the only one who has shown no outward sign of deterioration since we came to Tetherstones. It is a very insidious evil, and it spreads—it spreads." He sighed. "I foresaw it before we came here. I was never in favour of the scheme, but—I was overruled. We have a tyrant among us whose will is law."

"Then you don't like Tetherstones?" Frances said.

She saw again an extraordinary gleam in his eyes as he made reply. "You might ask a convict how he likes Princetown," he said. "My place is at Oxford, but I have been torn from it and made to endure life in the desert all these years."

"But a very beautiful desert," suggested Frances.

He made a wide gesture of repudiation. "What is that to an exile? When you have been made to eat stones for bread, you will not notice if they are beautiful to look at."

"I can understand that," she said. "Yet a sense of beauty is sometimes a help. At least I found it so when I was at Burminster."

"Ah! Burminster!" He repeated the name thoughtfully. "Did you ever meet anyone there of the name of Rotherby?"

"Why, yes." She started a little, remembering Arthur's attitude. "I was with Dr. Rotherby who is the Bishop of Burminster."

"Yes—yes." He nodded gravely. "We were at Oxford together. He left and I remained. So he is at Burminster! You were not happy with him?"

Frances hesitated. "Not very," she admitted.

He nodded again. "A hard man—a hard man! And did you ever meet his nephew—Montague?"

She felt the colour leap to her face. "Yes, I have met him," she said.

"Ah! He is a friend of yours," said the old man, with quiet conviction. "A close friend?"

She did not know how to answer him. No words would come. But in that moment to her intense relief she heard a step outside. The door opened, and Mrs. Dermot entered.

"Arnold," she said, "I am sorry to disturb you, but Dr. Square is here. He will be down immediately to see you. May he come in?"

The old man turned towards her with a fond smile. "My dear," he said, "any pretext is welcome that brings you to my side."

Frances got up, thankful for the interruption. "I will go to the kitchen if I may," she said. "Maggie is there."

"We need not drive you away," protested Mr. Dermot.

But she was already at the door. "Perhaps—later," she said, and was gone before he could say any more. The closing of the door behind her gave her a sense of escape from something terrible which she told herself was utterly unreasonable.

CHAPTER VI
THE CHAIN

The kitchen-door was half-open. She pushed it open and entered. Then sharply she drew back. It was raining and the place was in semi-darkness. Only a red glow from the great open fireplace lighted it, throwing into strong relief the old black rafters. And in this glow, seated at the table facing her, but with his head upon his hands, was a man.

He did not stir at her entrance. It was evident he did not hear her, and for a moment her impulse was to go as suddenly and silently as she had come. But something in that bowed silvered head checked her. She stood still, and in a second a whine of greeting from under the table betrayed her. Arthur sat upright with a jerk, and Roger came smiling out from his place at his master's feet to welcome her.

It was Roger who saved the situation. She stooped to fondle him, and in so doing recovered her self-possession. Standing up again, she found that Arthur also was on his feet. They faced each other once more in the firelight, and the beating of the rain upon the thick laurel bushes outside mingled with the dirge-like monotony of the dripping eaves filled in that poignant pause.

Arthur spoke, his voice low and constrained. "Come and sit down! I'm just going."

The awful pallor of his face, the misery of the eyes that avoided hers, went straight to her heart. She moved forward, urged by the instinct to help, forgetful of everything else in the rush of pity that surged through her.

"Don't go because I am here!" she said.

He had turned already to the outer door. He paused with his back to her, and took up his cap from a chair.

"It was not my fault you were sent for," he said. "It was done against my wish—without my knowledge."

The words were curt, emotionless. Why did she feel as though she were in the presence of a sorely-wounded animal?

"Don't go!" she said again, and somehow the words seemed to utter themselves; she was not conscious of any effort of her own by which they were spoken. "There is no need for you to go."

"No need!" He still stood with his back to her. His hand was on the door, but he did not go. "Did you say that?" he said, after a moment.

"Yes." She came forward slowly, and still it did not seem to be of her own volition that she moved or spoke. "I haven't come back to make trouble—only to try and help—if I can."

"Yes. I understand," he said, and his voice came half-strangled, as though he fought some obstruction in his throat. "Square told me."

She stopped at the table. "Have you been having tea? I thought Maggie was here."

"She has gone out with Elsie. Milly went upstairs to Dolly. I don't know where the others are."

Again curiously something in his voice pierced her. It had a deadened quality—was it utter weariness—or smothered pain?

"Have you had tea?" she asked.

His hand wrenched at the door-handle. The door opened and a drift of rain blew in. But still he paused.

"I haven't had mine," said Frances.

He turned almost with violence and the door shut behind him. "Why haven't you had yours? I thought Elsie brought it to you. I told her to."

He looked at her, heavily scowling, for a moment, then again averted his eyes.

"Don't be angry!" she said gently. "She did bring it, but I didn't stay to drink it because your mother said the doctor was here. Do you mind if I have some now?" She looked round the table that had been cleared, then turned to the fire. "The kettle is quite hot. It will soon boil."

He came back into the room. There was something about him at that moment upon which she could not look. He went to the dresser, and she heard the clatter of cups and saucers. She knew he was laying the table behind her, but she remained with her face to the fire.

Suddenly he was beside her. He took up the simmering kettle and forced it down into the heart of the fire, keeping his hand upon it.

"You will burn yourself!" she said.

He answered nothing, merely stood doggedly bent over the glow till the kettle spluttered and boiled. Then he lifted it, and turned back to the table.

Frances turned also. Mutely she watched him pour water into the old metal tea-pot. The haggardness of his face, the grim endurance of his set jaw, struck her afresh. She wondered if he were ill.

He set down the kettle and drew up the horse-hair chair with the wooden arms that she so well remembered.

"Sit down!" he said.

She obeyed him, finding no words.

He cut a slice from a loaf and began to toast it, Roger pressing closely against his gaitered legs.

Very suddenly his voice came back to her again, hollow, strained, oddly vibrant. "I should like you to know one thing. Though you have come back here against my will, you have—nothing to fear. I recognize it was—an act of—charity—and, so far as I am concerned, you are safe. I will never get in your way."

"Thank you," Frances said quietly. "I am not afraid of that."

He made a jerky movement, but instantly checked himself, and turning the bread upon the fork, maintained his silence. She wondered what was passing behind that tensely restrained front, what torment was at work within him to produce the anguish of suffering which she sensed rather than saw. But he gave her no clue of any sort. He remained bent and silent till his task was finished.

Then he brought the toast and set it before her. "Can you pour out your own tea?" he said.

She looked up at him, gravely resolute. "Mr. Dermot, please join me!"

He made a sharp gesture that was more of protest than refusal. "Afraid I can't stay. I've got to see Oliver."

"You can if you will," she said steadily. "That isn't your reason. You can see Oliver afterwards."

He gave in abruptly, in a fashion that surprised her. He dropped down on to the wooden chair he had occupied at her entrance, and propped his head on his hands.

"My God!" he said, under his breath. "My God!"

Then she knew that his endurance was very near the breaking-point, and the woman's soul in her rose up in strength to support his weakness.

She got up to take another cup from the dresser, then poured out some tea and took it to him on the other side of the table. He did not attempt to stir at her coming, but the hands that supported his head were clenched and trembling.

She bent over him, all thought of fear gone from her. "Here is your tea," she said. "Can you drink it?"

He moved then, reached out suddenly and grasped her wrist, drawing her hand over his face till her palm was tightly pressed upon his eyes.

"My God!" he said again, almost inarticulately. "Oh, my God—my God!"

A dreadful sob broke from him, and he caught his breath and held it rigidly till the veins in his temples stood out like cords.

Frances looked on mutely till she could bear it no longer. Then very gently she laid her other hand upon his shoulder.

"Ah, don't!" she said. "Don't! Let it come! It will be easier to bear afterwards. And what do I matter?"

She felt a great shiver go through him. His hold upon her hand was as the clutch of a drowning man, and suddenly she felt his tears, slow and scalding, oozing between her fingers. He bent his head lower and lower, striving with himself, and she instinctively turned her eyes away, averting them from his agony.

So, for what seemed an interminable space of time, they remained. Then at last the man spoke, jerkily, with difficulty, yet with returning self-mastery.

"It's no good crying out. It's got to be endured to the end." He paused; then: "I don't often cry out," he said and she thought she caught a note that was almost of appeal in his voice.

"We are all human," she said.

"Are we?" He raised himself abruptly with the words, and leaned back in his chair, looking straight up at her, her hand still grasped in his. "Are you human?" he said, as if challenging her. "I don't believe you are."

His eyes were burning. They had the strained look that comes from lack of sleep. A brief misgiving assailed her, but she put it firmly away. She met his look unflinching.

"Yes, I am human," she said.

"Then how you must hate me!" he said.

She shook her head in silence.

"Why do you do that?" he said. "Are you afraid to tell me so?"

"No," she said. "I don't hate you."

"Why not?" he said.

She hesitated momentarily. Then: "It may be because I don't know you well enough," she said.

There was something in his eyes that besought her. Again involuntarily she thought of a wounded animal. "Not well enough to hate me?" he said.

"Not well enough to judge," she answered quietly.

She saw his throat move spasmodically. His eyes left hers. "I would rather be hated—than tolerated—by you," he said, almost under his breath.

His hold upon her had slackened; she slipped her hand away. "Won't you have your tea?" she said. "I am sure you will feel the better for it."

He made an odd sound that might have been an effort at laughter, and stretched out his hand for the cup.

She stood beside him while he drank, and took it from him when he had finished. "Eat some toast while I pour you out some more!" she said.

"I made the toast for you," he said.

"It doesn't matter," she returned.

"It does matter." He leaned across the table for the loaf. "Bread will do for me. And you will drink some tea yourself before you give me any more."

She heard the dominant note returning in his voice. "I shall do as I think best," she said, but she complied, for something in the glance of those fevered eyes compelled.

They ate and drank together thereafter in unbroken silence until he rose to go. Then, his cap once more in his hand, he paused, looking across at her.

"So you have decided to reserve judgment for the present?" he said.

She met his look steadily, though her heart quickened a little.

"For the present—yes," she said.

He still looked at her. "And if you find—some day—that I can behave other than as a brute-beast, will you perhaps—manage to forget?"

To forget! The word, uttered so humbly, brought the quick tears to her eyes. She turned her face aside.

"Why don't you ask me to—forgive?" she said, her voice very low.

"Because I won't ask the impossible," he answered. "Because you tell me you are human, and—well, some things are past forgiveness. I know that."

He swung round with the words. She heard him open the door, heard again the drip and patter of the rain outside, heard the heavy tread of his feet as he went out.

Then, when she knew that she was alone, her strength went from her. She covered her face and wept.

In that hour she knew that she was chained indeed, beyond all hope of escape. Brute-beast as he described himself—murderer at heart as she believed him to be—yet had he implanted that within her heart which she could never cast out. Whatever he was, whatever he did, could make no difference now. She loved him.

CHAPTER VII
THE MESSAGE

"The doctor says it can't possibly go on much longer."

"But if it does—if it does——"

"Oh, Lucy, do stop crying! What's the good? You'll make yourself ill, child, if you go on."

"I can't help it—I can't help it. Mother looked like death just now."

"That's only because of something the Beast said. Oliver told me——"

The voice sank to a lower whisper as in the old days behind the screen, and Frances, seated in a low chair beside the bed, tried not to strain her ears to listen. She wished the two girls would leave the adjoining room and go to bed, but they had been placed there by Dolly while she snatched a brief rest, and she did not like to intervene. So she sat there motionless, watching a great moth that had come in from the night and was fluttering round and round the ceiling in the arc of light cast upwards by the shaded lamp at her side, and listening to Lucy's fitful sobbing in the other room and Nell's somewhat rough and ready efforts to comfort her.

The very thought of tears seemed out of place in that quiet room, for Ruth was as still and as peaceful as an effigy upon a tomb. She was not asleep; of that Frances was fully convinced. But she was utterly at rest, content so long as her friend remained beside her to lie in that trance-like repose and wait.

The soft night air blew softly in upon them, laden with the scent of the moors. The magic of it went to Frances' inmost soul. She felt as if in some fashion the message of which the child had spoken was being wafted in from those star-lit spaces, but as yet it had no words. Only the burden of it was already in her heart.

A long time passed thus; then there came a movement in the adjoining room. The whispering was renewed for a moment, and ceased. The white-haired mother entered, and as before, Ruth spoke.

"My dear Granny!" she said softly.

Mrs. Dermot motioned to Frances not to move. She came to the other side of the bed and knelt down. "Shall we say our prayers, darling?" she said.

Abruptly Frances realized that someone else had entered also, though she had heard no sound, and looking up she saw Arthur standing just within the doorway between the two rooms.

He stood there motionless until his mother began to murmur the Lord's Prayer, then noiselessly he crept forward and knelt close to the foot of the bed.

It came to Frances then, and she never questioned the impulse, to slip to her knees beside him. And in the hush of that quiet room, she prayed as she never prayed before.

Mrs. Dermot's gentle voice went unfaltering on to the evening hymn.
"Abide with me, fast falls the eventide,
 The darkness deepens; Lord, with me abide,
 When other helpers fail and comforts flee,
 Help of the helpless, O, abide with me."

Verse after verse very softly she repeated to the dying child, and at the last Ruth's voice joined hers, low and monotonous, murmuring the words.
"Hold Thou Thy Cross before my closing eyes,
 Shine through the gloom and point me to the skies,
 Heaven's morning breaks and earth's vain shadows flee,
 In life—in death—O Lord, abide with me."

The two voices ceased, and there fell a deep silence. How long it lasted Frances never knew. She was as one kneeling in a holy place, too near to the spiritual to reck of time. But gradually, as she knelt, there dawned upon her the consciousness of another presence in that chamber of Death. It did not surprise her when Ruth's voice, quiet and confident, spoke in the stillness. "This is my mother!" she said. "She came to me that night at the Stones and stayed with me so as I shouldn't be frightened. She said she would come again if God would let her. Isn't He kind?" An odd little quiver of rapture ran through the words.

"He is always kind to His little ones, my darling," said Mrs. Dermot very tenderly. " 'He shall gather the lambs with His arm and carry them in His bosom.' "

"That is what my mother told me," said the child. "She says—she says—that if we only knew how beautiful it is on beyond, we should never mind going, or cry—ever—for those who went. You won't cry when I've gone, dear Granny, will you?"

"Not for you, darling," Mrs. Dermot whispered back.

"Nor for my mother any more," said little Ruth. "She is quite happy. Do you see her? She is standing close to you and smiling. Don't you see her, Granny?"

"I know that she is here," said Mrs. Dermot.

"She is very, very pretty," said Ruth in a hushed voice, "much prettier than anyone else I know. Her hair is dark, and her eyes are lovely, like hare-bells. No one else has eyes like that." Again the thrill of gladness was in her voice. "I can see her, Granny! I can see her!" said little Ruth. Then in a lower voice, slightly mystified: "I wonder why Uncle Arthur and Miss Thorold are so unhappy. I can see them too, but they are not so clear. I wish they were happy. I should see them more easily then."

Frances raised her head, but the blue eyes were fixed upwards; it was the eyes of the soul that saw her, the voice of the soul that spoke.

"Miss Thorold," said the child, "the Stones are waiting for you. Don't ever be afraid! They are going to give you something that you're wanting—something that you've wanted always. I don't know what it is, but that doesn't matter. You'll know it when you find it, because it's very big—bigger even than the Rocking Stone. And if you can't find it by yourself, Uncle Arthur will help you. Only you'll have to ask him—because it's the only way." Her voice began to drag a little. "He's so lonely and so sad, and he never thinks anybody wants him. Often when you think he is cross, he is just unhappy. He has been unhappy for ever so long, and it's getting worse. Grandpa doesn't understand, but then he is so often away now. He has been away ever since that night I went to look for you at the Stones. I don't know where he goes to, do you?"

Frances hesitated, but at once Mrs. Dermot spoke in answer.

"Granny knows where he is, darling. He is coming back soon. Don't trouble your little head about him!"

"Give him my love!" said Ruth. "I shan't see him again, but he is too old to mind, and I am not big enough to matter. Will you ask Uncle Arthur to come quite close to me just for a minute? I want—I want to tell him something."

Arthur rose from his knees and moved to the head of the bed. His arm went round his mother as he stooped to the child.

"I am here, Ruth. What is it?"

There came a little gasp from the bed. "Will you—hold my hand?" said Ruth. "I—can't see you quite well yet. Thank you, Uncle Arthur. Now I can tell you. Do you remember that night I found my dear Miss Thorold—up by the Stones—when she was frightened—and lost?"

"I remember," he said.

"I found her—for you," said the child. "God sent me and I went. I brought her back to Tetherstones—for you. I told her it was home because you were here—because I knew—somehow—that you wanted her. You do want her, don't you, Uncle Arthur?"

"It doesn't matter what I want," he said.

"It does matter," said Ruth very earnestly. "Because when people want each other and haven't got each other they are very unhappy—same as you, Uncle Arthur. And I don't think she'll ever find that big thing by the Stones unless you help her. You see—you see—" again the child's voice flagged, she seemed to seek for words—"You see, there is—someone else. And if—if anyone else helps her, p'raps they won't find the real thing at all, but something—something quite different. Don't you see, Uncle Arthur? Don't you understand? It's hidden, and you'll have to hunt and hunt before you find it. I shall know when you find it. But I shan't be able to tell you how pleased I am. I shall only—be able—to send you—my love."

The tired voice trailed off drowsily. Frances was anxiously watching the little white face on the pillow, but suddenly something drew her look upwards. She met the man's eyes across the bed, and was conscious of a sense of shock. They were grim with a desperate endurance that pierced her like a cry. Though they met her own, they were fixed and desolate. Scarcely even did they seem to see her.

Then again Ruth spoke with that soft thrill of gladness that made her think of the first faint call of a bird in the dawning.

"My mother is waiting for me," she said. "She is going to take me out to the stars. Do you mind if I go, dear Granny? I would like to go so much."

There was a brief pause. Then: "I don't mind, my darling," Mrs. Dermot answered very softly, and added as if to herself, "God knows best."

"I shall always be happy with my mother," said little Ruth. "And when you come, we shall all be happy together."

She sank into silence again, and for a space no one moved or spoke. Frances realized that Ruth's breathing was getting feebler, but there was no distress of any sort. Like the flame of a spent candle the little life was slowly flickering out.

She heard the soft stirring of the night-wind in the trees of the garden and the patter of falling rain-drops. And the great peace in which the world was wrapped came into the quiet room like a benediction, so that presently she was scarcely aware of any other presence there than that of the Angel upon the threshold.

It seemed to her a long while before Ruth spoke again, and then it was to utter her own name.

"Dear Miss Thorold, are you there?"

She rose up quickly. "Yes, darling, yes. What is it?"

The blue eyes with their mysterious fire gazed straight up to hers. "You'll find it up by the Stones," said the child, "where the giant hare-bells grow. That is the message, dear Miss Thorold. And when you find it, keep it—always—always—always!" Her breath caught suddenly, stopped, went on again with a gasp. "Because God sent it for you—and He wants you to have it. Do you understand? If you don't, it doesn't matter—so long as you keep on looking. You'll know it when you find it, because it's—it's the most precious thing in the world." She broke off, and for a few seconds it was as if she had forgotten to breathe, so still was she, so utterly without any suggestion of pain. Then, very faintly, her voice came again.

"I'm very tired. Is my dear Granny there?"

"I am here, darling," came the patient answer from the bedside.

"Will you kiss me good night?" said little Ruth. "I am going to sleep now."

On either side of the bed the man and the woman drew back, making way for the older woman. She bent and kissed the child, clasping her closely, murmuring fond words.

So for a time they remained. Then there came a soft, fluttering sigh, and afterwards a great silence. And Frances knew that the child was asleep.

CHAPTER VIII
THE MIRACLE

"You won't leave us?" said Maggie tremulously. "Please, you won't leave us?"

"If I can be of the slightest use here of course I will stay," Frances answered, "for a time at least. But I can't live on your kindness any longer. That is absolutely certain. I am beginning to make money by my sketches, and I must be allowed to pay my way."

"You will talk that over with Mother, won't you?" said Maggie. "I know she doesn't want you to go. None of us do." She smiled tearfully. "Somehow we feel as if all the luck of Tetherstones would go with you, and there's never very much of it at any time, as you may have noticed."

"I shouldn't say that," said Frances. "Fortune favours the brave, you know. You mustn't let yourself lose heart."

"I try not," said Maggie. "But it's very difficult sometimes. That night you went away to Fordestown was so terrible, and then—and then losing little Ruth! We thought there would have to be an inquest, but Dr. Square is so good, and he managed everything for us. Of course our darling was not like other children. We all knew that, and that we shouldn't have her always. But that doesn't make it any easier, does it?"

"My dear, don't cry!" said Frances gently. "I am sure there is a happy time in front of you. Just keep looking up! You will see very soon that the clouds are breaking."

"I wonder," whispered Maggie. "Well, I must go. There's heaps to be done. Poor Mother is so tired when Father is ill."

"Is he better this morning?" Frances asked.

"No, not much. He fainted three times during the night. Dolly of course is splendid. She and Mother and Arthur divide the nursing between them. At least, Arthur—or Oliver—is always within call in case of need. But the rest of us are not much good. So we just run round the farm," said Maggie, preparing to depart.

"Is he fretting for little Ruth?" asked Frances.

Maggie's eyes opened wide; she looked startled for a moment. Then: "Oh, no! I doubt if he even thinks about her," she said. "He never loved her as we did. He doesn't love anybody except Mother. That's what makes it so difficult."

"I wonder if I could help with him," said Frances.

"Oh, don't think of it!" said Maggie. "It wouldn't be fit for you."

But Frances did think of it notwithstanding. The serious illness of the old man, so quickly following the death of little Ruth, had stirred her deepest pity for them all, and she longed to be of any use. They had done so much for her in her hour of need, and it seemed to her a heaven-sent opportunity to make some return.

The work of the farm went on as usual now that little Ruth had been laid to rest. The general routine was unchanged. There was no sign of mourning. It was only in their hearts that the child's passing had left a blank. The girls whispered together of her and sometimes wept, but no special corner was empty because of her. Like a will-o'-the-wisp she had dwelt with them and now had flitted away. All had loved her, all had cared for her, all missed her. But now that she was gone not one of them, save perhaps the white-haired grandmother, could say that the removal of her daily presence had made any material difference. She had ever been a thing of the spirit, flower-like, contented, asking nothing of those around her, clinging closely only to one. And that one was the least likely of all to make any outcry. Patient and steadfast, she went her quiet way, and if she suffered, none knew it.

Frances had come to regard her with a deep reverence. She understood now something of the nature of the bond that existed between mother and son. They were cast in the same mould. They faced life with the same determined fortitude. But whereas the one had definitely passed the age of rebellion and unrest, the other was still in the prime of life,—a gladiator to whom defeat was cruelly hard to bear. He might come to it in time, that stillness of resignation, but not till the fires of life had died down in his veins and there was nought of paramount importance left to live for. Then she could imagine such a state of mind supervening, but her whole soul revolted at the thought. And there were times when she was fiercely glad that he had not been able to hide his suffering from her.

She saw but little of him during that time, but on the day of her talk with Maggie, she came upon him unexpectedly towards evening, leaning upon the garden-gate in the gloaming, his pipe in his mouth.

He straightened himself to let her pass, and, the last glow of the sunset being upon him, she saw again that sleepless look in his eyes that had before so moved her.

She paused with the half-formed intention of making some casual remark; but words that were wholly different from those she had intended to utter came to her lips instead.

"How tired you are!" she said.

She saw his mouth take the old cynical curve. "But still not down and out," he said.

She realized at once that the subject was unwelcome, but she did not turn from it. Some impulse moved her in the face of his distaste.

"I am wondering," she said, "if perhaps I could be of use—relieve you and your mother a little. I should be very proud if you would let me try."

He caught at the word as though it stung him. "Proud! Miss Thorold, your pride is easily satisfied!"

She faced him steadily. "Mr. Dermot, I mean what I say—always. I owe you a debt. I should like to repay it. But if you refuse to accept payment, I will at least not add to it any further. If you will not allow me to be of use to you, I shall leave to-morrow."

His attitude altered on the instant, so suddenly that she was disconcerted. He leaned towards her with an odd gesture of surrender. "It is not a question of my allowing or disallowing," he said. "You have me in the dust. Do whatever seems good to you—now and always. You come or go at Tetherstones exactly as you will."

His manner had a baffling quality, but she did not question the sincerity of his words; for she sensed a certain anxiety behind them that thrilled her strangely.

"In that case," she said, "will you let me stay—and help you?"

He did not answer immediately, and in the brief silence she realized that he was putting strong restraint upon himself. Then: "You will stay," he said, "if you will deign to do so. As to helping me—as to helping me—" he paused as if at a loss.

Something moved her to fill in the gap. "If you will trust me in the sick-room," she said, "I think I could be of use. May I not try?"

He drew a hard breath and turned half from her as though he would go away. Roger, standing by and eagerly watching his every movement, prepared to accompany him, and then, realizing his mistake, drooped his head dejectedly and resigned himself to further inactivity.

Arthur spoke with his face averted. "It is not a question of trust, Miss Thorold. It is you yourself that I have to consider. You don't quite know what you are asking, and it is difficult for me to tell you."

"You need not mind telling me," she said.

He made a gesture of impotence. "I've got to tell you. That's the hell of it. If you stay here, you've got to understand one thing. My father is suffering from heart-disease, and, as you know, the heart and brain are very closely connected. His brain is affected."

"I am not surprised at that," Frances said. "In fact, I had suspected it before."

He turned upon her with that goaded expression which but for its suffering, might have intimidated her.

"What made you do that? What has he said to you?"

"Oh, nothing very much," she answered gently. "I have thought him a little vague from time to time. I noticed that he never seemed to regard little Ruth as an actual belonging, for one thing."

"Go on!" he said grimly. "You have noticed more than that."

She faced him candidly. "'Yes, I have. I have noticed a great lack of sympathy between him and his family for which I could not imagine they were to blame."

"You never blamed me?" he said.

She hesitated. "I think I always knew that you were very heavily handicapped in some way," she said.

He nodded. "Yes, damnably. But I won't attempt to deceive you of all people, so far as I am concerned. I have a brutal temper, and I hate him! I hate him from the bottom of my soul—just as he hates me!"

"Oh, stop!" Frances said, shocked beyond words by the deadly emphasis with which he spoke.

He uttered a sound that was half-laugh and half-groan. "You've got to know it. Yes, he is my father, but I only endure him for my mother's sake. I have wished him dead for years. I wish it more than ever now."

"Oh, hush!" Frances said. "Please don't say it! Don't think it! You will be so sorry afterwards."

"Why should I be sorry?" he said sombrely. "Do you think I shall ever regret him? He who has all my life stood in the way of my gaining anything I hold worth having? It's too late now. My chances are gone. And I don't complain—even to you. As I say, his brain is affected. He suffers from delusions. I have got to bear with him to the end. So what is the good?"

She could not answer him. Only, after a few seconds, she said quietly, "I think I should be too sorry for him to—hate him."

"I wonder," said Arthur.

He stood for a few moments looking at her. Then, very abruptly: "Is that by any chance the reason why you don't hate me?" he said.

She met his look unflinching. "No," she said. "At least not entirely."

"There is another reason?" he questioned.

She bent her head.

"And I am not to know what it is?" His voice was low but it held urgency.

Her hand was on the catch of the gate, but still she met his look. "Mr. Dermot," she said, "there is a French saying that applies very closely to you and to me. Do you know what it is?"

" '*Tout comprendre est tout pardonner*,'" he said.

She opened the gate. "Even so," she said. "When that happens, you will know why I have not hated you."

She left him with the words, but not before the sudden fire of his look had reached her soul. As she went away down the garden-path, she knew that her limbs were trembling. But there was that in her heart which filled her with a burning exultation. The stones were turning to bread indeed.

CHAPTER IX
THE INVALID

"Don't take any notice of anything he says!" whispered Nurse Dolly. "Just sit beside him and keep him quiet! He's got some queer fancies, poor old man. Sure you won't mind them?"

"Of course not," Frances murmured back.

"That's right. And give him some bromide if he gets tiresome! Otherwise, that digitalis stuff. You understand, don't you?"

"Perfectly," said Frances.

"Then I'll go," said Dolly. "Be sure to call if you want anyone! I shall only be in the next room. I expect he'll be quite good. He likes you. But don't stand any nonsense from him! Because if once he gets the upper hand, he's difficult."

"I am sure he will be good," Frances whispered, with a pitying glance towards the pallid face on the pillow.

"I daresay he will," said Dolly. "He's tired now. He may get a little sleep. It's very good of you, Miss Thorold. He won't stand anyone else near him, you know, except Mother. And it's killing work for her."

"If you only knew how glad I am to be of some use to you at last!" Frances said.

Dolly smiled. "You've made all the difference to this establishment already. There, I'll go. Sure you've got everything you want?"

"Everything," said Frances.

"Then good-bye! I'll be back in two hours unless you call me sooner."

She nodded a cheery farewell and departed, softly closing the door behind her, leaving Frances to wonder at her endurance. For it did not take more than the most casual glance to tell her that the girl's eyes were drooping with weariness.

"They are all amazing," she said to herself, as she sat down in a low chair within sight of the bed. "They never give in."

It was the afternoon of the following day and she had gained her end after a very brief talk with Mrs. Dermot who, somewhat to her surprise, had put but slight obstacle in her way. The fact that she herself was nearly dropping with fatigue possibly had some influence with her, but Frances was inclined to think that Arthur had already given his vote in her favour. For she had shown no surprise, only a wan gratitude that went to her heart.

So for that afternoon the invalid was in her charge, and Frances was strangely elated by the trust reposed in her. The grimness of Tetherstones seemed to be mellowing day by day into a homely warmth that was infinitely precious to her.

She had another reason also for elation on that golden afternoon of late summer, though with regard to this her feelings were decidedly mixed. A letter had been forwarded to her from Fordestown bearing a London postmark, containing a further cheque for ten pounds from Montague Rotherby, and a few words scrawled within telling her that her sketches were sold and that the purchaser desired to see her in town with a view to commissioning more. The message was of the briefest, wholly business-like in tone. He wrote from a club, but he gave her an address in Mayfair at which his friend—a Mr. Hermon—was to be found, and offered to meet her himself and conduct her thither if she would fix a date convenient to her.

It was an offer which she well knew she could not afford to refuse, though she would have given much to have received it from any other quarter. But since the means could not be of her choosing, since, moreover, it was inevitable that she should meet and finally convince Montague Rotherby that the concession he had so hardly won from her must be relinquished, she braced herself to face the situation with a stout heart.

"They are all so brave here," she said to herself. "I mustn't be the one to shirk."

And then rather wistfully she smiled at the thought of classing herself as one of the inmates of Tetherstones—she who had fled in terror not so very long before. She wondered how it was that they had all with one consent refrained from any species of questioning upon that night's doings. Arthur again, no doubt! But Arthur himself—how had he come to change his mind concerning her? Arthur who in his fury had so nearly taken another man's life!

She lacked the key to the puzzle and it was futile to turn it over and over. The fact remained that in some fashion she had been vindicated, and Arthur's remorse was a thing upon which she could not bear to dwell. She wondered if she would ever understand all, but she knew that already she had pardoned.

The afternoon sunlight slanted in at the open window. From where she sat she could see the steep rise of the moor that led up to the Stones. She pictured them in their stark grandeur—those mystic signs of a bygone age—the tetherstones of the prisoners and the terrible Rocking Stone that none might move out of its place, but that even a child might sway. How many of those striving ones had been ground to death in their desperation, she wondered? And now the sun shone upon that fatal place of sacrifice, and the giant harebells bloomed where the child who had never known darkness had wandered and lain down to sleep. Her thoughts dwelt tenderly upon little Ruth and her harebells—the flowers she had never seen yet knew and loved so dearly—the flowers to which she had likened her mother's eyes!

A feeble voice spoke in the stillness and her mind flashed back to her surroundings.

"Nan, my dear, is that you?" it said.

She heard the words and sat motionless, uncertain as to whether they were intended for her or not. Then she saw that the tired old eyes were looking straight at her, and she softly rose and went to the bed.

"Is there anything I can do for you?" she asked.

He looked up at her, frowning a little, as if there were something about her that he could not wholly understand. "Yes, dear, yes," he said finally. "Bring your little sketching-block and sit down beside me! I should like to lie and watch you."

"I haven't been doing any to-day," she said. "But I have a book here. Would you like me to read to you?"

He shook his head restlessly. "No, no, no! I am too tired for books. Bring your sketching! I should like that better than anything. The light is good enough, isn't it?"

"Oh, quite," she said, "if you really wish it. But—" She stood hesitating, uncertain whether to comply with his request; for the sketch upon which she was just then engaged was one of little Ruth in the corn-field. She was making it while the memory was still fresh within her, and she planned to give it to Mrs. Dermot.

The old man broke in upon her irresolution. "Go and fetch it! Go and fetch it! You know how I love to see you at work. They have kept you away from me for a very long time, my darling. Run and fetch it and come straight back!"

His manner was urgent though he smiled upon her with the words. She decided swiftly that, whatever his delusion, it was better to humour him. She went quickly from the room, and ran down the passage to her own. Here she hastily collected her sketching materials, and was back again within two minutes of her departure.

She found him anxiously watching the door, and she saw his eyes kindle afresh at the sight of her. "How like you, my dear!" he said. "There is no one else in the family who would have left me alone for a single second. They are always watching me, always watching me. I don't know why."

He spoke querulously.

She returned to her seat by his side.

"I expect they think you might want something and there would be no one to give it to you," she said. "Do you really want to see my latest sketch? You are sure it interests you?"

"Yes—yes." A touch of impatience sounded in the answer, but the next moment a thin old hand came out and patted hers. "My little daughter!" he said very fondly. "I can't spare you to that brother of mine again. He keeps you too long—too long."

"I am very glad to be back," said Frances gently.

She looked down at the ivory-coloured hand with its nervous, clutching fingers, and was irresistibly reminded of the talons of a bird. When it closed upon her own, she was conscious of a sense of chill that almost amounted to shrinking. But still pity was uppermost in her mind, pity for this frail old man whose hold on life was so weak and yet who seemed to cling to it with such persistence.

His clasp relaxed after a moment. "Well, dear, let me see what you have been doing!" he said wearily. "I must not talk very much to-day. My heart is very tired. Have you more than one to show me?"

"No, only one," she said. "There hasn't been a great deal of time just lately."

"Ah!" He smiled. "The pomps and vanities! Is that it? You have been very gay, I hear? And that handsome youngster—your cousin—what has he to say for himself? You will never contenance any serious attention from him, my darling, promise me! He is in love with you, of course. They all are. You are so lovely—so lovely. But cousins, you know, cousins are only brothers and sisters once removed. Uncle Theodore would never permit it for a moment. Neither would I, dear. You know that. You are so beautiful. You will look higher than a near relation with a wild record like his. Pshaw! I am talking nonsense. You would never dream of marrying him."

"Never!" said Frances very decidedly, as he paused for her assurance.

"Thank you, dear, thank you," he said. "Now let me see your sketch!"

She held it up in front of him, propped as he was upon the pillows, and there fell a long silence while he scrutinized it. The picture was of Ruth standing among the sheaves in the sunlight, with her flower-like face upraised, and in her little hands a trailing bunch of the golden corn.

The old man looked at it intently with drawn brows. Finally, with a deliberation that was almost painful, he looked at her.

"Who is that child?" he said.

She hesitated for a second; then: "Don't you remember little—Ruth?" she said gently.

His frown deepened. "Little Ruth! You mean the blind child, I think—the little girl who lives with us?"

"Yes," said Frances.

"And this is that child?" He turned again to the sketch, gazing at it fixedly. "But why have you made her like Nan?" he said, in a troubled voice. "Nan wasn't blind. She had eyes like bluebells." His look came back to her. "Thank you, Miss Thorold," he said courteously. "You have a very charming talent. Some day I hope you will allow me to conduct you to the Stones. I should much like to see a sketch of them from your brush, most especially of the Rocking Stone, regarding which there are some very interesting traditions. You have heard of some of them perhaps?"

"I have indeed," said Frances, laying her sketch out of sight with a feeling of relief. "I think it is rather a gruesome spot myself."

"It is—it is," agreed Mr. Dermot. "The Rocking Stone has even been called the Slaughter Stone before now. If you ever visit it at sunset you will see a curious phenomenon. It is streaked here and there with crimson strata, to which the sunset light gives the appearance of freshly shed blood."

"Shall we talk of something else?" said Frances quietly.

He lifted his brows. "Certainly," he said, with a touch of hauteur. "I have no desire to discuss anything distasteful to you. In fact, our worthy doctor has warned me that conversation of any description should not be indulged in too freely. So pray take up your sketch and work, and I will lie and watch you."

There was a certain imperiousness in his tone which reminded her of Arthur. She would gladly have left her sketch untouched, but she realized that to do so would not make for peace. She took it up again therefore without further words, and opening her box prepared to put in some minute touches.

The consciousness of the old man closely watching her did not tend to help her, but after a few minutes the fascination of her art asserted itself, and she began to forget him. She worked for some time without looking up, and the little blue-clad figure in the corn-field began to stand out in delicate outline. She knew, as her brush moved dexterously fashioning the image of her brain, that this was the best work she had ever done, and the delight of it quickened her blood. The thought of Rotherby's letter came to her, and she made a mental note that she would answer it that very day and accept the suggestion he had made. Now that her chance had come to her, she could not afford to let it slip. She must seize and hold it with both hands.

Her thoughts wandered back over the random words that old Mr. Dermot had just uttered. The name of Theodore had stirred her memory. It was the name of the Bishop of Burminster. She remembered how once in conversation with Arthur she had spoken of him and discovered that he knew him. Was it possible that they were related?

Another memory suddenly flashed across her—a vivid and strangely compelling memory. The eyes of the blind child with their deep blue fire of the spirit—the eyes of a visionary which had so pierced her that she had almost turned away! She felt as if a scroll, hitherto sealed, were being unrolled before her eyes; and so strong was the impression that her fingers ceased from their task and she looked up.

In a moment she was aware of a startling change in the old man in her charge. He had sunk down on the pillows, and his face was ghastly.

She got up quickly, seizing a bottle of restorative as she did so. Then she saw that his lips were moving and was partially reassured.

As she poured a dose into the medicine-glass, he spoke aloud. "You need not be alarmed. My heart is a little tired—a little tired. But it will not stop yet."

She bent over him, holding the glass to his pallid lips.

He drank and paused. "I shall soon be better," he said, and gasped for breath. A faint colour began to show once more in his face. He smiled at her and drank again.

"I am so sorry," she said, with deep self-reproach. "I ought to have seen."

"No—no," he said, in his kindly, courteous fashion. "You must not blame yourself for that. I think I will have a little sleep. I shall not last much longer, but I shall live to see the Stones again—just once again—my Stones—the place of sacrifice—where my three-fold vow has been accomplished." His voice began to trail off indistinctly. He closed his eyes. "The place of sacrifice—" he murmured again, and then followed an odd jumble of words in which "mother, father, and child" came with unintelligible frequency until his utterance ceased altogether.

Frances stood by his side, listening to his uncertain breathing while other words sprang up all-unbidden in her mind, almost finding their way to her lips.

"From all evil and mischief, from sin, from the crafts and assaults of the devil,—Good Lord deliver us!"

CHAPTER X
THE WOMAN'S RIGHT

"He is still sleeping very peacefully," said Mrs. Dermot, with a grateful look at Frances. "You had a very composing effect upon him this afternoon. I hope it did not tire you very badly."

It was supper-time, and they had met at the table in the old farm-kitchen, which Lucy and Nell had been spreading with the home produce. It was the one meal of the day at which the whole family as a rule assembled, but Dolly and Milly were absent on this occasion in the sick-room, and Arthur and Maggie had not entered.

"It did not tire me at all," Frances answered. "I was very, very glad to be of any use. I hope you will let me do it again."

"You are very good," said Mrs. Dermot. "He will be better after this for a time. A long, unbroken sleep always brings him back. Won't you sit down?"

"Did you sleep?" Frances asked.

"Oh, yes, Mother slept," said Lucy. "I took in her tea, and she never even knew."

"She needed it badly enough," put in Elsie. "She's been up three nights running."

"Ah, well, I expect I shall rest to-night," said Mrs. Dermot, with her tired smile. "Oh, there you are, Arthur! I was just wondering. And Maggie,—where is she?"

He had entered from the scullery. He stopped beside her chair. "Maggie? I don't know where Maggie is. Somewhere about, no doubt. How are you, Mother? Better?"

She looked up into his face, and Frances saw the flash of sympathy between them, realized for an instant the closeness of the bond at which till then she had only guessed, and felt as if she had looked upon something sacred.

"I am all right, dear," said Mrs. Dermot. "I have had a most refreshing sleep, thanks to Miss Thorold's kindness. Your father will be much better when he wakes."

"Sit down, Arthur!" said Nell. "We want to begin."

He glanced round with a quick frown. "Where is everybody? Maggie—Oliver! Why don't they come in? Go and call them, Elsie!"

"I don't know where they are," said Elsie. "I've milked the cows and fed the horses and locked up. They went to market this morning, and I haven't seen them since."

"Oh, rot!" he said. "They must have come back long ago. They are probably dawdling round somewhere. Has no one seen them? Nell, haven't you?"

Nell shook her head. "We've been busy in the dairy, Lucy and I. Only came in in time to get the supper. What's it matter? They'll turn up."

He turned again to Elsie. "You say you locked up. Was the brown cob back?"

"I didn't go that way," she said, with a touch of defiance. "It was only the cart-horses I saw to. Joe was there too. Oliver always does the cob."

"What does it matter?" Nell said again. "Maggie can have her supper when she comes in. There's no reason to wait for her."

"It does matter," he returned sternly. "I won't have any of you out on the moors after dark, and you know it."

"My good man!" said Nell. "What do you think we're made of?"

He whirled upon her in a sudden tempest of wrath. "Don't you dare to gainsay me! I mean it. I—will—not—have—you—out—after—dark. Is that plain enough? Damn it! Do you think I'll be defied to my face?"

"My dear!" said Mrs. Dermot very gently.

He looked down at her and curbed himself. "I'm sorry, Mother. But a chit like that—not eighteen!"

"I am eighteen," asserted Nell, crimson-cheeked. "And I won't be kept in order by you. So there!"

He turned his eyes upon her, and she shrank in spite of herself. "You will be kept in order by me," he said. "You will go up to your room now—do you hear?—and stay there for the rest of the night."

"I!" said Nell. "What—now?" She stood gripping the back of the chair in which she had been about to seat herself. Her face had gone from red to white. Her eyes stared straight across the table at her brother.

He answered her without moving, but his single word fell like a blow. "Now!"

There followed a terrific silence, during which it seemed to Frances that the wills of the man and the girl were in visible conflict though neither stirred or spoke. In the end there came a faint gasp from Nell, and she turned to obey.

Lucy started up with hysterical crying. "I'm going too, then—I'm going too!"

"You will stay where you are," Arthur said, without turning his gaze from the younger sister.

She dropped back sobbing in the chair, and Nell went wordlessly to the door. Slowly she opened it, slowly passed out and closed it again.

Mrs. Dermot looked up at her son. "Elsie may take up her supper," she said.

He shrugged his shoulders. "She can do as she likes." He moved to his own place and sat down. His look came to Frances. "Sorry to treat you to this exhibition," he said. "But discipline must be maintained."

She met his look with the utmost directness. "Did you say discipline or tyranny?" she said.

She expected anger, was prepared for it, even desired it. But he only smiled.

"Yes, you may call it that," he said. "But it's in a good cause. Nell is getting above herself. She has got to learn. Lucy, sit up and behave yourself! You've nothing whatever to cry about. Good heavens, child! Why all this fuss?"

Lucy sobbed some inarticulate words into her handkerchief, and abruptly Frances leaned forward. She spoke in a low tone, very urgently, to Arthur.

"Let her run after Nell and fetch her back!" she said.

She could not have said exactly what prompted the request. It was not primarily pity for either of the two girls. It was the man himself who held her attention at that moment, and an overwhelming desire to move that iron will out of its undeviating course.

But his reception of her interference was disconcerting. Instead of displaying the opposition she had anticipated, he spoke again to the still sobbing girl.

"Dry your eyes, you silly girl, and go tell Nell to come back!"

Lucy looked up with a gasp of sheer amazement, and Frances found herself gasping too at the utter unexpectedness of his action. Arthur's face wore a cynical expression, but he showed no sign of impatience. "Go on!" he said. "Go and fetch her back and be quick about it!"

Lucy got up and slipped from the room.

"Miss Thorold, may I give you some ham?" said Arthur.

Their eyes met, and she caught a quizzical gleam in his that sent an odd feeling as of tension relaxed through her.

"Thank you," she said.

He proceeded to carve the ham in silence, and as he did so there came the sound of wheels and a horse's feet outside.

"Here they are!" said Mrs. Dermot in a tone of relief.

"I knew they wouldn't be long," said Elsie.

Arthur's face took an inscrutable look. He said nothing whatever.

Elsie carried round the plates and they began the meal. After a brief pause Nell and Lucy came back into the room and silently resumed their places; but a considerable interval elapsed before the opening of the outer door into the scullery told of the entrance of the latest comers.

Maggie came in looking flushed and nervous. Oliver entered behind her, swaggering a little, his bold eyes somewhat fierce.

"Hullo!" he said. "That's right. I said you'd begin. We'd better sit down as we are."

Maggie's place was next to her mother. He pulled out the chair for her, and she dropped into it speechlessly.

"What have you been doing?" said Arthur.

He spoke quietly, but his tone was ominous. Maggie threw him one swift glance and then lowered her eyes.

"Everything's all right," said Oliver, with a touch of aggressiveness. "We thought we'd make a day of it. I'll tell you all about it presently."

"You'll tell me now," Arthur said.

"Oh, all right." Oliver stood with his hand upon the back of Maggie's chair. He bent suddenly over her. "Sure you want me to tell, Maggie?" he said.

She put up a trembling hand in answer. Abruptly he stooped lower and kissed her before them all.

The violent overturning of Arthur's chair as he sprang to his feet brought him upright again with a jerk. He broke in upon the other's furious oath with quick speech that yet was not wholly uncontrolled.

"Yes, you can damn as much as you please," he said. "It won't make a ha'porth of difference now. She is mine—for better for worse—and you can't undo it. We were married to-day at Fordestown—after we'd sold the pigs."

"Married!" The single word fell with frightful force from Arthur's lips. He put his hand suddenly to his head.

Maggie crouched against her mother, and Mrs. Dermot, pale as death, put her arm about her without a word.

Then across the silence, shrill as the piping of a bird, came Nell's voice. "Well played, Oliver! I wish you luck!"

He turned to her with his winning boyish smile and gripped her outstretched hand across the table.

"Thanks, little 'un! You're a brick, and I'll always remember it."

Elsie left her end of the table and came round to Maggie. Lucy cowered in her chair and hid her face.

Arthur's hand fell and clenched at his side. He spoke—not to Oliver, but to Maggie.

"Is this true?"

She looked up at him with an effort. Through quivering lips she answered him. "Yes."

"You are—actually married—to this—damned—clod?"

Oliver straightened himself sharply. "I'll answer that question," he said. "Come outside and I'll show you the exact stuff he's made of!"

But at that Maggie left her mother's sheltering arm and got up. She stood between the two men, breathing very fast.

"You shan't fight about me," she said. "You've nothing to fight about, for I belong to Oliver and always shall, from now on. I've the right—as every woman has—to choose my own mate, and I've chosen. That's all there is to it."

There was a simple dignity about her as she uttered the words that carried an irresistible appeal to Frances. Shaking as she was with agitation, the girl asserted her right of womanhood with a decision that none might question.

Arthur did not attempt to question it. He merely lifted a hand and pointed to the door.

"All right," he said. "You can go—you and your mate. And you will never enter Tetherstones again."

He did not look at Oliver. He had scarcely looked at him from the outset. But at that the young man's wrath boiled over, and he compelled attention.

"You think that you and your blasted Tetherstones count a couple of damns with either of us, do you?" he said. "You think that because poor Nan broke her heart here, we'd be pining to do the same! You're a damn' fool, Arthur, that's what you are. And now I've got what I want, I take pleasure in telling you so. You're too grand a swell to fight the likes of me. You don't fight your own labourers! No, I thought not. But you can't prevent 'em telling you the truth or taking a woman out of your family and giving her happiness—common or garden happiness—in place of this infernal mass of corruption you're pleased to call your family honour. I've got my honour too, but it's not your sort, thank God. I'm just a plain man, and I've no frills of any kind. But I've got the right to marry the girl who loves me, and there's no one on this earth can come between us now. If they think they can, well, let 'em try, that's all. Just let 'em try!"

He moved with the words, and pulled Maggie to him, pressing her close to his side. But his eyes remained upon Arthur, hot with anger and superbly contemptuous of the other man's superior strength.

Arthur stood motionless. His look was turned upon Oliver, but he made no attempt whatever to check the fierce torrent of words so forcibly poured out. To Frances he had the look of the gladiator sorely wounded yet holding his ground for the sake of that honour which Oliver so bitterly denounced. And her heart went out to the man in sudden wild rush of sympathy that seemed to sweep away all rational thought. She found herself on her feet and quivering with a burning desire to help him in some way, though how she knew not. The deadly pallor of his face, the awful fixity of his eyes, were more than she could bear.

He spoke—this time to Oliver but he did not deign to waste a single word in answer to the furious challenge hurled at him.

"Let me see your marriage certificate!" he said.

His words fell with the utmost calm and Frances wondered if she were the only one in the room who knew how cruelly deep was his wound.

Oliver drew a hard angry breath, as though he found himself unexpectedly held in check by some force unknown. He stared for a moment, then with a sullen air thrust a hand inside his coat. He brought out a paper which he flung down in front of Arthur.

"There you are. You'll find it all in order," he said. "You won't undo that knot in a hurry."

Arthur picked up the document, opened and scanned it, then held it in silence before his mother. She laid an imploring hand upon his.

"Arthur—Arthur!" she said, an anguished break in her voice. "Don't do anything in a hurry! I can't lose another of my girls like my darling Nan."

"I'm afraid you have lost her, Mother," he replied, with a species of grim gentleness, "since she has chosen to go."

"I haven't chosen to go!" burst from Maggie. She turned and flung her arms closely about her mother. "If I have to go, it'll be your doing, not mine and not Oliver's. He's willing to stay. He's told me so. In fact, he was willing to go on here in the same old way, and not to tell, only I felt I couldn't bear it. He's thought of me and my happiness all through—all through. And we've loved each other for years. You don't know what love is. You can never possibly understand. But Mother knows—Mother knows."

"Yes, I know," said Mrs. Dermot, and the tragedy of the quiet utterance was as though she stood beside one dead.

There was a brief pause as of involuntary reverence, then Oliver spoke, his voice steady and deferential. "It was only for the mother's sake we came back," he said. "I'd sooner have gone to the other end of the world myself. But—well, Maggie's happiness was at stake, so I couldn't."

"Maggie's happiness!" An exceedingly bitter note sounded in Arthur's voice. "Was it for Maggie's happiness, may I ask, that you persuaded her to do this thing?"

Oliver's look flashed back to him. He stiffened himself afresh for battle. Couldn't he see, Frances asked herself desperately? Were they all blind to the agony of this man's soul?

"Yes, it was," he flung back hotly. "It was for her happiness. Don't you dare to question that, Arthur Dermot! You're not in a position to question it. There's not a woman on this earth who would trust her happiness to you. And you know it."

The blow went home. Frances felt as if it had been directed against herself. She did not need to see the stricken look in Arthur's eyes. She knew without seeing, and on the instant she acted, for further inaction was unedurable.

Before he could make any reply to the thrust, she was in the lists beside him.

"You are wrong!" she said, and her voice rang clear and triumphant before them all. "You are utterly wrong! I would!"

She turned to him quivering with the greatness of the moment to find his eyes upon her with that in them which thrilled her to the soul.

She stretched forth a trembling hand. "I would!" she repeated, and this time she spoke to him alone. "You know I would!"

He caught her hand and closely held it. "Yes, I know—I know!" he said. Then curtly to Oliver, "That's enough for the present. Sit down and have some supper, you and Maggie too! We'll discuss this thing in the morning. Frances, sit here!"

He pulled forward a chair and she sat beside him at the head of the table. But save for that one brief command he did not speak to her or look in her direction again.

No one else ventured to address a word to her. Only Mrs. Dermot leaned forward and gently pressed her hand.

CHAPTER XI
THE PERFECT GIFT

The thing was done. Frances stood alone in the old ivy-covered porch looking out into the faint starlight and asked herself how she had come to do it. It had been the impulse of the moment, and she well knew that if she had taken time to consider she would never have acted upon it. But a power that was infinitely greater than herself had urged her, and she had had no choice.

Now it was over. The inspiration had departed, and she waited with a certain chill apprehension for the coming of the man she loved. He had gone up to the sick-room with his mother, and she had slipped away from the rest, for she wanted to be alone when he came. He generally smoked his pipe upon the porch when the day's work was done, and evidently Roger expected him to-night; for he shared her vigil, alert and friendly, his head within reach of her hand.

It was a very peaceful evening, full of that wonderful moorland fragrance so dear to her heart, so quiet that she could hear the cart-horses munching the hay in their mangers in the stable across the yard. From the kitchen quarters in the house behind her came the homely clatter of dishes being washed up, accompanied by the chattering of girlish voices. Elsie, Lucy and Nell were evidently discussing the dramatic events of the evening. She wondered what they all thought of her, if Maggie and Oliver imagined that she had made that amazing declaration for their sakes. She wondered what Arthur thought. . . . A curious feeling of depression came upon her. She felt as if she were faced by an immensity too great to gauge. What had she done? What had she done? Ah! His step at last! She turned with a hard-beating heart and met him face to face.

She could not read his expression in the dimness, but she realized in an instant that there was none of the lover's ardour in his coming. And the soul within her shrank like a frightened child. She stood before him trembling.

He came to her and paused. "Shall we go into the garden?" he said. His voice was low, constrained. She turned mutely, and they passed down the winding path between the hollyhocks and sunflowers side by side.

On they went and on in utter silence till they came to the door in the wall that led to the lawn and the cedar-tree. He opened it and she passed through. The door closed with a thud and he walked beside her again.

The silence widened and became a gulf between them. The dew lay like a silver veil upon the lawn. She turned aside to the path leading to the nut-trees. And here at last in deepest shadow he spoke.

"Frances!"

She paced on, as though some remorseless Fate compelled. She knew then—it seemed to her that she had known all along—that the gulf was such as could not be bridged.

She answered him with absolute steadiness. "You needn't say any more. Let us go back!"

He made a gesture with one hand that was almost violent. "It isn't always possible—to go back," he said.

"It is quite possible in this case," she said quietly. "Perhaps it will make matters easier if I tell you that I found out by accident some time ago that Maggie and Oliver were contemplating this step, and my sympathies have been entirely with them all through."

He gave a sharp start. "Maggie! Oliver! But why tell me this?"

"Doesn't it make it easier for you?" she said.

"Why should it?" he demanded. And then abruptly, realizing the loophole she had made for him, "Oh, damn it, Frances! Are you trying to throw dust in my eyes—at this stage?"

"Not in the least," she returned, and now her pride came back to her and she lifted it grandly like a banner. "I am telling you the truth. My sympathies are, and always have been, entirely with Maggie and Oliver. I may be very presumptuous, but I can't stand by and see a great wrong done without making a very great effort to avert it. I have made my effort, and whether successful or not I have at least managed to prevent your acting in this matter without consideration. That is all I have to say."

She was holding her banner bravely now, masking her own humiliation and his anguish of spirit also. For herein, it seemed to her, lay salvation for them both. If she could check the flood-tide of passion which she sensed in his restraint, if she could hold back the wild words that were fighting for utterance, she would be doing him service. And in serving him, she served herself. For thus has Love the Omnipotent ordained, that in the service of another we should find our own deliverance.

Again the silence fell between them. They were walking more slowly now in the gloom of the nut-trees. She realized that the tension was partially relaxed, but she did not dare to lower her flag.

He spoke at last, his voice very quiet and sombre, with something of the old iron ring. "What do you want me to do?"

They reached the end of the nut-walk and she turned. Her agitation was wholly past, but her heart felt deadly cold within her.

"I want you," she said, "to try to understand that Maggie and Oliver have done no wrong, and to treat them with kindness."

"Is that all?" he said.

She did not understand his tone. "Is it too much to ask?" she said.

"No, it is very little—less than nothing. Do you think I care a damn what happens to either of them now?" His voice shook a little.

She turned her face towards him as she walked. "Yes, you do care," she said. "And that's why it isn't easy. But, Arthur, listen! There is no one on this earth who has the shadow of a right to interfere between a man and woman who love each other. When I say love, I don't mean the mere physical attraction which so many mistake for love. I mean that holy thing, the love of the spirit, which nothing can ever change or take away. That is too sacred to be tampered with, and no third person should ever presume to touch it. It comes from God, and it should command our utmost reverence,—even our homage."

She spoke very earnestly, for somehow—in spite of that terrible coldness at her heart—it seemed essential that he should see this thing with her eyes. It lay with her—she knew it lay with her—to save him from committing a great wrong, and to avert another sorrow from Tetherstones.

But as they paced on towards the open starlight in front of them, his silence seemed to hold but little hope. And the coldness grew and spread within her, paralysing her. She knew if this effort failed, she could not make another.

Arthur spoke at last. "Are you suggesting that they should go on exactly as if this had not happened? If my father came to know of it,—it would drive him crazy."

"Your father need not know," she said. "He is an old man. It rests with you, not with him."

"Ah!" He stood still suddenly. "That's true. He can't live for ever. How many years have I told myself that, and yet I always forget it. Frances!" His voice thrilled suddenly, and then as suddenly he stopped himself. "No! I won't say that to you. I'll say just this. I see your point, and—I'll act on it if I find I can. Does that satisfy you?"

"Thank you," she said.

"Don't!" he said sharply, and swung round to go on. "Don't ever thank me! Just—believe in me—if you can!"

"I can," she said. "And I do."

They came out upon the path that wound about the dewy lawn, and walked back along it in silence.

To Frances it was as if there were nothing more to be said, and yet it was in the words that had been left unspoken that the true meaning of the interview lay. In some fashion she felt that a chapter in her life had been closed. She knew what lay before her. Her only course was to go, and she would not flinch from taking it. She would meet unswervingly the difficulties and trials of the way. She would keep her banner flying. For in that one word, her own name spoken as he had spoken it, the coldness had melted from about her heart, and whatever came to her now, she knew that, though inexplicably bound hand and foot like the prisoners of the tetherstones, he had poured out to her that which is greater than all things—the love of his whole soul—the perfect gift.

CHAPTER XII
THE PARTING

"I'll never forget what you've done for us," said Maggie. "And I'm very sorry you're going." She spoke with great earnestness but the lilt had come back to her voice and the light to her eyes. She held Frances' hand very tightly between her own. "You'll come back some day?" she said.

"I shall certainly come back to the moors," Frances said, "to make my sketches."

"Oh, that's all right," said Maggie. "Then you'll let us know where you are. I couldn't bear not to. You're going up to London now?"

"Only for a day or two—to see a friend who has found a purchaser for my work. I shan't stay," said Frances.

"A friend?" Maggie gave her a curious look. "Is it—it isn't—the friend you went away to see at Fordestown?"

"Why shouldn't it be?" said Frances.

"Oh, I don't know." Maggie coloured suddenly and vividly. "I just wondered, that's all. And then you're coming back? You will come back, won't you?"

"I shouldn't wonder if I came back to Mrs. Hearn," said Frances. "But, Maggie, tell me what makes you ask about Mr. Rotherby! What do you know about him?"

"Oh, I can't tell you that," said Maggie quickly. "I shouldn't have asked. But Arthur knows him—and hates him. Please don't let's talk about him—and I wouldn't go to see him if I were you. He's a bad man. Ah, here comes Oliver to fetch you! Good-bye, dear Frances, and just a hundred thousand thanks for everything."

She responded warmly to Frances' embrace, and returned to her butter-making with a song on her lips and gladness in her eyes.

"Yes, I should just think we are grateful," said Oliver, as he followed Frances out. "Arthur has been as decent as he knows how, and it's all thanks to you. Hope you'll make a match of it before long, Miss Thorold, when better times come. You won't want to wait as long as we did."

They all treated her thus, as if her marriage to Arthur were a foregone conclusion, cheerily disregarding the fact that neither she nor Arthur had given them any justification for so doing. They had in fact barely seen one another since that night in the garden, now two days past; and she had even begun to wonder if he would let her go without a word of farewell. Old Mr. Dermot was better, would soon be downstairs again, they said, and his son had returned to his work on the farm, appearing only at meals and then for very brief intervals.

She had taken leave of everyone else, save Oliver who was to drive her to the station, and time was too short for lingering. She gave up hope at last, as she climbed into the cart. Roger was nowhere to be seen, so evidently his master was not in the vicinity. Perhaps he had not grasped the fact that she was going! Perhaps he had forgotten the hour! Perhaps—and somehow this was a supposition to which she clung instinctively for comfort—perhaps he had decided that he could not face the parting. In any case, he was not there, and her heart was heavy as they trotted out on to the moorland road. She felt she could have endured anything more easily than to be suffered to go without a sign.

The sky was dark with clouds that drove rapidly but unendingly before a west wind. The chill of coming rain was in the air, and the great heads of the tors were wrapped in drifting mist-wreaths. The scent of the bogs came to Frances with a poignant sense of regret.

"I shall be home-sick for this when I get away," she said.

"It does take hold of you, doesn't it?" said Oliver.

Homely words that almost brought the tears to her eyes! Yes, it did take hold of her. She was bound with a chain that she could never break. She could not speak in answer. Her heart was too full.

She had said to Maggie that she expected to be in town for but a few days, but a strong conviction was upon her that her absence would be much longer than this. She even wondered if she would ever return. The future was as a blank wall before her which she was utterly powerless to penetrate. But she had regained her health, and she knew that courage would return as soon as the last of her farewells was spoken.

So they trotted on over the moor with the clouds gathering thickly on every side.

Rounding the curve of a hill, they came at length within sight of the spot where she and Roger had sat together on that summer morning that seemed so long ago, and she had first seen Roger's master. Vivid as a picture actually before her eyes, came the memory of that day, of the solitary horseman riding in the blinding sunlight, of the brief incident that had been their first introduction. She remembered her indignation—her sweeping condemnation of the man. But he had done worse things since, infinitely worse. Did she condemn him now? As if in answer, another memory smote her—the memory of this man bowed to the earth by a burden too great to be borne—the dumb agony of which she had been a witness—and his tears—his tears!

Her own eyes suddenly swam in them. She turned her face away. She must not break down now. She must not.

Some seconds passed before she could command herself to look again. They were nearing the bend in the road by which she and Roger had sat.

"Hullo!" said Oliver suddenly.

She started. "What is it? Ah!"

A great wave of feeling, tumultuous, overwhelming, surged through her and she could say no more. Arthur was waiting on his horse, motionless as a statue, at the very spot that meant so much to her. Roger was with him with pricked, expectant ears.

Oliver gave a chuckle and checked the cob. "Somehow I thought—" he said. "Have I got to pull up?"

She did not answer him, for Arthur with an imperious wave of the hand did that for her. He walked his horse forward as Oliver reined into a standstill.

"You can ride my animal back," he said. "I will take Miss Thorold to the station."

"You haven't too much time," said Oliver.

"Then get down and be quick about it!" said Arthur briefly.

To Frances he said nothing, and she attempted no word of greeting, even when he mounted to the seat beside her.

A hasty farewell to Oliver, the starting forward of the cob, a cheery bark from Roger scudding in front, and they were rounding the bend of the road and alone. Before them, the drifting clouds parted suddenly like a rent curtain, and a great shaft of light descended. They drove straight into the brightness; but as they reached it the clouds drew together again, and they were once more in gloom. The moor stretched all about them like a wilderness.

Arthur spoke at last. "Why are you going?"

His voice was quiet; it held no special thrill of interest. She even wondered as she made reply if he were greatly interested.

"It is better for me to go," she said. "I am going to take up work in earnest. I have had some encouragement. Several of my sketches have been bought."

"I have seen the one you gave to my mother," he said. "It was good of you to part with it."

"I did it for her," said Frances simply.

He nodded. "Nothing could have pleased her more. You say you have found a purchaser for the others. You are hoping to get commissioned work?"

"I am hoping," said Frances.

"And if you succeed, that will bring you back?" he said.

She hesitated. His tone told her so little.

"It might," she said at length.

He drove on for some distance in silence. Then, with a restraint so evident that she could not fail to realize that he was putting strong force upon himself, he said, "I hope you will succeed. I hope you will make your fortune. It's a difficult world, but there are always some lucky ones. You may be one of them. In any case, whether you are or not, may I give you one word of advice?"

"What is it?" she said.

He answered her briefly, with a certain recklessness that somehow hurt her. "Forget you ever met me! It's no good—no good! Don't weight yourself with a burden that can only handicap you! If it's your fate, as well as mine, to grind your bread from stones, you'll need all your strength to do it. People like you and me can't afford to waste any time over—dreams."

He cut the horse a savage flick over the ears with the last word and they went forward on a downward slant at a startling pace.

Frances attempted no rejoinder of any sort. She understood him too well. He had warned her not to return, at what cost to himself she would never know, though possibly it was for his own sake as well as for hers that he had done it. There was an insuperable barrier between them, and he was not a man with whom any compromise would be possible. There were in his nature fires which, it was evident, even he could not always keep under control. Perhaps he realized that he could not. But he had spoken, and she felt that he had spoken finally. It was not for her to question his decision. She could only go onward now through a wilderness of utter desolation.

Not till they had reached the outskirts of Fordestown and the grey moors were left behind, did he speak again, and then it was to say in his customary, clipped style, "We'll not make a tragedy of this. Life's too short. It's just good-bye and good luck! And that's all."

She forced herself to smile. "Except many, many thanks!" she said.

He stopped her quickly. "No, not that! Never that! Do you mind if I don't get down at the station? I don't like to leave the horse."

"Of course not," she said.

They finished the journey in silence. He did not so much as help her to descend. A porter came for her baggage, and at the last moment she stood on the path, looking up at him.

"Good-bye!" she said.

He looked down at her, his face like an iron mask. "Good-bye—and good luck! You haven't any time to spare."

He did not see the hand she began to offer, and it fell instantly. He touched his cap with his whip and lifted the reins. In another moment he was driving swiftly out of the yard.

She turned into the station with a curious sense of groping her way, and heard the porter's cheery voice at her shoulder. "It's all right, miss. You've got ten minutes to spare."

"Thank you," said Frances, and drew a hard, deep breath.

Ten minutes to spare! And then to take up the burden of life again!

PART IV

CHAPTER I
THE LAND OF EXILE

London and a cold grey pall of fog! Frances looked forth from the carriage-window and suppressed a shiver. The grim ugliness of the great buildings that bordered the line seemed to lay a clammy hand upon her. The sordid poverty of the streets was as a knell sounding in her heart. Somehow it seemed to her that there was a greater loneliness here than could be found in any solitude of the moors. It was like a gaunt spectre, menacing her.

The autumn day was fading into twilight, and a dreary drizzle had begun to descend from the smoke-laden sky. She saw the gleam of it on the platforms as the train ran into the teeming terminus. And the spectre at her elbow drew closer. This was the land of exile.

She shook herself free, summoning to her aid that practical spirit which had stood her in such good stead in the old days of her slavery. Was she weaker now than she had been then, she asked herself? But she did not stay to answer the question, for something within her uttered swift warning. She knew that there were weak joints in her armour of which she had never been aware before.

In any case it was not the moment to examine them. The long journey was over, and she had reached her destination. The time for action had arrived. She had made her plans, and it now remained for her to carry them out. With the money that Rotherby had sent for her sketches, she had enough to provide for that night at a hotel, and in the morning she was determined to find a cheap lodging where she could remain pending the settlement of the business that had brought her thither. Beyond that, her plans were vague, but if the matter went favourably she hoped to leave London again immediately. To live somewhere in the country—anywhere in the country—where she could breathe pure air and work; this was all she asked of Fate now. The reek of the town nauseated her; it filled her with an intolerable sense of imprisonment. She had an almost unbearable longing to turn and go back whence she had come. And then suddenly a voice spoke at her side, greeting her, and she looked round with a start.

"Didn't you expect me?" said Rotherby.

He smiled his welcome in the glare and noise of the great station, and two utterly antagonistic sensations possessed Frances at the sight of him, a feeling of dread and a feeling that was almost gladness. Little as she had desired to see him, the unexpected appearance of a familiar face in all that host of strangers sent a quick thrill of relief through her. The spectre that haunted her drew a little away.

She smiled back at him, and after a moment gave him her hand. "I never expected you. What made you come?"

He laughed with a hint of exultation. His hand-clasp was close and possessive. She drew her own away with a sudden, stabbing memory of that which had been denied her that morning.

"You said you were coming," he said.

"Yes, but I never said the train."

He laughed again. "There was no need. Come along! Any luggage? I've got a car waiting."

"My things are all here," she said. "But I am not going any further to-night. I am going to get a room at the station hotel. To-morrow I can find something cheaper."

"Splendid!" he said lightly. "I'll come and see you safely installed, may I?"

She could not refuse, but she made her acceptance of his escort as business-like as possible. Not for worlds would she have had him know that any company just then was preferable to that of the spectre of her desolation that stalked so close behind.

They went into the hotel, and she booked a room for the night, Rotherby standing by her side, amused, not, it seemed, greatly interested, until the business was accomplished.

Then, as she turned, he became at once alert and ready. She thought the cynical lines were more deeply marked than ever about his mouth and eyes, but his smile was wholly friendly.

"Look here!" he said. "You must dine with me and we'll do a theatre to-night. You're looking like the maiden all forlorn, though I'm relieved to see you've left the cow behind! I'll be round about seven. Will that do?"

She hesitated. "Do you know I think I would rather have a quiet talk with you somewhere?" she said, with something of an effort. "I want to hear all there is to hear—about my work."

"Oh, there's plenty of time," he said. "As a matter of fact, the dealer chap isn't in town at the moment. I heard on the 'phone this morning. He'll soon be back though, so you needn't be anxious."

The news chilled her. "I had hoped to see him to-morrow," she said.

"He'll soon be back," said Rotherby again, with careless confidence. "Now what about this theatre? You'll come? It'll pass the time away."

It was in her mind to refuse. She would have preferred to refuse. But in the end she accepted. Perhaps it was the dread of a long evening of solitary speculation and its attendant misgivings that actuated her. Perhaps his insistence weighed with her; or perhaps like a child she was overwhelmed by the sheer loneliness of her position. Whatever the motive, she yielded, and having yielded, she thrust all regrets away. It was as though after her long journey she had entered another world, and she determined almost fiercely to take the advice that had been offered her that morning and fling all handicaps aside. He had said it was no good. He had told her not to return. Then she would go forward on this new path and stifle the pain at her heart. It might be that in time she would forget. O God, if she could but forget!

She parted from Rotherby in the vestibule of the hotel and went up to her room. They were to meet again in little more than an hour, and she spent the time in a feverish effort to banish thought and to banish also that appearance of forlornness of which he had jestingly spoken.

She was very tired, but she would not own it, and when she met him again she had captured that reserve of strength which dwells at the back of jaded nerves, and an almost reckless charm was hers.

He gave her flowers, carnations and lilies, and she pinned them at her breast, revelling in their sweetness, exotic though she knew them to be. He took her to a restaurant, and the feeling of unreality followed her thither, throwing a strange glamour over all things. He did not again taunt her with being forlorn; for she held herself like a queen, and not even the simplicity of her attire could make her insignificant.

"Gad!" he said to her once. "How wonderful you are!"

And she uttered a little laugh that surprised herself. "It is all make-believe," she said.

He did not ask her to explain, but his eyes followed her perpetually with a kindling flame which mounted steadily higher, and when they left the table his hand closed for a moment upon her arm.

She shook it off with a laugh and a shrug. "Every game has its rules," she said.

He laughed also, answering her mood. "Every woman makes her own," he said.

They went out into the gleaming streets and entered the waiting car. The unaccustomed luxury was like a dream to Frances. It was no longer an effort to put the past away from her. It had sunk of itself into the far dim distance. Very curiously the only memory that remained active in her mind was that of the purple flower that bloomed upon the coping of the cloisters in the Bishop's garden. The vision of that was fantastically vivid, as it had been on that day of her first talk with Montague Rotherby.

The pain at her heart had wholly ceased, and she wondered a little, barely realizing that she had stilled it temporarily with this anæsthetic of unreality. But a sub-conscious dread of its return made her steep herself more and more deeply in its oblivion. After all, to whom did it matter except herself? This man with his cynical eyes was too experienced a player to be made a loser in one night. And she had so little left to lose.

She sat in a box with him at the theatre, and though she quickly absorbed herself in the play, she was aware of his undivided attention from the beginning.

It even exasperated her at last, so that she turned to him after the first act with a movement of impatience. "Does it interest you so little," she said, "that you can't even be bothered to glance at the stage?"

"I have seen it already three times," he made answer, "and I am more interested at the present moment in watching the effect it has upon you."

She uttered a laugh, but the words gave her an odd feeling of shock. The play was a fashionable one, but though it compelled her deepest interest, it held moments of disgust for her as well.

"I should never want to see this more than once," she said at the end of the second act.

Whereat he laughed. "Your education has been neglected," he said. "We all think like this now-a-days. The puritanical atmosphere of Tetherstones has spoilt your taste."

She was silent. Somehow the very word sent a pang to her heart.

He leaned slightly towards her, looking at her. "Tell me about your sojourn at Tetherstones!" he said. "Were the farm people decent to you? Were you happy there?"

There was a slighting note in his voice that she found intolerable. She turned deliberately and met his look.

"You know the Dermots," she said. "You know quite well that they are not just—farm-people. Why should you conceal the fact?"

He made a careless gesture. "I know that one of them shot me in mistake for a rabbit that night I waited for you," he said. "I was never more scared in my life. That was the son, I presume? Did he ever mention that episode to you?"

"Never," she said.

"No? Perhaps he wasn't very proud of it. Perhaps he realized that the rabbit fallacy wouldn't carry him very far in a court of law. I fancy he imagined that I was poaching on his preserves." Rotherby spoke with a sarcastic drawl. "Very unreasonable of him, what?"

She felt the burning colour rise in her face under his eyes, and she averted her own. "Not being in his confidence, I really can hardly give an opinion," she said.

"Oh, you're not in his confidence?" said Rotherby. "Somehow I didn't think you were, or you would hardly be so ready to take up the cudgels in his defence. He's a curious fellow. I knew him years ago. He had brains as a young man, then somehow he got touched in the upper story and got condemned to the simple life. That was how he came to take up farming. An awful blow to the old man, I believe! I heard he was never the same again afterwards. That is about as far as my information takes me. I must admit that from a personal point of view I am not vastly interested in the family. Did you find them interesting?"

"They were kinder to me than I can possibly say," Frances said.

The careless information he had given her was like an obnoxious draught that she had been compelled to swallow. But somehow, in spite of herself, she had assimilated it. It explained so much which before had been inexplicable. She remembered how she had more than once asked herself if the lonely gladiator on that Devon moor were always wholly responsible for his actions. And was this why he had told her only that morning that it was no good—no good—that her love was nought but a handicap to be overcome and cast aside?

Again she was conscious of the pain she had stifled waking within her. Again she felt the chill presence of the haunting spectre. Then Rotherby's voice came to her again, and she turned almost with relief.

"They were decent to you, were they?" he said. "I presume that was why you went back to them from Fordestown?"

She thrust her pain away out of sight of his mocking eyes. "No," she said quietly. "I went back to be with the little girl before she died. She wanted me."

He gave a slight start. "What? The blind child that used to run about the lane? Is she dead? What from?"

"She was very fragile," Frances said, and instinctively she spoke with reverence. "She had a fall which caused an abscess at the base of the brain, affecting the spine. The doctor had always known it might happen at any time. She didn't suffer—dear little soul."

"A tragic family!" commented Rotherby, and dropped into silence.

He leaned back in his chair with his face in shadow, and for a space she felt that his attention was no longer focussed upon her.

It gave her a certain sense of relief, for her thoughts would turn back to those few cynical words of his and she needed time to recover from the shock of them. Was it true? Was it true? Was this the key to the riddle that had so often baffled her? Was it for this that she had seen him writhing in agony of soul?

The curtain went up, and she jerked herself back to her surroundings. She tried to immerse herself anew in the play, but her interest was gone. The glamour had faded, and she knew that she was terribly, overwhelmingly tired. A desire for solitude came upon her and with it, inseparable from it, an intolerable sense of exile, a longing that was almost anguish for the peace of the open moors, for the scent of the bog-myrtle, and the rain. . . . She closed her eyes, and drew her memories about her like a mantle. . . .

CHAPTER II
THE NIGHTMARE

Someone was speaking to her. A hand touched her. She looked up with a start.

Rotherby was leaning over her. His eyes met hers closely, lingeringly, with a caress in them which her tiredness barely comprehended.

"How tired you are!" he said. "Shall I take you home?"

Home! For a few moments her weary brain clung piteously about the word. Then the pressure of his hand brought swift awakening. She sat up with a jerk.

"Oh, is it over? Yes, I am very tired. Forgive me! Let us go!"

His hand still held her. He slipped it under her elbow, helping her to rise.

She got up quickly, and freed herself. He put her cloak about her in silence. They passed out of the box into the crowd that filled the corridor.

"It's pouring with rain," said Rotherby, as they emerged into the vestibule. "Wait while I get the car!"

He left her, and she took her stand at a corner of the steps, idly watching the press of people that thronged past her on to the pavement. Her sleep had left her slightly dazed, physically cold. The thought of the dear Devon she had left only that morning had sunk very far below the surface of her consciousness. It was as if years as well as distance separated her from it, and all she knew now was the ache of weariness and a certain dull disgust with everything about her. A man on the pavement below her, wearing an ulster with a cap drawn down over his eyes, evidently waiting for a conveyance, caught her passing attention because the set of his shoulders was somewhat reminiscent to her of the lonely horseman who had awaited her coming on the moor, but she was too apathetic to bestow more than a cursory glance upon any, and she shrank at the moment with something like panic from all things that might pain her. She was too tired to endure any more that night.

Out of the press of hurrying people Rotherby detached himself and came to her. "It's all right. Take my arm! The car is just here."

She obeyed him, for the throng was great, and her only desire to escape the vortex of humanity and find the rest she so sorely needed. He piloted her through the crowd. For a few seconds she felt the rain beating upon her uncovered head, and then she was sunk upon the cushions in the darkness of the car with Rotherby beside her, and the glittering streets slipping past with kaleidoscopic rapidity.

The slashing of the rain upon the window-panes penetrated her consciousness. "What a wet night!" she murmured.

"Yes, fiendish," said Rotherby. "But I'll soon have you out of it. You're dead beat, aren't you?"

"Very, very tired," she answered, and dropped back into silence.

The car slid on through the night. They turned out of the glaring streets, and in the dimness Frances closed her eyes again. She did not want to talk; and

Rotherby's mood seemed to coincide with hers, for he sat in utter silence by her side.

She was hardly aware that the car had stopped when suddenly he spoke. "You'll come in here for a few minutes? I'll tell the man to wait."

She roused herself. "In where?"

He was opening the door. "It's a half-way house where you can get some supper. I have ordered it specially for you."

"Supper!" She echoed the word, slightly startled. "Oh, really I don't want any. I would rather go straight back."

He was already out of the car. He stood in the doorway, laughing. "Please don't keep me here in the rain to argue! Let's do it inside! I can't let you go supperless to bed. It's against my principles."

He took her hand with the words, and his own had an imperative touch to which she yielded almost before she realized it.

"I really don't want anything," she protested, but she was getting out of the car as she spoke. "I never thought of such a thing."

"Nonsense!" said Rotherby. "Then it's a good thing I'm here to think for you. I've got something rather interesting to tell you too. I've been saving it up all the evening. Confound this rain! Let's get into shelter!"

He spoke a word to the man, and then took her arm and led her swiftly up some steps to a lighted portico. They were actually inside before Frances found her breath to speak again. "What is this place?"

"It's a hotel of sorts," he answered lightly. "I hope it meets with your approval. It's somewhat after the French style. Come up in the lift!"

She went with him, still possessed by that feeling of unreality which had held her tired senses in thrall throughout the evening. The flowers at her breast were crushed and faded, but the scent of them had all the sweetness of a dream. Certain words floated through her memory—had she heard them only that morning? "People like you and me can't afford to waste any time over—dreams." Ah well, the night would soon be gone, and she would wake in the morning to the old grim struggle. But till then—like the memory of the purple flower upon the wall in the days of her slavery—she would hold to her dream.

She passed out of the lift with Rotherby, and he unlocked a door that led into a tiny hall.

"Take off your cloak!" he said; then, as she fumbled, unfastened it himself and slipped it from her shoulders.

She felt his eyes upon her again, and was stabbed, as a dreamer is sometimes stabbed, by a curious feeling of insecurity. Then he had turned away, and was taking off his own hat and coat.

He closed the door by which they had entered and she heard the snap of a patent lock. "We don't want anyone else in," he said.

She paused. "But isn't it public? I thought you said it was a hotel."

He opened another door, and switched on a light that showed her a luxurious red-curtained apartment, with a polished table spread with refreshments of all kinds, and an electric stove that burned with a hot glow before a deep settee.

"This isn't public," he said. "It belongs to me."

"Belongs to you!" She looked at him with eyes that were beginning to see that which her numbed brain till then had failed to grasp. "What do you mean?"

He made an airy gesture. "I mean that I have paid for it, that's all. See what a disappointment you would have given me if you had refused to come in to supper!"

She stood staring at him. "I—don't understand. You said—you did say—it was a public place?"

He smiled his scoffing smile. "Did I? I don't seem to remember it. It doesn't matter, does it? Sit down and have something! I prepared this as a little surprise, my Circe. You're not vexed?"

"Vexed!" she said, and paused, considering. "But—it's so extraordinary. I never dreamed——"

"No?" he said. "Well, you've been dreaming hard enough all the evening anyway. Come, sit down! Sit down and let's enjoy ourselves! There's no law against that, is there? Let's see if I can open this champagne!"

He proceeded to open it, and she watched him pour it foaming into two glasses on the table. The feeling that she had in some fashion been tricked was gaining ground with her, and yet in his careless demeanour she could detect no reason for alarm. He so evidently regarded the whole affair as a joke.

He turned round to her suddenly. "I say, don't look so shocked! There really is no need. You can always marry me afterwards, you know, if you feel so disposed. In fact, I think you are practically committed to that, so let's make the best of it!"

"What do you mean?" she said.

He lifted his brows cynically. "That's what I have brought you here to explain. But never mind that now! Drink some of this stuff! You'll find it quite good."

He motioned her to the table, but she held back. If she had dreamed all the evening, she was awake now, most suddenly and terribly awake. Her brain felt strangely clear, as if it had been focussed upon one thing only till it had crystallized to an amazing penetration. The vision upon which she had gazed uncomprehendingly for so long had resolved itself into a thing of horror which filled the whole of her consciousness.

She saw herself helpless as a prisoner chained to a rock, but superbly she gathered her strength to meet the situation. She faced him like a queen.

"You have made a mistake," she said. "Let me go!"

He straightened himself sharply. She saw an ugly look cross his face—the look of a man who is debating at which point to drive his weapon home. Then again, carelessly, he laughed.

"Do let's have supper first!" he said. "We can talk afterwards for any length of time. I am sure you will find that sound advice. A good meal is always a help."

She stood motionless, her eyes unwaveringly upon him. "Let me go!" she said again.

He came to her then, and though the smile was still upon his face, she knew that, like herself, he was braced for battle.

"Why this tragic attitude?" he said. "And to what end? Don't spoil the occasion, my Circe! We are going to enjoy ourselves to-night."

She flung down the gauntlet with a supreme disregard of consequences. "You hound!" she said.

He shrugged his shoulders. "I like you for that. Yes, I am a hound, but I don't appreciate an easy prey. I'll conquer you now I've got you. But I'm in no hurry. Sit down and let's talk it over!"

Somehow that weakened her more than any violence. His utter assurance, his easy acceptance of her contempt, his almost philosophical attitude in the matter, all made her realize the hopelessness of her position. He had deliberately trapped her, and he was not ashamed that she should know it. She stood before him speechless.

"That's better," he said. "You're getting a grasp of the situation, bringing that business-like mind of yours to bear upon it. Now listen to me! I love you. I can't tell you why, but I do. I've always wanted you, and I made up my mind a long while ago that I would have you. We began well, and then you broke away. But you won't break away this time. You belong to me, and I am going to enforce my claim. Is that quite clear?"

"You have no claim," she said through white lips.

"That is merely your point of view," he rejoined, "and I do not share it. You gave yourself to me, remember, and I never gave you any cause to regret your action. If you had behaved reasonably, we should have been married by this time, and all your troubles would have been at an end. As it is,—" He paused.

"Well?" she said.

She saw his face harden. "As it is," he said, "you have tried my patience to the utmost limit, till I have come to the pitch when I will stand no more trifling. Do you understand? To-night I am your master. To-night—for the last time—I ask you, will you marry me? Think well before you decide! To-morrow—possibly—you may be not only willing, but anxious, but," he shrugged his shoulders again—"I may have other plans by that time."

"Ah!" she said, and put a hand to her head.

The floor had begun to sway under her feet. His face, with its cruel, set smile, had receded into distance. She was cold from head to foot, with an icy coldness, and she thought her heart had ceased to beat. She felt herself totter.

And then there came the grasp of his hand, holding her back as it seemed on the very edge of the abyss. And instinctively she clung to the support he offered, with gasping incoherent entreaty.

"Oh, hold me up! Save me! Don't let me fall!"

"Sit down!" he said. "Here is a chair! Now drink! It's all right. You'll be better in a minute."

She felt the rim of a glass against her chattering teeth, and she drank with her head against his arm.

The wine was like fire in her veins; the awful numbness passed.

"Better?" said Rotherby. "Come, this is rather a terrible fuss to make, isn't it? Drink a little more!"

She drank again, and then, as he released her, bent forward over the table, hiding her face. A great shiver went through her and passed. She sat bowed and silent.

After a few seconds he spoke again, his tone quite friendly, but with that hint of mastery which made her realize how completely she was at his mercy.

"Sit up and have some supper! You will feel much better for it. Afterwards we will sit by the fire and talk."

She raised herself slowly, propping her chin on her hands. She spoke, haltingly, with difficulty, almost as if it were in a foreign language.

"If I give my promise—to—to—to—marry—you, will you—let me—go?"

"To-night?" he said.

"Yes, to-night." She did not look at him; she was staring before her at a picture on the opposite wall—a picture of heather-clad moors and running streams—but with eyes that saw not.

There was a brief pause, then very suddenly the man behind her moved. He bent and took her head between his hands, compelling her to face him.

"Why should I do that?" he said.

She met his look, though an irrepressible shudder went through her at his touch. "Because," she said, in the same slow, uncertain way, "you are a man—and I—am a woman. I am at your mercy—now, but I shall not always be. If you want to—to—hold me by any means—except force—then—you will be merciful. No! Listen! I am at your mercy. I know it. I own it. But—you are not all beast. If you will let me go, I will promise to marry you—as soon as you wish. If you will not let me go, you will have your way to-night. But after to-night—after to-night——"

"Well?" he said, awed in spite of himself by her voice, her words, her look, yet half-mocking still. "After to-night?"

"After to-night," she said, and drew herself from his hold, facing him with a gesture of freedom that was even regal, "you will never see me again, because I swear to you—before God—that I shall be dead."

He blenched a little, but in a moment recovered himself. "Pshaw! Words are easy—especially with women. That threat doesn't move me."

"No." She got up from her chair with a strange calmness. "It may not—yet. But it will—it will. If you were all beast, you might not care. But you are a man at heart, and so you will never forget it. And you will care—terribly—afterwards."

She turned from him with the words, walked to the settee before the stove, and sat down, holding her hands to the warmth, ignoring his presence utterly.

He did not follow her. There was that about her that made it impossible just then. He had not thought that she had the strength so to dominate the situation. It had been completely in his own hands, but somehow it had passed out of his control. Wherefore? The sight of her weakness had made the conquest seem so easy that he had almost despised her for it. And now?

He turned sullenly from her, took up a glass and drank.

After many seconds he spoke. "The last time I saw you, you gave me to understand that it was only your pride that kept you from marrying me. That is not the reason you want to back out now."

"I gave you my reason then," she made answer, without turning. "I did not love you."

"You loved me once," he rejoined, "before you threw me over."

She uttered a short, hard sigh. "I hadn't even begun to know the meaning of the word."

He flung round savagely. "There's someone else in the field. I suspected it before. Who is it? That maniac at Tetherstones?"

She leaned forward a little further to the glow. "It doesn't really matter," she said. "Even if it were so, it wouldn't really count, would it?"

"It would not," he rejoined curtly.

"So why discuss it?" said Frances.

Her weariness sounded again in her voice, but there was no weakness with it, rather a species of solitary majesty upon which he could not intrude. Yet, baffled, he still sought to penetrate her defences.

"You loved me once," he repeated doggedly. "What did I ever do to forfeit your love?"

She turned suddenly as she sat, and faced him, pale, with burning eyes of accusation.

"I will tell you what you did. You desecrated my love. You killed it at birth. You treated me then—as you are treating me now—dishonourably. You gave me stones for bread, and you are doing it still. I think you are incapable of anything else. Love—real love—is out of your reach!"

The fire of her words scorched him; he drew back. "Gad!" he said. "If you'd lived in the old days, you'd have been burnt as a witch."

"There are worse fates than that," she answered very bitterly.

"There are!" he returned with a flash of anger. "And hotter hells! Well, you've made your conditions. I accept them. You are free to go."

He flung the words with a force and suddenness that struck her like a blow. She sat for a few moments, staring at him. Then, with an effort, she rose.

"Do you mean that?"

He came close to her. His face was drawn. Somehow she felt as though she were looking at an animal through the iron bars of a cage.

He spoke, between his teeth. "Yes, I mean it. I will let you go—just to show you that—as you kindly remarked just now—I am not—all—beast. But—I hold you to your promise. Is that understood? You will marry me."

She lifted her head with a certain pride. "I have said it," she said, and turned from him.

He thrust out a hand and grasped her shoulder. "You will say it again!" he said.

She stopped. That grip of his sent panic to her heart, but she stilled it with a desperate sense of expediency. Yet, for the moment she could not speak, so terrible was the strain, and in that moment, as she stood summoning her strength, there came the sound of an electric bell cleaving the dreadful silence so suddenly that she cried out and almost fell.

"Damnation!" Rotherby said. "See here! I shall have to go to the door. You don't want to be seen here. You'd better go into the other room."

He indicated a door at the further end of the one in which they stood, and she turned towards it instinctively.

He went with her, and opened it, switching on a light. She glanced within, and drew back.

"Go in!" he urged. "I can't help it. It's only for a few seconds. I won't let anyone in. Quick! It's the only way."

She turned to him like a hunted creature, wildly beseeching quarter. "You will let me go afterwards? You promise it? You swear it?"

"Of course I will let you go," he said. "There goes that damn' bell again. You'll be all right here, and I won't keep you long."

He almost pushed her into the room, and shut the door upon her. The bell was pealing imperatively. She sank into a chair at the foot of the bed, and wondered if this nightmare would ever pass.

CHAPTER III
THE AWAKENING

The door was shut, but there came to her the sound of voices in the distance, and she listened intently, holding her breath. At any moment he might return, at any moment the dread struggle might be resumed. He had given her his word, but she did not trust him. She never had trusted him; and the memory of his grip upon her shoulder gave her small cause for confidence now. She glanced around her for a possible means of escape, but the only other door in the room led into the little hall in which even now Rotherby was parleying with his unwelcome visitor. The impulse came to her to brave all risk of observation and walk straight out while he was thus occupied, but a more wary instinct bade her pause. If the visitor were an old friend, he might enter uninvited, and if that happened the outer door would be left unguarded, and she could make her escape unobserved, before Rotherby could get rid of him. This would be far the easier course, and would offer fewer difficulties later. So, with stretched nerves, prepared for immediate flight, she waited.

The opportunity came even sooner than she expected. Very suddenly she heard the tramp of feet in the room she had just quitted, and in a second she was on her feet.

But in that second she heard a voice raised abruptly like the blare of an angry bull, and she stood rooted to the spot, listening, listening, listening, with her hands clasped tight upon her heart.

Words reached her through the tumult of sound, words and the sounds of a fierce struggle.

"Damn you, I'll have an answer! I'll kill you if you don't speak. What? You infernal skunk, do you think I'd stick at killing you? There's nothing I'd enjoy more."

There followed a dreadful series of sounds as of something being banged against the wall by which she stood, and then suddenly there came a terrific blow against the door itself. A cry followed the blow—a gurgling terrible cry, and it did for Frances what nothing else could have done; it gave her strength to act.

She could have made her escape in that moment, but the bare thought was gone from her mind. She sprang to the door, and threw it open. Then she saw that which she had already beheld that evening, but with unseeing eyes—the big man in the ulster who had waited just below her in the rain at the theatre steps half-an-hour before.

He was holding Rotherby between his hands as he might have held a sack of meal, and banging his head against everything hard in the vicinity. Rotherby was struggling with gasping, broken oaths for freedom, but he was utterly outmatched. As Frances flung open the door he fell backwards at her feet, and the man who gripped him proceeded furiously to stand over him and bang his head upon the floor.

"Oh, stop!" Frances cried in horror. "Oh, for God's sake, stop!"

He stopped. Her voice seemed to have an almost miraculous effect upon him. He stopped. But he knelt upon Rotherby, holding him down, and his face, suffused with passion, was to her the most appalling sight she had ever beheld.

There followed an awful silence, during which he remained quite motionless, bent over his enemy. Rotherby was bleeding profusely at the nose, but he was half-stunned and seemed unaware of it. His arms were flung wide, and his hands opened and shut convulsively, in a manner that made the onlooker shudder.

How long that fearful silence lasted she never knew. It seemed to stretch out interminably into minutes so weighted with dread that each was like an hour.

At last, when she could endure no longer, huskily, with tremendous effort, she spoke. "Do you want—to kill him?"

He raised his head slowly and looked at her. His eyes were bloodshot and the veins of his temples visibly throbbing, but the rest of his face was ghastly white.

He looked at her, and she felt a quick, piercing pain at her heart that made her catch her breath.

"I have wanted to kill him for years," he said. "Do you value his life? If not——"

It was terrible, it was monstrous; but it was real. He was asking her—actually asking her, as a victorious gladiator in the arena—for permission to despatch his victim. And even as he spoke, she saw his right hand move towards the throat of the prostrate man.

She cried out wildly at the sight, in an anguish of horror. "Arthur, no—no—no! That's murder! Arthur,—stop!"

"He is worse than a murderer," Arthur said in the same fatalistic tone.

"Ah, no!" she made gasping answer. "And you! And you!"

"And—you!" he said, with terrible emphasis.

She broke in upon him desperately, for the need was great. "He has done me no harm. Let him go! You must—you must let him go."

"Why?" he said.

"Because I ask you—I beg you—because—because—" She halted, frantically searching for adequate words. "Oh, wait!" she besought him. "Wait!"

His eyes regarded her immovably. "For your sake?" he said at last.

She wrung her hands together. "Yes—yes!"

He got slowly to his feet. "For your sake then!" he said. "Now tell me—what you are doing here? And why did you cry out just now when I rang the bell?"

His manner was absolutely quiet, but there was that in his look that warned her that the danger was not past. She did not dare to tell him the truth.

"I cried out," she said, "because—I was startled. I hid in this room for the same reason."

"And—you came here—for what?" he said.

She glanced away to the spread table, for she could not meet his eyes. "We had been to the theatre. I came in—for supper."

"And he has behaved towards you absolutely as a gentleman should?" he questioned, in the same level voice that made her think of a weapon poised for striking.

"Yes—oh, yes!" she answered.

He was silent for a moment or two, and she knew that his look searched her unsparingly. Then: "I don't believe you are telling me the truth," he said. "But I shall soon know."

He turned abruptly to the man on the floor. "Get up!" he said.

Rotherby had drawn his hands over his face. He rolled on to his side as the curt command reached him, and in a few seconds, grabbing at a chair, he dragged himself to his feet. But his face was ashen and he could not stand. He dropped into the chair with a groan.

Frances went to the washing-stand, squeezed out a sponge in cold water and brought it to him. He took it in a dazed fashion and mopped the blood from his nose and mouth.

Arthur stood by, massive and motionless, his face set in iron lines. He was like an executioner, grim as doom, waiting for his victim. He made no comment when Frances brought towel and basin to Rotherby's side and helped him.

But at length, as Rotherby began to show signs of recovery, he waved her to one side.

"Now, you! Let's have your version! What are you and Miss Thorold doing here?"

Rotherby looked at him through narrowed lids. His face was very evil as he made reply. "I chance to live here."

"I know that. And you'll die here without any chance about it if you don't choose to give me a straight answer to my questions. What did you bring her here for?"

"What the devil is that to you?" said Rotherby sullenly. "You go to hell!"

Though he was beaten so that he could hardly lift his head, he showed no fear, and for that Frances, who knew something of the temperament of the man who had beaten him, accorded him a certain admiration. To be punished as he had been punished, and yet to refuse submission proved a strength with which she had hardly credited him.

At Arthur's swift gesture of exasperation, she moved forward, intervening. "Let me speak!" she said. "I will answer your questions."

She stood between the two men, and again, vesting her with a majesty which was not normally hers, there came to her aid the consciousness of standing for the right. Whatever the outcome, she recognized that the protection of Rotherby must somehow be accomplished. To save the one man from death and the other from committing a murder, she braced herself for the greatest battle of her life.

Arthur's look came back to her. He regarded her sombrely, as though he recognized in her a factor that must be dealt with.

"You say he brought you here for supper," he said. "Did he give you no reason for believing that he meant to keep you here all night?"

She faced him steadfastly. The man's life hung in the balance. It rested with her—it rested with her.

"I was on the point of leaving when you arrived," she said.

"Is that the truth?" he said.

"It is the truth," she answered quietly.

"You honestly believe he meant to let you go?"

"Yes." Her eyes looked straight into his with the words. She realized that the tension was slackening, but she dared not relax her own vigilance. The danger was not yet past. Not yet had she accomplished her end.

"He has never given you any cause to distrust him?" Arthur said.

She hesitated momentarily. "I am trusting him now," she said finally.

"Why?" He flung the word with a touch of fierceness. "You are saying this to bluff me. It is not true."

"It is true," she said resolutely, paused a second, then very firmly made her position secure. "I am trusting him because—because I have promised to be his wife."

The declaration fell between them like a bombshell. She did not know how she uttered it, and having done so, there came a mist before her eyes which seemed to fog all her senses, making it impossible for her to gauge the result—to realize in any sense the devastation she had wrought. She thought she heard him draw the breath between his teeth as though he repressed some sign of suffering. But she was not sure even of this, so desperate for the moment was her own extremity.

It could not have lasted for long, that wild tumult of emotion, but when it passed she was trembling from head to foot as though she had merged from some frightful conflict. She wanted to protest for very anguish that she could not endure any more, she could not—she could not! But her voice was gone. She stood waiting, wondering how soon her strength would utterly fail.

Arthur's voice came to her at last, low, hoarse with restraint. "So that is why you came to town!"

She could not answer him. There was no reproach in his tone, but the pain of it was more agonizing to her than any suffering of her own. As in a vision she saw him beaten and thrust aside—the mighty gladiator to whom, for some mysterious reason, victory was eternally denied. Her whole soul cried out against the fate that dogged him, but she stifled the cry. She could not—dared not—give it utterance.

She yet stood between him and his victim, and she must continue to stand. She clung to that thought before all else. To save him from himself—it was all that counted with her just then.

He spoke again at length, and in his voice was a subtle difference that told her the end was within sight—the battle almost won.

"I am beginning to understand," he said. "I thought—somehow I thought—I had misjudged you—that night at Tetherstones—you remember? Well, I know better now. I shall never make that mistake again. If he marries you, no doubt you will consider yourself lucky. But—just in case you don't know—I had better warn you that he doesn't stick at letting a woman down if it suits his purpose."

His voice grew harder, colder; it had a steely edge. "You may have heard of a sister of mine who died some years ago—Nan? He ruined her deliberately, intentionally. He never meant to make good. She was young. She didn't know the world as you know it. She—actually loved him. And she paid the penalty. We all paid to a certain extent. That is why—" his tone suddenly deepened,—"I have sworn to kill him if he ever comes my way again—as I would kill a poisonous reptile. Perhaps it seems unreasonable to you. Your ideas are different. But—the fact remains."

He ceased to speak, and still she stood between them, past speech, almost past feeling, yet steadfast in her resolve. The battle was nearly over—the end within sight.

Again there fell a silence, and she counted the seconds, asking herself how long—how long? Somewhere within her she seemed to hear the echo of the words that he had spoken on that terrible night at Tetherstones. "I loved you—I—loved you!" And now as then she felt that the fires of hell were very near. But she would not faint this time. O God, she must not faint!

He spoke again—for the last time—and there was a sound of dreadful laughter in his voice.

"It seems I have come on a fool's errand," he said. "I can only apologize for my intrusion, and withdraw. No doubt you know best how to play your own game. I only regret that I did not realize sooner what it was."

That was all. He turned from her with the words, and she knew that the awful battle was over. Because of her, he would let his enemy go free.

But as she stood numbly listening to the heavy tread of his feet as he went away, she knew no sense of conquest or even of relief. The battle was over, but she herself was wounded past all hope. And she thought her heart must die within her, so bitter was the pain.

CHAPTER IV
THE VICTORY

He was gone. The clang of the outer door spoke of his departure.

He was gone, and the dread struggle was past.

She came to herself like a dazed mariner flung ashore by the breakers, hardly believing that the peril was over. A great weakness was upon her and she knew that she could not stand against it. Of Rotherby's very existence at the moment she was unaware. Mechanically, gropingly, she made her way to the settee before the stove and sank down upon it. She was shivering violently.

The warmth came about her, and she stretched out her hands to it, seeking its comfort, thankful for the physical relief of it, yet hardly conscious of her surroundings.

"It is dead—it is dead!" she kept saying to herself over and over. "It is quite—quite dead!"

But for a long time she could not bring herself to realize why she said it or what it was that was dead.

At last by slow and painful degrees it began to dawn upon her that there was a meaning to the words. Something was dead. Something had died by her hand in that very room. What was it?

Now it came to her in all its immensity, crushing her down. She had slain his love. She had killed her own romance. From that night onwards he would never think of her again save with reviling and bitterness of soul. She had taken that which was holy and flung it in the dust. She had desecrated the perfect gift, had made a hideous travesty of that high vision which had been vouchsafed to her. More, she had dragged the man she loved down to the very gates of hell, and had made him know the tortures of the damned.

The warmth was beginning to ease her exhausted body, but her spirit found no comfort. Almost she preferred that numbness of all her faculties. For the misery that was taking its place was more than she could bear.

She still sat with her hands outstretched, but hot tears were rolling down her face, unheeded, unchecked, the tears of a great despair.

"It is dead," she said to herself over and over in the desolation of her soul. "It is dead. It is dead."

There came a voice behind her—Rotherby's voice, and she started slightly, remembering him. It was curious how little he counted now.

"Frances," he said, and with her outer consciousness she noticed an odd embarrassment in his tone and faintly wondered. "I've made a pretty poor show of this. Don't cry! You're perfectly safe."

"Am I crying?" she said, and put a hand to her face.

He came and sat beside her. "Listen!" he said "I've been a damned cad. And you're a topper. I never knew you had it in you—or any woman had for the matter of that. There's nothing I won't do for you after this. Understand?"

"I don't want you to do anything," she said wearily.

He made an odd sound as of some irony suppressed. "You're nearly dead," he said. "So am I. Come and have supper! And trust me—will you trust me?"

Something in his tone reached her. She turned slowly and looked at him. His face was very pale, and his eyes looked drawn and strained; but except for this she saw no traces about him of the recent struggle. He met her gaze with a faint smile.

"I've had all the nonsense knocked out of me for to-night," he said. "But I suppose I'm damned lucky to be here at all. That fellow has the strength of an ox. The back of my head is like a jelly, damn him!"

"I thought he meant to kill you," she said dully.

"He did," said Rotherby. "You saved my life."

"Did I?" Her look fell away from him. "It wasn't for your sake," she said, after a moment. "It was for his."

"I gathered that," said Rotherby. "That's what makes you so wonderful."

"I don't feel wonderful," she said.

He leaned towards her. "Don't cry!" he said again. "You are wonderful. And you've made me feel a cur of the very first magnitude. That's something to accomplish, isn't it?"

"I don't know," she said. "I wasn't thinking of you."

"You're worn out," he said. "Have some food, and I'll take you back. You're going to trust me, aren't you? I swear I won't let you down after this. You're not afraid of me?"

"Oh no, I am not afraid of you," she said.

In a detached, impersonal fashion, out of the depths of her despair, she wondered how he could imagine that he or his actions had the slightest importance for her. Could anything in the world really matter after this cataclysm? He might have been a total stranger, ministering to her, so small was his significance now.

But she was in a vague fashion grateful for his kindness, and when he brought her food, she forced herself to eat lest he should think her unappreciative. It revived her also, lifting the awful weight of inertia from her senses, so that after a while she was capable of coherent thought again.

"That's better," Rotherby said presently. "Look here! You won't believe me, but I'm most damnably sorry for all this."

"I do believe you," she said, with a wan smile.

"Oh, I don't mean the hammering," he said. "I'm actually thinking of you for a change. I've been a rotter all my life, and I don't count. But you—you're straight. I always knew you were. And I've found out something more about you to-night. I've found out why you turned me down."

He got up abruptly, and began to walk about the room.

"I half-guessed it long ago. I know it now. You love this hairy-heeled chap who nearly killed me to-night. You needn't bother to deny it. You love him and he loves you. And yet—and yet—you let him believe—that of you! Good God! There isn't another woman on earth would have done it."

"I had to do it," Frances said with simplicity. "He would have killed you."

"Yes, he would have killed me—and swung for it. You didn't want him to swing. Listen!" He came suddenly to her and knelt by her side. "You told me a little while ago that I was not all beast, that I was a man at heart. And you're right. I am—I am. Frances, I swear to you—I'll never let you down after this."

The earnestness of his tone moved her somewhat. She put out a hand to him. "I know," she said.

He gripped her hand fast. "You don't know what a brute I am," he said. "I'm going to tell you. That fellow—Arthur Dermot as he styles himself—is my cousin. His father is Dr. Rotherby's brother. We were friends once, he and I—sort of brothers, you understand. He had a sister—a lot of sisters—one in particular—a lovely girl—Nan." He paused. "Somehow you have always reminded me of Nan, so dainty, so queenly in your ways, so quick of sympathy—so full of charm. Well, I loved her—she loved me. It was a midsummer madness—one of those exquisite dreams that one revels in like a draught of wine, and then forgets."

"That isn't love," said Frances.

He lifted his shoulders. "Isn't it? Well, perhaps you are right. I never wholly forgot. But we were young. She was only twenty. No one suspected us of falling in love until the thing was done. Then there was an outcry—first cousins—no marriage. We hadn't even begun to think of marriage, but I swear—I swear—I never meant to let her down. If they had left us alone, the thing would probably have fizzled out, but the fuss somehow worked us up to fever pitch. We met—by stealth—at night. She was young and very ardent. I was a damned cad. I own it. But she—she was like a flame, and in the end—well, you know what happened in the end. We came to our senses very early one summer morning. She was scared, and when I tried to calm her she flew into a passion. I got angry too. We quarrelled and separated. That very day the old Bishop, my trustee he was then, sent for me and told me he had a mission for me to execute in Australia. It was a trumped-up job. I knew it at the time. But I was hot-headed, and there had been talk of foreign travel before. I took it for granted that our dream had come to an end. I accepted and went."

"How could you?" Frances said.

He raised his shoulders again. "I told you I was a brute. But at the time it seemed the only thing to do. The dream was over. One doesn't sit over the cards in broad daylight."

The cynicism habitual to him sounded in the last words. She shrank a little and withdrew her hand.

"Yes, I know," he said. "You are a woman. You take the woman's point of view. But I'm not defending myself. I'm just telling you the plain truth. I didn't know when I went about poor Nan's trouble. I had a letter from her three months after, telling me. She wanted to run away, to come and join me. It was a wild, hysterical sort of letter. It had taken six weeks to reach me, and it seemed likely she had changed her mind by that time. In any case I was just starting for an expedition into the Blue Mountains. I put her letter on one side to answer, but somehow I never did answer it. I thought she had probably exaggerated the whole thing. So I hoped for the best and let it slide."

"How wicked!" Frances said. "How contemptible!"

The condemnation in her voice was all the deeper for its quietness. She sat before him cold, impersonal as a judge, her eyes fixed straight before her.

A curious shiver went through the man. He got up to cover it, and resumed his pacing of the room.

"I was away for over two years," he went on, speaking as one impelled. "I never heard from her during that time. I almost forgot her. Then I came home. I found they had left Oxford. Did I tell you old Dermot Rotherby had held a professorship there, and Arthur was reading for the Bar? No one seemed to know where they were. Old Theodore, the Bishop, had been appointed to Burminster. I went to him, asked him for news. He said Dermot's health had broken down, and they had taken a farm in the country. They had never been much to one another. He spoke very vaguely of them. It was Aunt Dorothea who let it out. She told me Nan had died mysteriously—that there had been a child—that they had changed their name in consequence—and then she got badly scared and begged me not to let the Bishop know she had told me, and not to dream of going near them as it was more than my life was worth. I must admit I didn't feel drawn that way, since poor Nan was past help. So I decided to let sleeping dogs lie, and cleared out of the country again. I stayed away for some time, sometimes drifting back to London, but never for long. Then at last I got tired of wandering and came home. I went to Burminster, and met—you. You caught me then. You've held me ever since. And I could have won you—I

178

could have won you—" He stopped abruptly. "What's the good of talking? I've lost you now, haven't I? You'll never look at me again."

"Never," Frances said.

Her hands were clasped as she sat. There was no longer any agitation about her. She might have been a carven image, so still was she, so utterly aloof and removed from all emotion.

He glanced at her once or twice as he walked, and finally came and stood before her.

"I haven't told you quite everything even now," he said. "There's one thing I'm almost afraid to tell you. Shall I go on—or shall I hold my peace?"

"Go on!" she answered in the same dead-level voice.

"You think nothing matters now," he said. "You think you won't care. You're wrong. You will care—horribly."

"I think I have got to know," she said, "whatever it is."

"All right," he said recklessly. "You shall know. After some damnable fate had taken you to Tetherstones, after they had tried to murder me and failed, after that night at Fordestown when you refused to come with me, the devil entered into me, and I made up my mind I'd get you—at any cost. And so I played you a trick. I lied to you." He bent down, trying to read her impassive face. "Do you understand? I tricked you—to get you up here."

She did not flinch or give any sign of feeling. "Do you mean about my sketches?" she said.

"Yes. That's just what I do mean. I have got them all here. No one has seen them but myself."

A faint frown drew her forehead. "But you paid for them," she said.

"I know. That was part of my damned scheme to get you into my power. You were always so independent. I thought when once you realized that you had been living on my money, it would break your spirit."

"How—odd!" she said.

And that was all. No word of reproach or condemnation; yet the man winced as if he had been struck in the face.

"My God!" he said. "If you would only curse me! Any other woman would."

"But why?" she said. "The fault was mine. I always knew—in my heart—that you were—that sort of man."

"My God!" he said again. "You haven't much mercy."

She looked up at him. "I am sorry for you," she said. "But—I don't blame you. You were made that way."

He struck his fist into his hand. "Frances, I swear to you—I swear to you—No, what's the good of swearing? I'll show you. Look here! We won't talk any more to-night. We're both dead beat. I'll take you back to your hotel. And in a day or two—if you will trust me—I'll show you that I am not—that sort of man. Will you trust me, Frances? Give me this one chance of making good? I'm a blackguard, I own it; but I can play the game if I try. Will you trust me?"

There was a hint of desperation in his voice, and, because she was a woman, that reached her where mere protestations had failed.

She held out her hand to him mutely, and as he took it she rose to her feet, looking him straight in the eyes. But she did not utter one word. She had spoken her condemnation and there was nothing left to say.

Out of her despair, tragically but fearlessly, she faced him. And to the man in his abasement there came a sense of greatness such as he had never before known.

Not by strength and not by strategy, but by purity of heart, she had conquered the devil in his soul.

CHAPTER V
THE VISION

London skies and ceaseless rain, and the roar and swish of London traffic over the streaming roads! The tramp of many hurrying feet, the echo of careless voices vaguely heard, and the grey, grim river flowing out to sea! How terrible it was! How inevitable! How—lonely!

She stood—a slim dark, figure—in the recess of the bridge leaning against the stone balustrade while the crowds passed by unheeding, and looked down into the dark-flowing water.

How long would it take, she wondered, how long a struggle in those dreadful depths before the soul rose free? And then—even then—would it be freedom, or slavery of another kind, a striving against yet more awful odds, a sinking into yet more fearful depths? Her tired mind wandered to and fro over the problem. So easy to die, if that were all! But after death—what then? Having shirked the one issue, could she possibly hope to be in any sense better equipped for that which lay beyond? Having failed hopelessly to prove herself in the one life, could there be any possibility of making a better bargain for herself in the next? Her brain recoiled from the thought. No, deliverance did not lie that way.

Perhaps it did not lie anywhere, she told herself drearily. Perhaps there was no deliverance. Like the prisoners of old, shackled to that stone of fate, perhaps it was her lot to wait until it descended upon her. She had sought so desperately for a way of escape, and now every channel was closed to her. Further seeking—further striving—were useless. God alone could help her now.

She looked up at the grey sky and felt the cold rain beating down upon her. Who was it who had once said: "Ask and ye shall receive, seek and ye shall find, knock and it shall be opened unto you"? Strange that such words as those could ever be forgotten! They came upon her now almost as if they had been uttered aloud. And with them, very suddenly, came the memory of her prayer from the Tetherstones on the night of her great need. "From all evil and mischief, from sin, from crafts and assaults of the devil, Good Lord deliver us!" And how wonderful—how God-sent—had been her deliverance! The thought of little Ruth shot across her mind like a ray of light. Again the childish fingers seemed to clasp her own, closely, confidingly, lovingly. It was like a message to her soul—the angel of her deliverance!

It was then that the power to pray came to Frances, there on the open crowded bridge between the grey skies and the grey river with the grey stone to support her. She could not have said whence or how it came, but it possessed her for a space to the exclusion of all else. And she prayed—as she had prayed by little Ruth's death-bed—with a fervour and a depth of faith that amazed herself. Not for deliverance, not for a way of escape, only for strength in her weakness—only for sustenance, lest the journey be too great for her! And when she ceased to pray, when the great moment passed—all too quickly, as such moments always must—when she woke again to physical misery and physical exhaustion, to the dripping skies and the leaden world and the dank uncleanness of the atmosphere, though no sign of any sort came in answer, yet she knew that her prayer was heard.

She turned and left the bridge, still with the feeling of that little hand in hers, and a sense of relief that was almost rejoicing in her heart. Though she had lost everything, though she trod the stones of the wilderness and the way before her was dark and steep and wholly unfamiliar, yet her fear had gone. The burden was lifted. For she knew that she was not alone. She went back through the rain-soaked streets, and still it seemed to her that that angel-presence went with her, guiding her feet. She had come out to seek a cheap lodging, but now that purpose had gone from her. She returned to the great station and the vast hotel as one led.

She passed in under the echoing glass roof where the shrieking of trains mingled with the noise of the scurrying multitudes. Everyone was in a hurry, it seemed, except herself, and she—she moved without haste and without lingering to a destination unknown.

She turned in to the hotel vestibule, leaving the noise and the seething crowds, conscious of a great quietness that came as it were to meet her and folded her round. It was late afternoon, and her intention had been to give up her room, but she had not done so, and she did not now turn to the office. She went instead to a settee in a corner and sat down there as one who waited. A few people passed to and fro, but no one accosted her. The place was dim and restful. She took no interest in them, or they in her.

Somewhere in the distance a page-boy was calling a number in a raucous voice. No one responded to it, and she vaguely wished he would stop; for he intruded upon the peace of the atmosphere like a yapping dog heard in the silent hours of the night. Now he was drawing nearer and becoming more obtrusive. Why did not someone stop him? If he had a message why couldn't someone take it and send him away? Or if he couldn't find the person for whom it was intended, where was the use of continuing that untuneful yell?

"*Two—four—nine! Two—four—nine!*" Now he had left the lounge and was coming down the corridor to the vestibule! The thing was beginning to get upon her nerves. She drew further back into the corner as he approached. Quite a small boy, with the sharp rat-like features of his type, and gleaming brass buttons all down his front that reflected little knobs of light from a distant lamp! His voice was stupendous, shattering the peace, piercing her brain with its insistence, pulverizing the vision that had brought her thither.

"*Two—four—nine! Two—four—nine!*" He came close to her, paused, yelled the number straight at her so that she shrank, and then passed on to the almost empty vestibule where he continued his intolerable cry without result.

His voice began to pass into the distance, to merge into the vague sounds that penetrated from without. Now she heard it no longer, and she breathed a sigh of thankfulness, and tried to return to the state of quiescent waiting which he had so rudely disturbed. But something had happened. She realized it with almost a sense of calamity. The little fingers no longer clasped her own, the feeling of peace had left her. The vision had fled.

She made a desperate attempt to call it back, to force her mind to grasp afresh the power that had so magically inspired her. But it was gone. The outer darkness came down upon her once more. The blackness of despair entered into her soul.

She sat for a space in blank hopelessness. Then it was all a myth, that strength so wonderfully bestowed, the trick of an overwrought brain—no more! Her prayer had been in vain. She was alone and sinking—sinking! A sound of great waters suddenly filled her ears. She saw again the grim, dark river flowing to the sea—so deep, so cold, so terrible! She lifted her face, gasping, as though those awful waters were overwhelming her. Her heart had ceased to beat. It felt like a stone within her, and she was cold to the very soul of her.

Ah, God, what was that? A cry in the distance—a voice that called! What was it? What was it? She grabbed her failing faculties to listen. It might be even yet the salvation for which she had prayed and waited. It might be—ah, what was it and why did it hold her so?

Breathlessly she listened, and for those moments she was like a prisoner on the very brink of death, hearing afar off the arresting cry that meant—that might mean—a reprieve. Now it grew nearer, it grew louder, it filled the world,—the universe—like a trumpet that could not be ignored. Words came to her through the wild chaos of her mind—three short words flung like a challenge far and wide—now a demand, now a menace—so that all must surely stop to listen!

"*Two—four—nine! Two—four—nine!*" That page with the fiery buttons was returning!

Along the corridor he came, and she caught back a burst of terrible laughter that rose from her stone-cold heart at the sight. A minute figure with a brazen voice that bawled trumpet-wise, and bearing a brass salver with a telegram upon it. Now he approached her again, and she marvelled at the noise he made. Surely he was made of brass, this messenger whom no one heeded!

"*Two—four—nine! Two—four—nine!*" He came to her, he stopped again. He shouted his challenge full at her. Then he ceased.

He thrust the salver towards her, and spoke in a husky, confidential undertone. "Ain't that your number, miss?"

She stared at him, amazed rather by the unexpected cessation of the noise than by the words he spoke.

He thrust the salver a little nearer. "Ain't that your number?" he said again. "Two—four—nine! Thorold! Ain't that your name?"

She put out a hand mechanically. "Is it? Can it be? Yes, my name is Thorold."

Her voice came mechanically too; it had a deadened sound.

The boy's sharp eyes scanned her with pert curiosity. As she took the telegram, he pursed his lips to a whistle, but no sound issued from them.

She read the message in a sort of suspended silence that was peculiarly intense.

"I am in need of secretarial help if you care to resume your position here as a temporary measure. Please come to-night or wire. Rotherby. The Palace. Burminster."

A voice out of the void! A forgotten voice, but none the less clear! She looked up as it were through thinning mists and saw the boy's bright eyes watching her. Why was he interested, she wondered? What could it matter to him?

"Any answer, miss?" he suggested helpfully, and now she saw a gleam in the little rat-keen eyes and understood.

"No, none," she said, "none. I shall answer it in person."

He looked pinched for a moment, and then he grinned cheerily, impudently, philosophically.

"That's right, miss," he said. "Don't you lose no more time about it! Time's money to most of us."

And with that he turned to go, but sharply, on impulse, she stayed him. "Boy, wait!"

He waited at once. "Yes, miss? Anything I can do for you?"

"No, nothing," she said, "nothing. You have already done—much more than you know." She pushed a hand down into the pocket of her rain-coat and found a halfpenny that had been there ever since the coat had been new. "I've carried this for luck," she said, and managed to smile. "It's all I can offer you. Will you have it?"

He stared at her for a second, then his shrewd grin reappeared. "Not unless you'll toss me for it," he said. "There'd be no luck without."

She accepted the sporting suggestion. Strangely, in that moment, it appealed to her. She needed trivialities as never before.

"You can toss if you like," she said.

He took the coin and spun it, caught it deftly, and looked at her. "Heads, miss?" he questioned.

"Yes, heads," she agreed.

He slapped it forthwith on to the tray and handed it to her. "Heads it is—and I wish you good luck!" he said.

She picked up her halfpenny, for there was a compelling look in his eye which warned her that she was expected to play the game.

"Thank you," she said, finding nothing else to say.

He drew himself up with a comic assumption of the grand manner. His little beady eyes twinkled humorous appreciation of her action.

"You're welcome, miss," he said ceremoniously, and turning, tramped away with his salver under his arm.

He left her laughing in a fashion that eased the tension of her nerves and took from her that terrible hysterical feeling of being off her balance that had so nearly overwhelmed her. She returned the halfpenny to her pocket and sat motionless for a few seconds to recover.

Yes, her vision had departed, but her prayer was answered. A way was opened before her, and, stony and difficult though it might be, she knew that the needed strength to take it would be given. Her heart was beating again and alive with a great thankfulness. It was not the way she would have chosen, but what of that? It was not for her to choose.

And so, as her normal powers returned to her, she did not stay to question. She rose to obey.

CHAPTER VI
THE INQUISITOR

"I have been given to understand," said the Bishop, "that circumstances have arisen which have made you not unwilling to return to me for a time."

"Yes, that is so," Frances said, "if you care to make use of me."

She stood before him in the book-lined study where so many of her hours had been spent in bitter bondage of body and spirit. The table with its typewriter was in its accustomed position in the window, and beyond the window she caught a glimpse of the grey stone of the cloister-arch, no longer decked in purple but splashed with the crimson of autumn leaves. The morning sun shone warmly upon it. It was a glorious day.

She had travelled down by a night-train, and not till the official hour of ten o'clock had the Bishop accorded her an interview. His austere countenance displayed no vestige of welcome even now, yet she had a curious conviction that he was not wholly displeased by her prompt reply to his invitation. His greeting of her, though cold, had been without acidity.

"Pray sit down!" he said, indicating a chair. "I have a few questions to ask you before we proceed any further. I beg that you will reply to them as concisely as possible."

"I will do my best," Frances said.

She took the seat facing him, the morning-light unsparingly upon her, and she knew that he looked at her with a closer attention than he had ever before bestowed upon her, as she did so.

"I will came to the point," he said, in his curt, uncompromising way. "You realize of course that my message to you was not the result of chance, that I was actuated by a motive other than the mere desire to suit my own convenience?"

"Yes, I guessed that," she answered quietly.

He nodded, and she thought that the ascetic lines of his face became a shade less grim as he proceeded. "I will not disguise from you the fact that as a secretary I have not yet found your equal, but that was not my reason for sending you that message. Now, Miss Thorold, kindly pay attention to what I am going to say, for time is short. I am due to conduct the service in the Cathedral in less than half-an-hour. I have a question to ask you primarily to which I must have a simple and unequivocal answer. When I discharged you some three months ago from my employment, I believed that an intrigue of an unworthy nature existed between my nephew and yourself. I ask you now—and you will answer me as before God—has there ever been any justification for that belief either before or since?"

He spoke with great solemnity and emphasis. His eyes—-those fanatical deep-set eyes—were fixed upon her with an intensity that seemed to burn her.

"You will answer me," he said again, "as before God."

And Frances answered him with the simplicity of one to whom shame was unknown. "There has never been the smallest justification."

Something of tension went out of the Bishop's attitude, but he kept his eyes upon her with a scrutiny that never varied. "That being the case," he said, "on the assumption that you have nothing to hide, I am going to ask you to give me a brief—really a brief account, Miss Thorold, of all that has occurred between the date of your dismissal and the present time."

He spoke with the precision of one accustomed to instant obedience, but Frances stiffened at the request.

"I am sorry," she said. "But I am not prepared to do anything of the kind."

He lifted his thin brows. "You think my demand unreasonable?"

"Not only that. I think it impertinent," Frances said, and still she spoke with that simplicity which comes from the heart.

"In—deed!" said the Bishop.

There would have followed a difficult pause, but very quietly she filled it. "You see, there are some parts of one's life so sacred, that no man or woman on earth has any right to trespass there. In fact, I personally could not admit you even if I wished to do so. If I gave you the key, you would not know how to use it."

"You amaze me!" said the Bishop. He got up and began jerkily to pace the room, much as his nephew had done on the night that she had sat in judgment upon him. "Are you aware," he said after a moment, "that many men and women also have come to me with their confessions and have eased their souls thereby of many burdens?"

She watched him with her clear eyes as he moved, and in her look was something faintly quizzical. "Yes," she said, "I can believe that many people find relief in throwing their burdens upon someone else. With me, it is not so. I prefer to bear my own."

He stopped and confronted her. "You presume to treat this subject with levity!" he said.

"Oh, believe me, no!" She rose quickly and faced him. "I have been through too much for that. But what I have been through only God—who has kept me safe—will ever know. I could not even begin to tell an outsider that."

The earnestness of her speech carried weight in spite of him. His face softened somewhat. "You are a strange woman, Miss Thorold," he said. "But I am willing to believe that your motives are genuine though your methods do not always commend themselves to me. Sit down again, and kindly answer the few questions I shall put to you, which, you may as well be assured, are dictated neither by curiosity nor impertinence. I have been placed in a very peculiar position towards you, and I am doing what I conceive to be my duty."

That moved her also. Perhaps for the first time in her life, she looked at him with a certain respect. "I will answer your questions to the best of my ability, my lord," she said.

"Enough!" said the Bishop, and waved her back to her chair prior to reseating himself. "First then, when you left me, was it alone?"

"Quite alone," said Frances.

"And you went—where?"

"I went to a village on the moors called Brookside. It is a few miles from Fordestown. I found a lodging there."

"Ah! And my nephew knew your whereabouts?"

"Certainly he did. He had offered to find me employment. I had practically promised to be his secretary in the event of his writing a book."

"You did not consider that in any sense an indiscreet thing to do?" questioned the Bishop.

She felt herself colour slightly, but she answered him without hesitation. "Yes, I did. But beggars can't be choosers. I tried to keep things on a business footing. I thought he was merely sorry for me. I did not realize—" she stopped abruptly.

"That he was strongly attracted by you?" suggested the Bishop.

"I did not think that I was sufficiently attractive for that to be possible," she answered with simplicity.

The flicker of a smile crossed his hard features. "You do not know human nature very well," he observed. "But to continue! You went to Brookside. And then?"

"He came to see me there," Frances said.

"And made love to you?"

"Yes."

"Against your will?" asked the Bishop.

She met his look with great directness. "No, it was not—at first—against my will. But I misunderstood him. And he misunderstood me.

Afterwards—very soon afterwards—I found out my mistake. That is all I have to say upon that subject. It is over and done with now, and I do not wish to think of it again."

"I fear it has led to various complications," said the Bishop, "which make it impossible to dismiss the matter in that fashion. However, we will pass on. May I ask you to give me the bald details of what followed?"

She hesitated. That he was already in possession of most of the circumstances attending her sojourn at Tetherstones was a fact which she did not question, but she had a strong repugnance to discussing them with him.

He read it, and in a moment, with a courtesy that surprised her, he tried to set her at her ease.

"You need not scruple," he said, "to speak freely to me upon this matter. Nothing that you may tell me will go beyond this room."

"Thank you," she said, but still she hesitated. She could not tell him of that terrible night with Montague upon the moors. At last, with an effort, "I had an unpleasant adventure," she said. "I was lost in a fog. A little blind girl from a farm near by called Tetherstones found me, and took me home with her. I was ill after that, and they nursed me."

"They?" queried the Bishop.

"The Dermots," she said.

"Ah!" said the Bishop.

He sat for a space lost in thought, his eyes still fixed upon her.

"Tell me about them!" he said at length. "Of what does the family now consist?"

She told him, and he listened with close attention.

"What is the father like?" he asked then.

"He is an invalid," she said. "The son works the farm, and the girls all help. The mother spends most of her time looking after the old man."

"Is he very old?" asked the Bishop.

"Very, I should say," she answered.

"And the child—she is blind, you say?"

"Not now," said Frances gently. "She is dead."

He bent his head. "How did she come to die?"

"It was an accident," Frances said. "It happened one night——"

She stopped. He was looking at her strangely, almost as if he suspected her of trying to deceive him.

"You are sure it was an accident?" he said.

She gazed back at him in amazement. "How could it have been anything else?"

He made a peculiar gesture as if to check her questioning. "And the old man? Tell me more about him! What form does his malady take?"

His manner was compelling. She found herself answering, though wonder still possessed her. "He suffers with his heart, and at times his brain wanders a little. He gave me the impression of being worn out, but I did not see a great deal of him."

"You never saw him when he was ill?" said the Bishop.

"Yes, once." She paused.

"Once?" repeated the Bishop.

"Yes. He was not quite himself at the time. I sat with him for an afternoon. He spoke rather strangely, I remember. He—" Again she paused. Memory was crowding back upon her. The inexplicable horror with which that day she had been inspired returned to her. And suddenly a strange thing happened. It was as if a curtain had been rent aside, showing her in a single blinding moment of revelation the phantom of terror from whose unseen presence she had so often shrunk in fear.

She uttered a sharp gasp, and turned from the hard eyes that watched her. "That is all I can tell you," she said.

He made no comment of any sort, refraining from pressing her upon the subject with a composure that left her completely at a loss as to his state of mind. Her own mind at the moment was in chaos, so sudden and so overwhelming had been her discovery. She marvelled at her previous blindness, but she asked no question even in her bewilderment. Her loyalty to her friends at Tetherstones held her silent.

She was conscious of an urgent desire to be alone, to trace this thing to its source, to sort and arrange the many odd memories that now chased each other in wild confusion through her brain, to fit together once and for all this puzzle, the key to which had just been so amazingly given her.

But the Bishop still sat before her, an uncompromising inquisitor who would not suffer her to go until he had obtained the last iota of information that he desired.

He spoke, with cold peremptoriness. "Well, Miss Thorold, there remains the matter of your further adventures with my nephew. Your sojourn at Tetherstones at the time of your illness did not—apparently—terminate these. Do you object to telling me under what circumstances you left the Dermots?"

"I left them finally to get work," she said.

"And in the first place?" said the Bishop.

She met his look again. "In the first place I left them at night with your nephew. We went to an inn at Fordestown. He went up to town the next day, and I took a lodging in the place. I went back to Tetherstones about a week later at the request of old Dr. Square who attended them. The little girl was ill and wanted me. She died that night."

"And you stayed on?" said the Bishop.

"I stayed on until two days ago, when I also went to town in the hope of selling some of my sketches. Your nephew had offered to help me."

"And that was your sole reason for going?" he said.

"No, not my sole reason." She spoke deliberately, and said no more.

"But the only one you are prepared to give me?" he said.

"Yes," she answered with decision.

He looked at his watch. "And you are not disposed to tell me how you came to run away—at night—with my nephew, a man with whom you wish me to believe that you had no desire to be associated?"

"No," said Frances quietly.

"My opinion in the matter carries no weight?" he suggested.

She knitted her brows a little. "I would certainly rather you believed in me," she said. "But—I cannot give you any convincing reason for so doing."

"You can if you wish," said the Bishop.

She shook her head. "I am afraid not."

He rose. "By answering two questions which concern yourself alone. First, why are you not willing to marry my nephew?"

She looked at him, slightly startled. "Because I don't love him," she said.

"Thank you," said the Bishop. "And is there any other man whom you would be willing to marry?"

His eyes held her. She felt the blood surge over her face, but she could not turn away. He waited inexorably for her reply.

For a space she did battle with him, then very suddenly, almost whimsically, she yielded.

"Yes, my lord," she said, and she spoke with a certain pride.

He held out his hand to her abruptly; there was even a glimmer of approval in his look. "Miss Thorold, you have convinced me," he said. "I have misjudged you, and I will make amends."

It was not an apology. There was not a shadow of regret in his words, scarcely even of kindness, yet, oddly, they sent a rush of feeling to her heart that swept away her self-control. She stood speechless, fighting her emotion.

"Enough!" said the Bishop, turning aside. "I must go to prepare for the service. Perhaps you would like to walk in the garden and find refreshment there. I will ask you later to resume your secretarial duties."

He was gone. She heard the door shut definitely behind him, and the garden with its old-world peace seemed to call her. Storm-tossed and weary, she went out into the warm sunlight, thanking God with her tears.

CHAPTER VII
FAIR PLAY

The deep tones of the Cathedral organ thrilled across the quiet garden. There came the chanting of boys' voices, and then a silence. She wandered on through the enchanted stillness, past the cloister arch, and so by winding paths down to the haunted water whither her Fate had led her on that summer night that seemed so long ago.

Her tears had ceased. She walked like a nun, her hands folded before her. The pain in her heart was wonderfully stilled. She was not thinking of herself any more, but of Tetherstones, and the grim secret that had so suddenly been bared to her gaze. She saw it all now—or nearly all—that skeleton which they kept so closely locked away, and she marvelled at her blindness. To have lived among them, and to have seen so little!

The gentle white-haired mother with her patient silence—the chattering girls darkly hinting yet never revealing—the sombre prematurely-aged man who ruled them all, grinding the stones for bread, bitterly trampling all his ambitions underfoot, refusing to eat of the tree of life lest he should fail in that to which he had set his hand! And little Ruth—little Ruth—who had lived and died among them in her innocence—the child whom none had wanted but all had loved,—the child whose passing had wrung those terrible tears from the man who had never seemed to care!

Yes, she held the key to it all—that agony of despair, that extremity of suffering. The Bishop's question: "You are sure it was an accident?" The old man's halting enquiries—his relief at her reply—and then later his wandering words that had awakened such horror within her! His three-fold vow! What had he meant by that? And the place of sacrifice—the place of sacrifice! Again she seemed to hear the mumbled words. And her mind, leaping from point to point, caught detail after detail in a stronger light.

Now the picture of that terrible night stood out vividly before her. That shot in the moonlight, and her own conviction of tragedy! The coming of little Ruth to her deliverance—the banging of the door! Only Grandpa! The child's words rushed back upon her. Only Grandpa! He had come in after those shots, had gone to the kitchen. How she remembered his weary, dragging gait! And she had fled—and she had fled! Again little Ruth's words came back to her: "Oh, please come!" Ah, why had she not stayed with Ruth that night?

And the child had set out to seek her. Possibly she had gone to the old man first to see if she had returned to the kitchen, and not finding her, had hastened out to the Stones to search.

She tried to turn her imagination at this point, but a power stronger than herself urged it on. She saw the child flitting like a spirit through the night, over the lawn and through the nut-trees, pausing often to listen, but always flitting on again. She saw a dark shadow that followed, avoiding the open spaces, but never pausing at all. And she remembered the eyes that once had glared at her through those nut-trees and she had deemed them a dream!

Now she saw Ruth again out in the corn-field, hastening over the stubble, drawing near to the Stones—that place where the giant harebells grew. And the Stones themselves rose up before her, stark in the moonlight, and the great Rocking Stone which a child could set in motion from below but which none might overthrow. And the flitting form was climbing it to find her—ah, why had she left little Ruth that night?

The place of sacrifice! The place of sacrifice! The words ran with a mocking rhythm through her brain. She saw it all—the childish figure poised in the moonlight—the lurking shadow behind—a movement at first imperceptible, gathering in weight and strength as the great Stone swayed forward—and perhaps a faint cry. . . . She covered her eyes to blot out the dreadful vision. Ah, little Ruth! Little Ruth!

When she looked up again, it had passed. Yet for a space her mind dwelt upon the old man and his helplessness—his pathetic dignity—his loneliness. And the mother with the eyes that were too tired to weep! She could understand it all now. Piece by piece the puzzle came together. She did not wonder any longer at the devotion that had inspired them all to sacrifice. They had done it for the mother's sake. Ah, yes, she could understand!

She reached the yew-tree by the lake where she and Montague had hidden together and stood still. The dark boughs hanging down screened the further side from her view, but the small fizz of a cigarette-end meeting the water awakened her very swiftly from her reverie. She drew herself together with an instinctive summoning of her strength to meet him.

But when he came round the great tree and joined her, she knew no fear, only a sense of the inevitableness of the interview.

He spoke at once, without greeting of any sort. "I've been waiting for you. You've seen the Bishop?"

"Yes," she made answer. "He has been—very good to me."

"I can hardly imagine that," said Rotherby dryly. "But he means well. Look here! I don't know whether you'll be angry, but I've told him everything. It was the only thing to do."

She stood before him with grave eyes meeting his. "Why should I be angry?" she said. "I think it was—rather brave of you."

"Brave!" he echoed, and his lips twisted a little as though they wanted to sneer. "Would you say that of the cur that takes refuge behind your skirt? No, wait! I'm not here to torment you with that sort of platitudes. It doesn't matter what you think of me. I don't count. You'll never see me again after this show is over. I promise you that. I've led you a devil's dance, but I'm nearly done. There's only one figure left, and you've got to step that whether you want to or not."

"What do you mean?" Frances said, arrested rather by the recklessness of his speech than by the words he spoke.

"I'll tell you," said Rotherby. "It'll be something of a shock, I warn you. But you have pluck enough for a dozen. First then, I've got to own up to a lie. You remember that affair at Tetherstones—when I was shot waiting for you?"

"Oh yes," she said. "Yes." She knew what was coming, yet she waited for it with an odd breathlessness. Somehow so much seemed to hang upon it.

"It was not Arthur Dermot who fired that shot," Rotherby said. "It was the old man, and he meant murder too. But Arthur and Oliver were both there and that put him off. They turned up unexpectedly from different directions and chased him, but somehow he got away. I bolted—with my usual bravery." Again she saw his twisted smile. He went on, scarcely pausing. "I didn't tell you the truth for several reasons. I daresay you can guess what they were. Arthur is sane enough except when he sees red. But the old man—well, the old man is a raving lunatic at times, though he has his lucid intervals, I believe. He ought to be shut up of course, but his wife has never been able to face it. Some women are like that. You would be. They keep him shut up when he goes off the rails. I believe he has only got one serious mania, and that is to kill me. So it has been fairly easy to guard against that until lately. It was poor Nan's trouble that sent him off his head in the first place, but if I had kept out of the way he would probably have remained harmless. You understand that, do you?"

"I am beginning to understand—many things," Frances said. But she could not speak of little Ruth to him.

He also seemed glad to pass on. "Well we needn't discuss that any further. He got wind of my coming, and he did his best to out me. He didn't succeed—perhaps fortunately, perhaps otherwise. Now to come to Arthur! He would have left me alone if it hadn't been for you. You realize that, of course?"

"Oh yes," Frances said, wondering with a faint impatience why he harped upon the matter.

He saw the wonder and grimly smiled at it. "I realized that too," he said. "It has simplified matters considerably. I told you I would play the game. Well, I've played it. After I had got down here yesterday and seen the Bishop, I wrote to Arthur. I told him the whole truth from beginning to end. He hasn't any illusions left by this time concerning you—or me either."

"Ah, what made you do that?" Frances said.

Strangely in that moment, deeply as his words concerned her, it was not of herself she thought, but of the man before her, with his drawn, haggard face in which cynicism struggled to veil suffering.

"I don't know why you did that," she said. "It was not necessary. It was not wise."

"It was—fair play," he said, and still with set lips he smiled. "I did more than that, and I shall do more still—unless you relieve me of the obligation."

"What do you mean?" she said. "What can you mean?"

A growing sense of uneasiness possessed her. Did he know Arthur Dermot's nature? Was it not madness to dare again that tornado of fury from which she had so strenuously fought to deliver him? It had not been an easy thing, that deliverance. She had sacrificed everything to accomplish it, and now he had refuted all. "I think you must be mad," she said. "Tell me what you mean!"

The bitter lines deepened about his mouth. "I will tell you," he said, "and once more seek the refuge of your generous protection. I told him that I should go to-day to Fordestown, and from Fordestown I would meet him at the Stones at any hour that he cared to appoint, to give him such further satisfaction as he might wish to demand."

"Montague!" The name broke from her, little accustomed as she was to utter it. "Are you really mad?" she said. "Are you quite, quite mad?"

"I am not," he answered briefly.

"But—but he will kill you if you meet again!"

192

She gasped the words breathlessly. This thing must be stopped. At all costs it must be stopped.

He was still smiling in that odd, drawn way. She did not understand his look. He raised his shoulders at her words.

"He may. What of it?"

"Oh, you mustn't go!" she said. "It would be madness—madness."

"I have had my answer," said Rotherby.

"You have?" She stared at him. "What is it? Quick! Tell me!"

He pulled a telegram from his pocket and gave it to her. She opened it with shaking hands. Three words only—brief, characteristic, uncompromising! "*To-night at ten.*" No signature of any sort—only the bald reply!

She gazed at it in silence. And before her inward sight there rose a vision of the man himself as she had seen him last, terrible in his wrath, overwhelming in his condemnation. Yet her heart leapt to the vision. He was the man she loved.

She looked up. "You mustn't go," she said. "Or if you do—I shall come too."

"No," said Rotherby.

She met his look. "Why do you say that? What do you mean?"

"I mean that you will never go anywhere with me again," he said.

"But—but—" she stumbled over the words, hearing other words ringing like hammer-strokes in her brain,—"he will kill you—he has sworn to kill you if you go his way again."

"Do you think you could prevent it," said Rotherby.

She crumpled the paper in her hand. "Yes, I could—I would—somehow."

"Very well. You can," he said.

His manner baffled her. She looked at him uncertainly. "Tell me what you mean!" she said again.

He made a curious gesture, as of a player who tosses down his last card knowing himself a loser. "I mean," he said, "that you can go in my place. Either that—or I go alone."

Then she understood him, read the strategy by which he had sought to prove himself, and a deep pity surged up within her, blotting out all that had gone before.

"But I couldn't possibly go," she said. "It wouldn't really help either, though—" she halted a little—"I know quite well what made you do it—and—I am grateful."

"One of us will go," Rotherby said with decision. "That I swear to God. It is for you to decide which."

There was indomitable resolution in his voice. Very suddenly she realized that the way before her was barred. She drew back instinctively.

"But that is absurd," she said. "You know quite well that there is nothing to be gained by going."

193

"Except a modicum of self-respect," said Rotherby. "It may not be worth much, but, strange to say, I value it. I will forego it for your sake, but for no other consideration under the sun."

He was immovable; she saw it. Yet in despair she made another effort to move him. "But how could I go?" she protested. "It is utterly out of the question. You know it is out of the question."

"Do I know it?" said Rotherby, with his faint half-scoffing smile.

"If you think at all, you must," she said. "I couldn't possibly face it. Not after—after——"

"After he has been told the truth in such a fashion that he cannot possibly doubt you," said Rotherby. "Forgive me, but I thought—love—was capable of anything. If it isn't, well—as I said before—I go alone. That is quite final, so we needn't argue about it. There is a train to Fordestown at five this afternoon. I shall go by that, and pick up a conveyance at the station."

"There are none," she said, clutching at a straw.

"Then I shall go to The Man in the Moon for one. Anyway, I shall keep my appointment—with time to spare," said Rotherby. "You might give us a thought before you turn in. It'll be an interesting interview—even more so than our last."

He swung upon his heel with the words, but Frances threw out a hand, grasping his arm.

"Montague,—please—you're not in earnest! You can't be! I mean—it's so utterly preposterous."

He stood still, the smile gone from his face. Very suddenly he threw aside the cloak of irony in which he had wrapped himself, and met her appeal with absolute sincerity.

"I am in earnest," he said. "And it is not preposterous. Can't you realize that a time may come in a man's life when just for his own soul's sake he has got to prove to himself that he is not an utter skunk? It doesn't matter what other people think. They can think what they damn' well please. But he himself—the thing that goes with him always, that sleeps when he sleeps and wakes when he wakes—do you think he can afford to be out with that? By God, no! Life isn't worth having under those conditions. I'd sooner die and be damned straight away."

He laughed upon the words, but it was a laugh of exceeding bitterness. And there came to Frances in that moment the conviction that what he said was right. No power on earth can ever compensate for the loss of self-respect.

Somehow that passionate utterance of his went straight to her heart. If she had not forgiven him before, her forgiveness was now complete and generous. She saw in him in the hour of his repentance the man whom once she could have loved, and she was deeply moved thereby.

"Are you satisfied?" he said. "Have I convinced you that I am playing the game—or trying to?"

She met his eyes though she knew that her own were wet. "Yes, I am convinced," she said. "I am satisfied."

"And what are you going to do?" he questioned.

Very simply she made answer. "I will go to Tetherstones."

He drew a hard breath. "You're not afraid?"

"No," she said.

He put an urgent hand on her shoulder. "Frances," he said, "you must make him understand."

"He will understand," she said.

He bent towards her. His voice came huskily. "It isn't only—for myself," he said. "You know that?"

"I know," she said.

"I want to win your forgiveness," he said, and there was appeal in the pressure of his hand. "Have I got that?"

"Yes," she said.

"You are sure?" Voice and touch alike pleaded with her.

She felt the tears welling to her eyes. "From my very heart," she said. "Yes, I am sure."

She offered him both her hands, and he took and held them closely for a space, then abruptly he let them go.

"You will never love me," he said, "but it may please you some day to remember that you taught me how to love."

And with that he turned and walked away from her, not suffering himself to look back. She knew even as she watched him go that he would keep his word and that she would never see him again.

Out of sheer pity it came to her to call him back, but a stronger impulse held her silent. She became aware very suddenly of the crumpled paper in her hand, and, as the solitude of the place came about her with his going, she spread it open once again and read.

CHAPTER VIII
THE PLACE OF SACRIFICE

An owl was hooting in the moonlit distance, and the ripple, ripple, ripple of running water filled in the silences. A vast loneliness—the loneliness of the moors at night which is somehow like an unseen presence—wrapped the whole world as in a mantle which the weird cry of the wandering bird pierced but could not lift. The scent of wet bog-myrtle with now and then a waft of late honeysuckle was in the air. And from the east, silver, majestic, wonderful, a moon that was nearly full mounted upwards to her throne above the earth.

The rough track that led to the Stones was clearly defined in its radiance, and the Stones themselves stood up like sentinels on the hill. A wonderful place! Yes, a wonderful place, but how desolate, and barbaric in its desolation!

A woman stood at the gate that opened from the lane on to that steep track. She had walked up from the village in the moonlight, and before her it was as clear as day, but she stood as one hesitating to emerge from the shadows. Her hands were folded together as if in prayer.

A vagrant breeze stirring the high hedges that bordered the lane made her turn her head sharply to listen, and a faint, vague sound from down the hill brought a further movement of attention from her. But the sound ceased—it might have been some scurrying wild thing—the wind died down, sighing sadly away, and all was quiet again, save for that unseen, trickling water, and the far, haunting cry of the owl on the hill-side.

But her own movement had given her courage, or perhaps she feared to remain; for she paused no longer at the gate. Noiselessly she opened it and passed through. Then closing it, she stood for a moment, looking back. Down the lane a light glimmered, fitfully, seen through tree-branches—Tetherstones.

Her eyes sought it with a certain wistfulness, dwelt upon it, then resolutely, with a sigh half-checked she turned and mounted the hill, walking rapidly and soundlessly over the short grass beside the track. Nearer and nearer she drew to the Stones in their gaunt splendour, and the spell of the place encompassed her like an enchantment; but she hesitated no more. Firmly, steadfastly, she pursued her way.

Once indeed she gave a great start as a horned creature blundered suddenly up in front of her, and dashed away with clattering feet over the scattered stones, but she checked her instinctive alarm with swift self-assertion. It was only a goat more startled than herself. What was there to fear?

She came at last into the great circle, pushing through coarse straggling grass till she reached the smooth, boulder-strewn turf where the sheep and the goats had grazed. And here she stopped and looked around her in the moonlight with the feeling strong upon her that she was being watched.

Again, with an effort of will, she dismissed the thought. It was the stark emptiness of the place that induced it; of that she was certain. For there was no sign of movement anywhere; only the great Tether Stones standing round, a grim challenge to the centuries. She turned slowly after a time and faced the Rocking Stone. More than ever now in the moonlight had it the appearance of rolling towards her, as though set in motion by some unseen hand. And she shuddered as she watched it. The eeriness of the place was beginning to fold itself around her irresistibly, almost suffocatingly.

"Why should I be afraid?" she whispered to herself, clenching her hands desperately to keep down the panic that was knocking at her heart. "There is nothing here to hurt me. They are only stones."

Only stones! Yet they seemed to threaten her by their very immobility, their coldness, their silence. She was an intruder in their midst, and whichever way she turned that sensation of being watched went with her, oppressed her. The hooting of the owl in the distance was somehow like the calling of a lost spirit, wandering to and fro, seeking rest—and finding none. . . . There was no other sound in all the world, though her ears were strained to listen. Even the music of the streams was hushed up here.

"They are only stones," she said to herself again, and began to walk down the centre of the circle towards the Rocking Stone, defying that engulfing, fateful silence with all her strength. Within a dozen yards of it something stopped her, as surely as if a hand had caught her back. She stood still, not breathing.

Was it fancy? Was it reality? The monstrous thing was moving! Like a seated giant giving her salutation it swayed slowly forward. And what were those long, crimson streaks upon it that gleamed as if wet in the moonlight?

She stood as one transfixed, possessed by horror. A devil's paradise! The words rushed meteor-like through her brain. Surely this gruesome place was haunted by devils!

Fascinated, she watched the great stone. Would it leave its resting-place, roll down to her, annihilate her? Had it started upon its dread course she knew she could not have avoided it. She was paralyzed by terror, possibly the more intense because of its utter unreason.

That some animal might have set the thing in motion was a possibility that did not even cross her mind. She knew, without any proof, that some evil influence was at work. She could feel it with every gasping breath she drew.

Downwards and yet further downwards rocked the great Stone, and at the last there came a grinding noise as though some substance were being pulverized beneath it. It was unutterably horrible to the looker-on, but still she could not turn and flee. She was as much a prisoner as though she were indeed tethered to one of those grim monsters that stood about her.

Spell-bound as one in a nightmare, she stood and watched, quaking and powerless, saw the thing begin to lift again like some prehistoric beast of prey rising from its slaughtered victim, saw it roll slowly back again soundlessly, as if on hinges, with the inevitable poise which alone kept it in its place, saw the dreadful crimson streaks and patches that dripped down its scarred front. And suddenly the bond that held her snapped. She turned from the dreadful sight and fled through the ghastly solitude as if she fled for her life.

Again the cry of the owl sounded, much nearer now, and she thought it was the shriek of a pursuing demon. Through that grass-grown place of sacrifice she tore like the wind, so goaded by fear as to be hardly conscious of direction. And now the shriek of the demon had become a yell of mocking laughter that died away with dreadful echoes among the Stones. . . .

She reached the open hill-side beyond that awful Circle, and here abruptly she was stayed. A maddening pain awoke in her side and she could go no further. The pain was acute for a few seconds, and she crouched in the grass in her extremity, fighting for breath. Then, gradually recovering, she began to tell her racing heart that she had fled from shadows. Yet it was no shadow that had moved that Rocking Stone.

Her strength returned to her at last and she stood up. But she could not return to that terrible trysting-place. Her knees were shaking still. There was only one course left if she would keep her tryst, and though her whole soul shrank from the thought of it, yet was she in honor bound to fulfil that pledge. Since she could not return, she must wait on the hill-side till he came. The appointed time must be drawing near now, and if she knew him he would not be late.

Even with the thought there rose a sound from the valley below her,—a clear and beautiful sound that went far to dispel that sense of lurking evil that so oppressed her—the church-clock striking ten. It renewed her courage, it stilled that wild, insensate fear within her. It gave her the power that belongs to purity.

No longer weak and stumbling, she left the spot where she had crouched and walked across the grass towards the track by which he would come. And as she went, there came to her the clang of the gate that led out of the lane. He was coming!

She realized abruptly that she could not stand and await him in the full moonlight. The shadows of the Stones fell densely not fifty yards away, and, conquering that instinct that urged her in the opposite direction, she directed her steps towards them. The consciousness of another human presence went far to disperse the ghostly influence of the place. The definite effort that lay before her drove the thought of forces less concrete into the background. At the very entrance to the arena, screened by the shadow of the first great Tether Stone she waited for him.

Immediately below her was the cattle-shed with its thatched roof, within which she and Montague Rotherby had found shelter on that night of fog when deliverance had so wonderfully come to her. Her mind dwelt upon the memory for a moment, then swiftly flashed back to the present, for, distinct in the stillness, there came to her the sound of his feet upon the track. Her heart gave a wild bound of recognition. How well she knew that sound!

Slow and regular and unfalteringly firm, they mounted the steep ascent while she stood waiting in the shadow. Now she could see him, a dark and powerful figure, walking with bent head, coming straight towards her, pursuing his undeviating course. Now he was close at hand. And now—

What moved her suddenly to look towards the cattle-shed—the flash of something that gleamed with a steely brightness in the moonlight, or an influence more subtle and infinitely more compelling. She knew not, but in that moment she looked, and looking, sprang forward with a cry. For in the entrance, clear against the blackness behind, she saw a face, corpse-like in its whiteness, but alive with a murderous malice,—the face of a devil.

Her cry arrested the man upon the path. He stood still, and she rushed to him with arms outspread, intervening between him and the evil thing that lurked in the shed.

She reached him, flung her arms around him. "Arthur—Arthur! For God's sake—come away from this dreadful place—this dreadful place!"

Wildly she poured forth the words, seeking with frantic urgency to turn him from the path. But he stood like a rock, resisting her.

"What are you doing here?" he said.

She tried to tell him, but explanation failed. "I came to meet you, but—there is—there is something dreadful in the barn. Don't go near! Come away! Oh, come away!"

But still he stood, resisting her desperate efforts to move him. "I have come to meet Rotherby," he said. "You go—and let me meet him alone!"

The curt words steadied her somewhat, but she could not let him go. "Arthur, please,—listen!" she urged. "He isn't here. I came in his place. But there is something terrible in the shed. I don't know what. I only know—I only know—that the whole place is full of evil, and the thing I saw—the thing I saw—is probably one of many."

She was trembling violently, and his hand came up and supported her. "Oh, why did you come?" he said, and his tone held more of reproach than questioning.

She answered him notwithstanding. "I had to come. There was no choice. But don't let us stay! I have seen the Rocking Stone move. I have seen—a thing like a devil in the barn."

"How long have you been here?" he said.

She was shivering still. "I don't know—a long time. But that awful thing——"

He turned towards the barn. "Your nerves have been playing you tricks," he said. "There is nothing here."

She hung back, still clinging to him, reassured by his confidence in spite of herself, yet afraid beneath her reassurance.

"It couldn't have been fancy. I am not fanciful. Arthur, don't go! Don't go!"

He stopped and looked at her, and in his eyes was that which strangely moved her, stilling her entreaty, overwhelming her fear, banishing every thought in her heart but the one great rapture of her soul as it leaped to his.

So for a long moment they stood, then his arm went round her. He turned aside.

"We will go to the Stones," he said, "and leave these banshees to look after themselves. It was probably a goat you saw."

She went with him, almost convinced that he was right and that her fancy had tricked her. She would have gone with him in that moment if all the ghosts of the centuries had awaited them among the Stones.

As they passed into the great arena, he uttered a groan, and his arm relaxed and fell. "This is absolute madness," he said. "I told you before. I am tied. I am a prisoner. I shall never be free." The iron of despair was in his voice.

"Then I will be a prisoner too," she said.

"No—no! Why did that scoundrel send you to me? Why didn't he come himself?" He flung the words passionately, as though the emotions surging within him were greater than he could control.

But she answered him steadfastly, without agitation. "Arthur, listen! He sent me to you because he is ashamed of all that has gone before—and because he wished to make amends. He has gone out of my life. But I have forgiven him, and—some day—I hope you will forgive him too."

"Never!" he said. "Never! I would have killed him with my naked hands if I had had the chance."

She suppressed a shiver at the memory his words called up. "That is not worthy of you. Forgiveness is a greater thing than revenge—oh, so much greater. And love is greater than all. You won't believe it, but—he was capable of love."

"He was capable of anything," Arthur said, "except playing a straight game."

"You are wrong," she said earnestly. "You are wrong. He has played a straight game now in telling you the truth and in sending me to you. He made me come, do you understand? I didn't want to—I would rather have done anything than come. But he would have come himself if I hadn't. And so———"

"You came to save his life?" suggested Arthur, with a bitter sneer.

She answered him with the simplicity that is above bitterness. "I came to save you both."

He looked at her with a certain grimness. "And why didn't you want to come?"

Again with absolute directness she answered him. "Because I knew how it would hurt you to send me away again."

He swung away from her and again she heard him groan. "This is well named the place of sacrifice," he said. "Do you remember the day I first brought you here? I loved you then, and I knew it was hopeless—utterly hopeless. It is more so than ever now. I can't go on. I won't go on. This thing has got to stop. God knows I have fought it. You have got to fight it too,—go on fighting till it dies."

"It will rise again," she said.

His hands clenched. "I've never been beaten yet," he said.

To which she made no answer, for she knew, as he did, that there is no power in earth or heaven so omnipotent as the power of Love.

They went on together, side by side down that great arena, the gaunt Stones all around them like monstrous idols in a forgotten place of worship. They drew near to the Rocking Stone, and very suddenly Arthur stopped.

He stood before it in utter silence, and she wondered what was passing in his mind. The moonlight shone full upon the face of the Stone. She saw again those strange red streaks of which old Mr. Dermot had told her. But her fear was gone, swallowed up in that which was infinitely greater—her love for the man at her side.

How long they stood thus she did not know. She began to realize that he was bracing himself anew for sacrifice, that he was battling desperately for the mastery against odds such as even he had never faced before. She saw him once more as a gladiator, terrible in his resolution, indomitable as the Stone he faced, invincible so long as the breath remained in his body. His last words kept hammering in her brain with the swing and rhythm of a haunting refrain: "I've never been beaten yet—I've never been beaten yet." And through them, faint, thread-like as a far-off echo, she heard another voice—whether of child or angel she knew not: "You'll find it up by the Stones, where the giant hare-bells grow. It's the most precious thing in the world, and when you find it, keep it—always—always—always!"

The giant hare-bells! There they grew at the foot of that grim Stone where the child had lain all night, unafraid because God was there. She saw them, pale in the moonlight, and in memory of little Ruth she stooped to gather one.

It was then that it happened,—so suddenly, so appallingly,—with a crash as if the heavens were rent above her. A blinding red flame seemed to spring from the very ground in front of her, the smell of burning choked her senses. The whole world rocked and burst into a blaze. She went backwards, conscious of Arthur's arms around her, conscious that they fell together . . . or were they hurled into space among the wandering star-atoms to drift for evermore hither and thither—spirits without a home?

"From all evil and mischief, from sin, from the crafts and assaults of the devil, from Thy wrath—and from everlasting damnation" (that dreadful irremediable doom in which she had never believed), "Good Lord, deliver us."

CHAPTER IX
WHERE THE GIANT HARE-BELLS GROW

Who was that whispering behind the screen—Lucy and Nell, could it be, audible as ever, though hidden from sight? It was like a long-forgotten story, begun years since and never finished.

"Dr. Square says she may just drift away and never recover consciousness at all; but her heart is a little stronger than it was, and she is able to take nourishment, so she may rally and sleep it off. I wonder if she will remember anything if she does."

"Oh, I hope—I hope she won't!" This was surely Lucy's voice, hushed and tearful. "She may have seen him lying dead, all torn by the explosion. It would be dreadful for her to remember that."

"Well, thank God he is dead!" Nell spoke stoutly, as one expectant of rebuke. "The life we have led has been enough to kill us all. Whatever happens, things must get better now."

"Oh, hush!" imploringly from Lucy. "It is wrong—it must be wrong to talk like that."

"I don't see why," combatively from Nell. "God must have arranged it all. And when you've carried a burden that's too big for you, it can't be wrong to be thankful when He takes it away."

"But think of Mother!" Lucy's whisper was broken with tears.

"I do think of her. And I know she is thankful too. My dear, you are thankful yourself. Why disguise it? It isn't wrong to be thankful." Nell spoke with vigorous decision. "If only *she* gets over this—and I don't see why she shouldn't, for it's only shock, nothing else—why, all our troubles will be over. The inquest was the simplest thing in the world—nothing but sympathy and condolences, no tiresome questions at all. I'm ashamed of you, Lucy, for having so little spirit. Don't you see what it means to us? Why, we're free—we're free—we're free!"

To which, sighing, Lucy could only answer, "It doesn't seem right. And she hasn't got over it yet, and even if she does——"

"Which she will!" Nell's voice arose above a whisper and ran with confidence. "Which she shall and will! How I would like to know what brought her there! I wonder if she will ever tell us."

"I wonder," murmured Lucy.

Thereafter for a space there was silence, and then there began that gradual groping towards the light which comes to a brain awakening. Who was it who was lying dead among the Stones? And why were they all so thankful? Then at last she opened her eyes to the soft sunshine of late autumn and awoke from her long, trance-like sleep.

Someone rose to minister to her, and she saw the white-haired mother with her patient eyes bending over her. She smiled upon her with a great tenderness.

"So you are awake!" she said, and Frances knew that she was glad. "Don't try to move too quickly! Just wait till your strength comes back!"

"Am I ill then?" Frances asked her, wondering.

And she answered gently, "No, dear. Only tired. You will be quite all right presently. Just lie still!"

So Frances lay still and pondered, fitting the puzzle piece by piece, slowly, painfully, till at length with returning memory the picture was complete. But who was lying dead among the Stones? And why—oh, why—were they thankful?

She could not ask the quiet woman by her side. The sad face bent over her work somehow held her silent, so deep were its lines of suffering. But the need to know was strong upon her. Someone was lying dead. Someone had been killed. Who? Oh, who? And what had caused that frightful explosion up there among the Stones?

There came to her again the memory of Arthur's arms holding her. And they had gone out together into the star-wide spaces. How was it that she had returned—alone?

Something awoke within her, urging her. She sat up, not conscious of any effort.

Mrs. Dermot came to her. "What is it, dear? Are you wanting something?"

Frances looked at her, but still she could not ask that dread question. Her lips refused to frame it. Not of anyone could she have borne to ask that which so earnestly she desired to know. She must find out for herself. She must go to the Stones. If he were dead—and in her heart she knew he must be—she would meet his spirit there.

And she must go alone.

She met Mrs. Dermot's gentle questioning very steadfastly. "I want to get up, please," she said. "I am going to the Stones—to look for something."

She expected opposition, but she met with none. Mrs. Dermot seemed to understand.

"Whatever you wish, dear," she said. "But don't overtax your strength!"

She helped her to dress, but she did not offer to accompany her. And so presently Frances found herself out in the misty sunshine, hastening with a desperate concentration of will towards the place of sacrifice.

She never remembered any stages of her journey later, so fixed was she upon reaching her destination. But as she sped up the steep track, her heart was racing within her, and, conscious of weakness, she had to pause ere she reached the top to give herself breathing-space.

Then she pressed on, never once looking back, passing the cattle-shed without a glance, reaching the Stones at length and moving fearlessly in among the long shadows cast by the setting sun.

A warm glow lay everywhere, softening the dread desolation of the place. She walked straight down the great circle, looking neither to right nor to left, straight to that point whence she had stood and watched the ghostly Rocking Stone sway before her like a prehistoric monster in dumb salute. And here she stood again, arrested by a sight that made her suddenly cold. The Rocking Stone was gone,—crumbled into a shattered heap of grey stones, around which the giant hare-bells still flowered in their purple splendour!

She caught her breath. This was where he was lying dead. This was where she would meet his spirit.

Again little Ruth's message ran like a silvery echo through the seething uncertainty of her soul. "You'll find it up by the Stones, where the giant hare-bells grow—something that you're wanting—that you've wanted always—very big—bigger even than the Rocking Stone. If you can't find it by yourself, Uncle Arthur will help you. You'll know it when you find it—because it's the most precious thing in the world."

The echo sank away, and the loneliness that was like an unseen presence came close about her. The silence was intense, so intense that she heard her own heart jerking and stopping, jerking and stopping, as the hope that had inspired her slowly died.

She stood motionless before that tragic heap of stones, and the unseen presence drew closer, closer yet. Then, rising clear from the valley, there came to her the sound of the church-clock striking the hour.

That released her from the spell. She lifted her clasped hands above the ruin before her and prayed,—prayed aloud and passionately, pouring forth the anguish of her soul.

"O God, let him come to me—only once—only once! O God, send his spirit back to me,—if only for one moment—that we may know that our love is eternal—that holy thing—that nothing—can ever change—or take away!"

The agony of her appeal went up through the loneliness, and she stood with closed eyes and waited for her answer. For she knew that an answer would be sent. Already, deep within her, was the certainty of his coming. Had she not told him on this very spot that their love would rise again?

And so she waited for that unseen presence among the barren and desolate stones, felt it drawing near to her, felt the surge and quiver of her heart at its nearness. And then—very suddenly—a great wave of exaltation that was almost more than she could bear caught her, uplifted her, compelled her. She turned by no volition of her own,—and met him face to face. . . .

"Arthur!" she said.

And heard his answering voice, deeply moved, deeply tender. "Frances! Frances! Frances!"

She was in his arms, she was clinging to him, before she knew that it was flesh and blood that had answered her cry. But she knew it then. His lips upon her own dispelled all doubt, banished all questioning. The rapture of those moments was the rapture which few may ever know on earth. He had come back to her, as it were, from the dead. Later, it seemed to her that no words at all could have passed between them during that wonderful re-union. Surely there are no words that can express the joy of those who love when at last they meet again! Is there in earth or Heaven any language that can utter so great a gladness?

She only remembered that when speech again was possible they were walking side by side through the chequered spaces of sunlight and shadow that lay between the Stones. And the desolation was gone for ever from her heart.

His arm was about her. He held her very closely.

"Why did you come up here?" he asked her.

And when she answered, "To find you," he drew her closer still.

"My mother told me. I followed you. She would have told you everything if you had asked, but the doctor said it must come gradually. She was afraid of giving you a shock."

"I was afraid to ask," said Frances.

He looked down at her. "You're not afraid now. Shall I tell you everything?"

She met his look. "I know a good deal. I know about—Nan, and about your father,—at least in part."

"You have got to know—everything," he said, and stopped where he had stopped once before to gaze out between the Stones to the infinite distance. "And you are to understand, Frances, that what has passed between us now can be wiped out—as if it had never been, if you so desire it. You know about—my sister Nan." His voice dropped. "I can't talk about her even to you, except to tell you that you are somehow like her. That was what made my father take to you. He didn't take to any strangers as a rule. Neither did I." Again she was conscious of the close holding of his arm, but he did not turn his eyes towards her. He went sombrely on. "We gave up everything and came here because the trouble over Nan had turned his brain. He wanted to tear across the world and kill my cousin. So did I—once. But—my mother—well, you know my mother. You realized long ago that all we did was for her sake. And so—since so far as we knew, my father had only the one mania and was sane on all other points—we came here. Nan's baby was born here. We settled down. My father never liked the life, but he got better. We hoped his brain was recovering. Then—one winter night—the madness broke out again. I was away on business. He got up in the early morning, went to Nan's room, and ordered her out of the house with her child. He terrified her, and she went. The next morning she was found up by the Stones in deep snow, dead. The child was living, but she was always a weakling, and she lost her sight. My father had a seizure when he heard that Nan was dead. In his delirium he told them what he had done. But when he came to himself he had forgotten, and his distress over the loss of Nan was heart-rending. Of course he ought to have been sent away. My uncle, Theodore Rotherby, had urged it from the outset; but my poor mother would not hear of it. And I—well, I hadn't the heart to insist. After that, I never left home again. Either Oliver or I kept guard day and night. But except for occasional outbursts of unreasonable anger he became much better, almost normal. He regarded me as his gaoler and hated me, but he always worshipped my mother. I believe it would have killed him to be parted from her. Better if it had perhaps, but—it's too late now. What I did, I did for the best." He uttered a heavy sigh. "It brutalized me. I couldn't help it. It didn't seem to matter. Nothing ever mattered till you came. I was harsh with the girls, I was harsh with everyone—except my mother. Life was so damnable. There were times when the burden seemed past bearing. The perpetual strain, year in, year out,—only God knows what it was."

"I can guess," whispered Frances.

His brooding eyes softened somewhat, but still he did not look at her. "Then you came. You changed everything. But that letter—you remember that lost letter? My father found it, recognized the writing, knew that my cousin was in the neighbourhood. That brought everything back. Somehow from the first he always connected you with Nan. There is a resemblance, though I can't tell you where it lies. On the night my cousin came to meet you at the Stones—that ghastly night—he broke out. I think you know what happened. He tried to murder him, but he got away. Oliver was there, but he ought to have been earlier. I blamed him for that. The mischief might have been avoided. However, my cousin got away, and my father dodged us and came back to the house. There he left his gun, thinking he had killed his man. Then he must have seen the child. Possibly she spoke to him. I don't know. But the lust for murder was on him that night. He followed her to the Stones, dodging us again, and saw her climb on to the Rocking Stone. He had made a great study of the Stones, and it was he who had discovered how to make the thing move. He used his knowledge on that occasion, and—and—well, you know what happened." His arm tightened about her convulsively.

"Oh, don't tell me any more!" Frances said.

He bit his lip and continued. "It all came out afterwards in his ravings, but we suspected foul play before. I was practically sure of it. Frances, it nearly killed my mother. I shall never forget her agony as long as I live."

"My dear—my dear!" Frances said. But she was thinking of the man's own agony which she had witnessed in the farm-kitchen on the night of little Ruth's death.

He drew a hard breath between his teeth. "Then, as you know, he was taken ill. And I hoped he would die. My God! How I hoped he would die! That night with you in the garden—do you remember? The night you offered yourself to me! I could have fallen at your feet and worshipped you that night. But—I had to turn away. You understood, didn't you? You knew?" A passionate note sounded in his voice.

"Oh yes, I knew," Frances said.

He went on with an effort. "I was nearly mad with trouble myself after that. And afterwards—when you were gone and I heard from Maggie that you had been inveigled into going up to town alone to meet that scoundrel, I couldn't stand it any longer. I had to follow you. I went to his rooms and I dogged him that night. I was like a man possessed—as much a murderer at heart as my father had ever been. If you hadn't stopped me, I should have killed him. But—oh, Frances,—" his deep voice broke—"nothing was worth while after that lie of yours. If it hadn't been for my mother I should have put an end to myself."

She laid her cheek against his shoulder. "Arthur! Do you think I found it easy—to lie? It nearly killed me too."

"Wait!" he said. "Hear it all! I came back. I found my father better. But I was at the end of my endurance. I couldn't go on. I told my mother so. I told her he must be certified insane and put away. She said I was quite right, though I know it would have broken her heart to have done it. I told her I must go right away too—to save my own sanity. And she—God bless her—she understood without any words. She just told me to go. Then I had my cousin's letter, telling me everything, vindicating you. I shouldn't have believed him if I hadn't known you. But—knowing you—I knew it was true. He asked for a meeting, and I agreed. Somehow I couldn't help it. It seemed inevitable. You know how sometimes one is pushed by Fate. I was bound to agree. I don't know what would have happened if I had met him. I might have killed him. I can't say. But I had only my hands to do it with. I didn't set out to kill him. And then—you came instead. You were frightened. You thought you had seen a devil. Do you know what it was you saw?"

"Your father!" she whispered.

"My father, yes. He had been wandering among the Stones, and I can only think that he had remembered about the child, and in a fit of mad remorse he had made up his mind to destroy the Rocking Stone,—possibly himself also. It is all surmise now. Anyhow, when you saw the Stone move, he must have been putting the charge underneath. And afterwards—when you and I were standing there—the murderous impulse must have seized him again. Perhaps he took me for Montague, and he may have thought you were Nan. I don't know. It is impossible to say. Anyway, he fired the fuse, and blasted the Stone. God only knows how we escaped unhurt. But he—but he——"

"He was killed?" said Frances.

"Yes, instantly. When I came to myself, you were unconscious and he was lying dead among the stones. Oliver and some of the men heard the noise and came up. We carried you back. I thought you were dead, but Dr. Square said it was only shock, that in a few days, given absolute quiet, you might recover."

"A few days!" said Frances, wonderingly.

"It happened a week ago," he said. "You were semi-conscious once or twice, and then you seemed to sleep. That was what brought you back."

"How amazing!" she said.

He turned for the first time and looked down into her upraised face. "I thought you would never come back," he said, and in voice and look she gauged the misery to which he gave no words. "I never had any hope."

The tears sprang to her eyes. She clung to him voicelessly for a few seconds. Then: "And I thought you were dead!" she whispered. "That was why I didn't dare to ask!"

He took her shoulders between his hands, holding her slightly from him. "Frances, listen!" he said. "I'm going to be fair to you. I won't take you—like this. You don't know what I am—a hard man, melancholy, bitter, the son of a murderer, not fit for any woman to love, much less marry. I am going away—as I said. Maggie and Oliver will run the farm. My mother will stay on with them. The girls will either stay or find their own way in the world. I've come to see that it isn't for me to hold them in any longer. Maggie made me realize that—you too. But I always had the thought of Nan before me. That was what made me so hard with them. But I'm going away now. And you will go back to the Bishop. He wants you. I believe he will be decent to you. I have heard from him about you. Some day—some day—you will find a man worthy of you. Not me—not Montague—someone you can give your whole heart to—and trust."

He paused a moment. His face was quivering. She saw him again—a gladiator fighting his desperate battle, conquered yet still not beaten to earth, holding her from him, defying the irresistible, ready to make the last and utmost sacrifice, that she might suffer no hurt.

And then, with a gesture of renunciation, he dropped his hands from her and let her go.

"That's all," he said, and there was a tremor in his voice which thrilled her through and through. "You are free. I am going. Good-bye!"

He turned away from her with the words. He would have gone. But in that instant Frances spoke—in the language that comes from the heart and speaks to the heart alone.

"I am not free," she said, "and you can never make me so. I am yours—as you are mine—for ever and ever. Nothing can ever alter that, because—God made it so."

Then, as he stood motionless, she went close to him, twining her arm in his, drawing him to her.

"Ah, don't you understand?" she said. "I love you—I have always loved you—I shall love you till I die."

And then he yielded. He turned with a low, passionate sound that was almost of pain, and held her to him, bowing his head against her, beaten at last.

"You are sure?" he said, and she felt the sob he stifled. "Frances, you are sure? Before God—this is for your own sake—not for mine?"

She held him to her, so that the throbbing of her heart was against his own. "But you and I are one," she said. "God made us so."

The church-clock struck the hour again, and they looked at one another with the dismay of lovers for whom time flies on wings. Down the hill at the farm they heard Roger's voice uplifted in cheery admonition. The cows were being driven back to pasture for the night, and Maggie's song came lilting through the gloaming.

"Shall we go back to Tetherstones?" Arthur said.

And Frances nodded silently.

They left the place of sacrifice hand in hand.

THE END

Printed in Great Britain
by Amazon